imagining transit

THEORY AND PEDAGOGY

Kristi E. Siegel
General Editor

Vol. 2

PETER LANG
New York • Washington, D.C./Baltimore • Bern
Frankfurt am Main • Berlin • Brussels • Vienna • Oxford

SIKIVU HUTCHINSON

imagining transit

race, gender, and transportation politics in los angeles

PETER LANG
New York • Washington, D.C./Baltimore • Bern
Frankfurt am Main • Berlin • Brussels • Vienna • Oxford

Library of Congress Cataloging-in-Publication Data

Hutchinson, Sikivu.
Imagining transit: race, gender, and transportation politics
in Los Angeles / Sikivu Hutchinson.
p. cm. — (Travel writing across the disciplines; vol. 2)
Includes bibliographical references.
1. Local transit—Government policy—California—Los Angeles.
2. Transportation and state—California—Los Angeles. 3. Race discrimination—
California—Los Angeles. 4. Sex discrimination—California—Los Angeles.
I. Title. II. Series.
HE4491.L75 H87   388.4'09794—dc21   2001038296
ISBN 0-8204-5586-5
ISSN 1525-9722

Bibliographic information published by **Die Deutsche Bibliothek**.
Die Deutsche Bibliothek lists this publication in the 'Deutsche
Nationalbibliografie'; detailed bibliographic data is available
on the Internet at http://dnb.ddb.de/.

Cover design by Lisa Barfield
Cover photo (Subway Terminal Building,
Downtown Los Angeles, 1925) by Sikivu Hutchinson

© 2003 Peter Lang Publishing, Inc., New York
275 Seventh Avenue, 28th Floor, New York, NY 10001
www.peterlangusa.com

All rights reserved.
Reprint or reproduction, even partially, in all forms such as microfilm,
xerography, microfiche, microcard, and offset strictly prohibited.

Table of Contents

Acknowledgments vii

Introduction: Crossings 1

Chapter One: Dreaming of La Plaza 17

Chapter Two: Whiteness and the City 33

Chapter Three: The Northern Drive: Black Women in Transit 59

Chapter Four: Driving While Black 77

Chapter Five: Little Patch of Green 103

Chapter Six: Station to Station 129

Chapter Seven: Waiting for the Bus 149

Chapter Eight: The Juggernaut 165

Notes 185

Bibliography 217

Acknowledgments

In appreciation of their support, encouragement, and fierce commitment to writing, I'd like to thank my parents, Earl Hutchinson and Yvonne Divans Hutchinson, for instilling me with the love of the word. For his enduring faith, wisdom, and insight my heartfelt appreciation goes to my grandfather, Earl Hutchinson, Sr., who always reminded me to keep my "eyes on the sparrow." The advisement of Senior Editor Dr. Heidi Burns and Production Editor Bernadette Alfaro was also instrumental to the completion of this book. The past year of my life has been greatly enriched by the mentorship and inspiration of Genethia Hudley Hayes, who graciously provided her recollections on growing up in Leimert Park for this book. The drudgery of revision was minimized significantly by the constant reinforcement of my friends Heather Aubry, Kamela Heyward-Rotimi, Sumitra Mukerji, Jennifer Fink, and Jack Wiren. Their sound critical feedback and unflagging interest in the many incarnations of this project took the edge off of much writerly angst.

INTRODUCTION
Crossings

> It is the stabilizing persistence of place as a container of experiences that contributes so powerfully to its intrinsic memorability...we might even say that memory is naturally place-oriented or at least place-supported.[1]
> —Edward Carey (1987, 24)

> November 30, 1925, was a truly great day in Los Angeles' history. Your editor was among the thousands who crammed into the Subway Terminal that day and perhaps his first-hand recollections would be of interest.[2]
> —Anonymous source (1925)

In 1951, five years before the passage of the Interstate Highway Act, my grandmother set out in her '49 Chevy for Los Angeles, the fount of possibility, the hybrid city. For white middle-class Americans it was the dawn of the Ozzie and Harriet era, rife with national imagery of apple-cheeked white children, dutiful white wives, and bootstrap red-blooded American male breadwinners swinging home to 5 p.m. suburbia in their guzzlers from
Detroit.

For my grandmother and many other black women who took part in the fifty-year exodus that encompassed the Great Migration, California was a more viable alternative to the white terrorism and economic exploitation of the South than the densely populated, heavily urbanized cities of the East Coast. Leaving close-knit urban and rural communities in segregated trains that dug past the Mason-Dixon Line, black women and their families struck out for the North in what would be the most influential in-migration in the country's history. Throughout the migration era, public transportation was a linchpin for the black struggle for democracy. It was during this period that blacks' peculiar relationship to the American city was fully articulated. Black migrants inherited the tradition of anti-urbanism that informed the dichotomy between city and suburb in American social thought. The American city has historically been reviled as representing the antithesis of American values of individualism and upward mobility. During the Migration era black in-migration enflamed white resentment, touching off a wave of brutal race riots. In flagship metropolises such as Chicago, Boston, and New York, segregation was one of the most insidious barriers to black mobility. Segregation, job discrimination, and race riots effectively "racialized" the Migration-era American central city. As Anglo American white "ethnics" took advantage of New Deal social programs and moved away from central cities, the inner city was indelibly linked to the downward spiral of the southern black transplant. Thus, even though the North was portrayed as the "promised land" in early Migration narratives, the pattern of de facto segregation that prevailed in urban centers established the black body as a space of containment.

It is through this narrative that I use transit as a lens for interrogating the social construction of urban subjectivity and collective memory. In this reading I do not presume to translate L.A. or parse the inscrutability of the city with "definitive" empirical research. Rather, I have chosen to explore the social history of Los Angeles transportation politics as a meditation on the ways in which transit is imagined. I have focused on the question of how transit reflects such themes as national identity, the American Dream, public and private space, collective memory, and the more elusive question of "being," particularly as it relates to the perverse seductions of autocentrism.

As social agent and author, L.A.'s transit landscape embodies the dialectic between the dead letter of the city's interurban railway and the romance of the automobile. Historically, transit has been a powerful means of stitching together the ontology of racial presence, urban public space, and racial subjectivity. In the South during the Great Migration, blacks resisted Jim Crow and de facto spatial apartheid by creating their own transit companies and staging protests on segregated buses and streetcars. The dynamic of racial embodiment that governed black movement in the Jim Crow South deeply influenced travel and transit to the North. The railroad was a particularly resonant figure in the black imagination. It was a symbol of hope and longing in migration testimonials, blues songs, and newspaper articles on the North.

Blacks' struggle against racial assaults designed to prevent them from migrating deeply informed the black urban consciousness that emerged after World War I. For migrants subjugated by the culture of terrorism that pervaded the rural South, cities in general, and northern cities in particular, represented possibility. This sense of possibility is compellingly reflected in such rhapsodic cautionary tales as Toni Morrison's *Jazz,* in which "the City" itself becomes an all-consuming, spectral presence in her characters' struggle for an emotional fulfillment and agency denied them in the rural South.

In the Migration-era city, public transit was a crucial political outlet for black women. The organized and unorganized acts of civil disobedience of

Rosa Parks and other black women on city buses and streetcars attest to the signal role public transportation played in the history of black female agency and resistance.[3] From trolley to highway, bus to subway, the Montgomery bus boycotts to the Freedom Rides, mass and private transit have been spaces of desire for black female subjects. As historian Paula Giddings notes:

> There had always been a tinderbox quality to the ill-treatment of Black women on public conveyances. As early as 1866 the millionaire activist Mary Ellen Pleasant sued the San Francisco Trolley Company after she was prevented from riding one of its car's...Treatment on the Jim Crow cars had been a catalyst in Ida B. Wells's activist career...and had been an issue Black women had put on the agendas of...the CIC and NACW. Yes, there was an old and special relationship between Black women and public transportation.[4]

This "old and special relationship" resonates throughout contemporary southern California, where 88 percent of all bus riders are people of color, and women of color represent the neediest users of public transit overall. How, then, has transportation influenced the inscription of race and urban public space in the United States? In order to answer this question I will examine how American cultural and racial identity was forged throughout the decline of the streetcar industry and the consolidation of the auto-industrial complex.

Blacks in Southern California were uniquely affected by the nation's cathexis on the automobile. The systematic devaluation of public transit deepened the divide in job, housing, and educational opportunities for African Americans vis-à-vis whites. In many respects the steady gains of European Americans during the post-World War II era were attributable to this divide. The regime of separate and unequal fueled the engine of white postwar prosperity. White veterans returning from the war were beneficiaries of a wealth of New Deal social welfare programs. Proto-suburban housing subdivisions like Long Island's 1948 Levittown development were expressly designed as havens for white veterans and their families. This period of triumphal capitalist consumption set the tone for late twentieth-century American national identity and the "universalization" of the ideal of the American Dream. The United States' ascent as a global first-world empire, its Cold War with the Soviet Union, and the rise of Fordist manufacturing intensified the racialization of African Americans as urban, pathological, and hence unassimilable. Tied to the consolidation of the welfare state, African Americans were perceived as being outside the pale of the American Dream. While the American Dreams of the white midwesterners who flocked to southern California after the Depression have become part of the regional canon of how the western United States is defined, black visions of the West as the Promised Land have been marginalized.

Part of the challenge of writing this book has been negotiating these competing visions of nationhood and collective memory. Collective memory speaks to a culture or group's sense of connection to the past, and is specifically reflected in the narratives that they construct to articulate their relationship to social history. The built environment is an especially important vehicle for collective memory. The transit scheme of L.A. County is the result of successive, and sometimes overlapping, stages of transit development that have been characterized as a transportation palimpsest. A drive down Crenshaw Boulevard, one of the main streets in Southwest L.A., in 1937 would have revealed a mix of car, streetcar, and pedestrian traffic. Today, hundreds of passengers on Crenshaw's 210 bus line ride over the bones of railway L.A. As one of those passengers, cursing the filth, abject slowness, and sheer perversity of the bus system in the 1980s, I fantasized about New York's battered subways and the Bay Area's sleek modern trains—wondering why L.A. did not have a train system of its own.

Looking back, the conventional wisdom was always that the city was too big, too unwieldy to accommodate rail. Belying this wisdom was a rich social history of rail, one that had helped articulate the Olympian sprawl of the city. As the Los Angeles Metropolitan County Transportation Authority (MTA) prepares to develop a right-of-way on Exposition Boulevard that has lain dormant for over a decade, collective memory becomes a critical issue in any reading of the cultural and psychic landscape of the city.

Downtown, at the corner of Hill and Sixth streets the Pacific Electric subway terminal building, remnant of L.A.'s old railway system, sits in eerie proximity to the new Red Line subway. After being open for many years, the building is boarded up, a blip on a rearview mirror, one of the many unoccupied older buildings of ambiguous provenance that haunt the schizoid landscape of downtown. When the building originally opened in 1925 a crush of passengers descended upon it each day, and its tunnels echoed with the burbled signals of passing trains switching tracks as they fumbled through the dark and out to the horizon to cities like Glendale, Hollywood, and Pasadena.

The subway terminal building was an integral part of Los Angeles's interurban streetcar system. Traversing the entire county, the Pacific Electric was established in 1901 by transit mogul Henry Huntington and had the distinction of being the most extensive railway system in the United States from its inception in the teens, to its postwar decline.[5] Filling in the gaps left by the Southern Pacific and Santa Fe railroads, the Pacific Electric helped write the map of modern-day L.A. Moreover, under Huntington's direction the company became a crucial part of real estate development within the county. Streetcar lines were often established in sparsely populated areas to spur further settlement.[6] This strategy was the cornerstone of the politics of development in early L.A. It continued the tradition of land speculation begun by railroads in the nineteenth century.[7]

The history of southern California's streetcar system is like a whisper from Atlantis, a figment unimaginable within the vaunted cultural and spatial dissonance of the city. It is there on a drive through downtown, on the I 110 Harbor Freeway, fenced in by the corporate swirl of the business district to the east, and the clutch of rambling old houses that bookend parking lots, condemned buildings, and strip malls to the west. During the 1920s, automobiles were already in neck-to-neck competition with streetcars for road space downtown. The subway terminal was intended to level the playing field between them, "saving approximately eight minutes of travel time."[8] The streets outside the subway crackled with electrified wires, spit-polished Packards and Fords, and rail workers and office clerks and domestics jumping on and off trolleys, hustling for those eight minutes of five-cent fare time.

In many respects this project is about the transporting quality of memory, in both a literal and figurative sense. Just as memory throws us back onto an uncertain past, a past that is constantly being reinvented, and that requires one to reexamine the very firmament of identity upon which one's sense of history rests, transit forces a reckoning with the nature of being. The spaces of driving and riding shape consciousness in myriad ways. The sense memories one has of a city street are not the same walking as they are driving or riding the bus. The things that catch our eye, that capture our imagination, incite memory, forge emotional connection, are different with each mode of conveyance. Twenty-first century Los Angeles, a city infamous for its paradoxes, richly exhibits this dynamic. As a symbol of postindustrial development, the seductions and dislocations of memory have deep resonance for the cultural landscape of the city. The city's segregated neighborhoods are not only a testament to the imprint of white flight and economic disinvestment but to the cultural richness that communities of color have historically drawn on under conditions of spatial apartheid. That most canonical depictions of Los Angeles communities of color have chosen to focus almost exclusively on "deficit" models of development, in lieu of an appreciation of this richness, exemplifies how colonial notions of people of color reinforce a historic American hostility toward collective memory. Memory is important to the social history of communities of color because it repudiates what bell hooks has called the "forgetfulness" encouraged by the dominant culture.[9] For hooks, memory "sustains a spirit of resistance."[10] Remembering counters the hegemonic traditions that portray social history as a teleological chronicle of the accomplishments of "Great Men" and "Great Women." Collective memory has the capacity to foreground other sites of knowledge, spaces that communities not included in the social history of the dominant culture have created in connection with the built environment. A vision of history based on the importance of collective memory is one that not only acknowledges history's drive to recuperate what has been lost (to make the invisible visible and the absent present), but recognizes the inherent contradiction of this proj-ect. This vision recognizes that history is narrative, informed by gaps and omissions that do not allow for easy truths.

The drive of history is in many ways homologous to the way in which transit functions as an agent of being and time. Both mediums hurl us from the past of our point of origin to the future of our point of destination; both mediums suggest the fundamental elusiveness of the present. What has fascinated me most about the social history of American transportation is the degree to which it has been shaped by forgetting. In the 1910s the automobile was decried as a dangerous flash in the pan by the streetcar industry. From the 1920s to the 1940s Los Angeles had the most extensive trolley network in the country. The conversations that neighborhoods, planners, developers, and city government are having about the place of rail in the city are haunted by the ramifications of the twentieth century's capitulation to the automobile. They are haunted by the internal combustion engine's power to shape not only modern urban development but modern bodies and modern time.

Throughout this work I will attempt to unpack how the social imaginary, "the collective memory of an event or place that never occurred but is built anyway," informs the envisioning of "transit-scapes" in Los Angeles.[11] Beginning from the premise that "city spaces and architectural landscapes...have been the active systemizers of memory," I will examine how these transit landscapes have influenced the city's development as a model for American postindustrial, posturban development.[12] My analysis will primarily be concerned with the implications this trajectory has had for the decline of public transportation, toward an assessment of the enormous impact this decline has had upon the racial landscape of the region.

When the last train left the Pacific Electric subway terminal in 1955, train systems nationwide had suffered major losses in funding, ridership, and right-of-way space. The degradation of rail and railway infrastructure set the stage for the highway architecture that would become the signature of modern urban space. It was the era of the Interstate Highway Act, the modern civil rights movement, McCarthyism, and the enshrinement of the white postwar nuclear family. It was the last gasp of streetcar-era Los Angeles, the country's full-blown intoxication with the automobile and the devaluation of public transit. Through interviews, analysis of social and economic commentary of the period, personal reflections, and theoretical exegesis, I embark upon a narrative of Los Angeles's transportation palimpsest.[13]

The problematic rebirth of urban rail in L.A. is the latest phase of what has been referred to as the region's transportation palimpsest. The metaphoric quality of the palimpsest—a document that is written over many times at successive stages in its history, thus losing the meaning or representational integrity of the original—underscores the non-teleological nature of history.[14]

The palimpsest, then, throws the process of a document's invention into relief. An example of the blurred boundaries of past and present, the palimpsest suggests a future contaminated by the protean nature of the original document.

In this respect, the model of the palimpsest provides a means for "understanding" and interrogating the contradictions of social history. The palimpsest suggests the possibility of positioning history beyond the limitations and biases of Western teleology, challenging the notion that time progresses linearly. The Western belief that past, present, and future are distinct from one another is disrupted within the text of the unfinished palimpsest, whose past emerges from its future.[15]

The future looms large in the mythos of Los Angeles, its language of accelerated time and sprawl, its Jeffersonian evocation of the divide between the individual and community having become the model for the nation. It was perhaps in recognition of this dynamic that writer Mike Davis subtitled his landmark L.A. tome *City of Quartz* "excavating the future of Los Angeles." For Davis, this paradox is critical to understanding the relationship between the built environment and collective memory because it bridges the city's segregationist social history and the "paramilitarization" of space that governs racial politics in contemporary L.A. Drawing on the work of Walter Benjamin, who articulated the essential foreignness of one's place of origin, the degree to which narrating home gains its power from the distance of the native, whose memory conjures a vanished, imaginary place in time, Davis embarks upon a reading of L.A. that challenges teleological visions of the city as the pinnacle of the American Dream. Reading the future of the city through an excavation of its development–driven, suburban frontier past,

Davis's analysis illustrates how the past shifts underneath our very feet. Thus, the segregated spaces that inform black urban imagination were equally as important to the articulation of white California dreamin'. Imbibing the suburban ideal and the myth of bootstraps prosperity, white Americans' sense of postwar national identity was shaped by post–Jim Crow spatial apartheid. Affordable single-family housing, well-paying jobs, quality education, and a prodigiously subsidized highway system were key to this identity. However the conventional wisdom has been that hard work and sacrifice got "us" here, not a tradition of democratic citizenship based on white privilege.

One of the key premises of this book is that transit is a metaphor for being, and that the restlessness, rugged individualism, and lust for new frontiers that made the postwar vision of first-world democracy possible has always been predicated on colonial notions of the Other. The shopworn myth of American ingenuity reflects the profound role movement has played and continues to play in shaping American character and American imagination. Indeed, the social construction of white identity from the early twentieth century into the postwar period is an example of the "ontological" boundlessness, the performative elasticity of American whiteness. As a category that is always in movement, race is informed by the particular social, cultural, and historical context within which it emerges. However, the rigid binaries of Western dualism and empiricism historically disguised the social construction of race under the edifice of scientific racism. For example, the boundaries of whiteness were still very much under contestation from the development of the first colony of English immigrants in seventeenth-century Jamestown to the mass emigration of poor white European immigrants to the United States at the turn of the twentieth century. While the advent of racial slavery by the Virginia Assembly in 1661 facilitated the transition of poor, unpropertied, disenfranchised whites (some of whom had been indentured servants) from serfs to citizens, it did not end the discussion on who was properly white. Whites of Jewish, Irish, Eastern, and southern European descent were all variously perceived as less than white within the context of Anglo American society. Indeed, attaining the class status of whiteness involved rituals of identification with the violent code/symbolism of racial apartheid that dehumanized blacks, Native Americans, Asians, and Latinos as culturally Other. In many instances these rituals often took the form of securing labor rights for white workers at the expense of workers of color. In the volatile period from the post–Civil War era to World War I, white workers from the Deep South to New England race-baited Chinese and African Americans brought in as replacement workers during strikes by segregated white unions.[16] These conflicts allowed white workers to demarcate class and race lines. By portraying workers of color as parasites who undercut the value of white labor by working for dirt cheap wages, white workers were able to claim a connection with the Protestant work ethic of hard work and sacrifice.[17]

The workplace was an important stage for the performance of white racial identities. Crossing from white "ethnic" to white, non-Anglo whites were able to draw on the full arsenal of racial apartheid to make their claim for assimilation. Transportation technology was a major force in this dynamic. Early streetcar systems enabled working-class whites to move from crowded inner cities to nascent suburban communities at the turn of the century. In the mid-1950s, the development of the interstate highway system refined patterns of white out-migration from urban areas, a phenomenon that would, of course, come to be known as white flight.

It is my contention that the nation's shift from public to private transportation had a significant impact on the inscription of postwar racial subjectivity. Indeed, how did the decline of public transportation allow posturban subjects to experience place differently?

As a sociology instructor at Seattle University, I required my students to keep transportation journals in which they documented their daily journeys on foot, bicycle, bus/train, and/or car. Asked to reflect on the communities they traveled through, the people they encountered, and the microsociological exchanges they observed and participated in, each student provided critical commentary on the race, gender, and class politics of urban and suburban transportation in their journal. Seattle is illustrative because it is experiencing the same crises of postindustrial development and segregation as L.A., having transmogrified into a hideously congested sprawl of exurbs yoked together by the I5 freeway. The solution of local government and city planners has been a costly rail system that has run over budget and elicited vociferous opposition from many community and environmental justice coalitions.[18] While Seattle awaits judgment day on its rail system, L.A. is re-envisioning its trinity of car, bus, and rail. The next chapters bear witness to this dialogue.

The racial axis of Los Angeles belies the "boundless city" fantasy that has often been associated with the city in the popular imagination. In her 1970 novel *Play It as It Lays,* Joan Didion evokes a city of desolation and ennui whose cultural center and "moral" compass are signified by the eternally available freeway. For the protagonist of the novel, Maria, a B-movie white actress whose major pastime consists of obsessively driving the freeway at ten o'clock each morning, the Los Angeles freeway system is a source of order and release. In Maria's view, "it was essential...that she be on the freeway at ten o'clock. Not on Hollywood Blvd. Not on her way to the freeway, but actually on the freeway."(15). The freeway becomes a means of both moving beyond and staying within an interiority of self that threatens to strangle her. In Didion's narrative the freeway is an existential figure, a means of homing in on the spatial and psychic economy of a "city" whose radical decenteredness transforms the freeway into its "most meaningful source of community." Maria's disaffection is both symptom and symbol of a cityscape whose most significant source of identity is the sense of being without boundary that the freeway confers upon drivers of a certain race.

According to David Brodsly, this sense derives from the freeway's "dissociation from the urban landscape."[19] Here,

> The freeway does not exist within the surrounding landscape. It is in this sense like a tunnel, boring through the city without physical or psychological obstacles, *a Los Angeles subway system* (emphasis added)[20]

From the conjuncture of the Santa Monica 10 and San Diego 405 freeways in the west, to the overlay of the 405 and the San Fernando 115 in the north, the freeways that lie near the more heavily white neighborhoods establish borderlines and clear paths of containment for motorists of color.[21] Some critics have argued that the freeway affords white motorists the privilege of passing up inner-city communities adjacent to the southern and eastern spurs of the system. By allowing white motorists to pass up these areas, the freeways contribute to a white hegemony of speed and transcendence.[22] While my work will be informed by this critique, I am interested in looking back from the reign of the freeway, from within the spatial logic of the interchange, the connector ramp, the center divider. I am compelled by the prospect of tracing the paths of desire that ferried—to hijack a term—both "restless" women from Southern black communities as well as the much mythicized Anglo "frontiersperson."

Within the course of this narrative I illustrate how transportation is a motive force in the spatiotemporal and ontological construction of race in the United States. The discussion is informed by a reckoning with how transit functions as a metaphor for being. By looking at transit as metaphor I make a connection between the *structure of metaphor* and the evolution of L.A.'s transportation palimpsest—tracing the path of transit from the transcontinental railroad lines out of the city in 1875, to the demise of the Pacific Electric Railway in the 1950s, to the development of the freeway system in the 1960s and 1970s, and finally to the embattled fixed and light-rail tributaries of the nineties. I link the mapping of this geography with the transfiguring power of metaphor, its transmuting of time and presence, its function as a means of conveyance.[23] I draw on Jacques Derrida's reading of metaphor (via Aristotle) where metaphor "risks disrupting the semantic plenitude to which it should belong...open[ing] up the wandering of the semantic." According to this view metaphor neither recovers nor illuminates the hidden meaning of the original, but questions the original's claim to self-identity.[24] Thus, my reading turns upon a consideration of how metaphor forces a reckoning with time; a saying "yes to time," rather than to infinity.[25] This recognition of the irreducibility of time runs counter to American/Western notions of time as progressive or teleological. By conferring presence upon the subject in question, metaphor disrupts the notion of time as progressive. Metaphor essentially brings the subject into being, thus highlighting the unstable temporality that informs the subject's claim to self-identity and self-presence.[26] The subject cannot exist without being rendered "present" by metaphor.

Throughout this work it is my contention that race has been inscribed through metaphor. I am interested in how American notions of whiteness are formed through a hijacking of time, through the fetishization of notions of progress vis-à-vis the racial determinism of city and suburb. Here, I refer to American social discourse that has constructed the inner city as abject racial Other. This construction emerges from the othering of the body of the free slave and the immigrant during the nineteenth and early twentieth centuries; culminating in the othering of the body of the black subject from the Great Migration to the present. In my view this form of racial determinism illustrates how race functions as a temporal category. The white subject ostensibly comes into being by surpassing the limits of racial presence as established by the segregated city. Race, then, becomes the province of the Other, and the "irredeemability" of the city becomes a function of race. The "raced" subject (I refer here to the manner in which people of color have been socially constructed as racial first and foremost) is fixed in time, while the "unraced" subject (white subjects who are assumed not to have a racial identity), as the universal subject, is subversive of time.

The extension of white privilege to include so-called white "ethnic" European immigrants during the postwar period exemplifies this dynamic. By allowing second- and third-generation European immigrants access to better housing, jobs, more equitable working conditions, education, and health care, New Deal programs and institutions (such as the Works Progress Administration and the Federal Housing Administration), as well as the labor movement, played an important role in integrating non-Anglo whites into the narrative of progress that informs American national identity. These horizons of opportunity enabled once reviled European immigrants such as Irish and Polish Americans to be included in the progress-driven telos of Anglo American subjectivity. In this respect whiteness came to be defined by its transcendence of racial or ethnic identity. Reliant on the Other to both affirm and disavow its racial "beingness," whiteness is ultimately constructed as a subject position that is radically subversive of the prescriptions of time and presence.

In teasing out the implications of this history for urban development, I focus on the subway system in New York City, using it as a counterpoint to the development of city space in Los Angeles. The racialization of turn-of-the-century and Great Migration–era New York is germane because it set the stage for the association of blackness with the inner city. With this in mind, I contrast the prototypical urbanism of New York with the anti-urbanism of Los Angeles. In the discourse of city planners, government officials, and many average citizens, who had imbibed the city's arcadian myth, L.A. was an antidote to the urban disorder of New York. It is my contention that city planning and transportation policy in Los Angeles did much to promote this myth.

Thus, I bring New York into the discussion to amplify the ways in which race and immigrant identity was elaborated within the context of public transportation. The relationship between New York and L.A. is evocative because it provides a means of examining the similarities and differences between the patterns of segregation and spatial apartheid that resulted from the development of an autocentric society versus that of a multimodal society.

The metaphorical nature of race and transit is compellingly illustrated in both cities. In using the notion of metaphor to support my argument, I examine how the history of transportation in L.A. is informed by the writing of racial subjectivity as a space of transit. To this end, I make two major claims. First, I argue that the way race is figured in the United States assumes the "transit-like" valences of metaphor. Second, I argue that whiteness, in its invisibility as a subject position/racial identity, mimics the drive of metaphor and is essentially *symptomatic*, unable to be truly revealed, always constituted as an anxiety of origin.[27]

Throughout the analysis I unpack the fascination and desire Los Angeles elicited within black migrants during the Great Migration and postwar periods. I proceed from Susan Anderson's observation that

> the urban ideal has been potent in black culture...rural life has meant, among other things, slavery, peonage, isolation and terror. It is not surprising that the city,

symbolizing escape from the racist excesses of the Deep South, is an object of black enchantment.[28]

For blacks, L.A.'s status as urban ideal and source of "enchantment" was double-edged. Here was a city that embodied many of the most odious aspects of rural Jim Crow while posing the potential for socioeconomic advancement. For example, from World War II into the postwar era, L.A. led the nation in black home ownership. During the war, blacks were able to obtain higher-paying manufacturing and defense jobs in industries that were heretofore closed to them. The violence of this peculiarly American disparity between the possibilities and limits of democracy resonates throughout black imagination of L.A., envisioned as "heaven" by Langston Hughes in the 1930s and as a terroristic hell by Chester Himes in the 1940s. It is a paradox that plays itself out in the driving culture of the city, where getting behind the wheel is both peril and pleasure for the black motorist, who must negotiate the regime of racial profiling that has increasingly come to govern exurban cities.

In each chapter of the work I have placed special emphasis on the role anti urbanism plays in racializing public and private space. Chapter 1 outlines some of the factors that influenced settlement in L.A., beginning with a consideration of the impact of railroad and streetcar development upon white Midwestern migration to southern California. Spatial apartheid informed the white migrants' "California dream." The chapter also examines how myths that shaped American national identity guided the automobile's ascent as cultural icon. I discuss this phenomenon vis-à-vis the construction of whiteness in the post urban city. In addition, I also explore its implications for racial being and presence. Finally, I discuss the influence that freeways have had on solidifying spatial apartheid in the city, concluding with an inquiry into the peculiar economy of race and time implicit in the motorization of L.A.

Chapter 2 traces the way in which the city was framed in turn-of-the-century urban planning criticism and American social thought. It begins with an analysis of the two competing models of national subjectivity expressed by the Jeffersonian and Hamiltonian ideals. These two models emphasized private property, the market economy, and the relationship of the city to the nation's telos of individualism and progress. Moving from these themes, the chapter examines how European immigrants were viewed as being in need of "redemption" from the squalor of the city. Urban reformers of the period believed that the potential for redemption lay in the achievement of so-called mainstream Anglo American values. Through an appraisal of the New York subway system's impact upon immigrant communities during the teens, the chapter considers the role that public transportation played in the European immigrant's redemption.

Chapter 3 examines black women's imagining of the city in the context of the Great Migration. While the example of the white immigrant in the urban "ghetto" informed the myth of American upward mobility, the parallel example of the Southern black migrant became the icon for urban pathology. Perhaps more than any event in the history of the American city, the mass migration of blacks from the South to the North would critically influence the direction of urban development. Using migration-era narratives such as Toni Morrison's *Jazz,* and Ann Petry's *The Street*, the chapter explores how black female subjectivity was shaped in the imagined landscape of the city street and early migrant communities. The North was the subject of considerable myth-making and lore for black migrants. The chapter looks at the resonance of this seduction with respect to the ontology of black female mobility. Thus, in attempting to evaluate how racial embodiment informed the construction of gender in the urban North, the chapter also considers how competing notions of black and white femininity informed the figuration of public and private space. The role that the automobile and the streetcar played in furthering notions of white female subjectivity and black female pathology is a key element of that story.

Chapter 4 focuses on the impact that the mass production of the automobile had on the nation as a whole and on Los Angeles in particular. It addresses how the automobile solidified American anti urbanism and the desire for the frontier of the single-family home. The chapter begins with a consideration of black female embodiment on the highway, foregrounding how the automobile has often been a conflicted symbol in the lives of working-class women. It proceeds with an appraisal of the failure of the city planning tradition, examining the role that it played in the decline of the streetcar industry, as well as in the rise of highway legislation. I also consider how the theme of the "open" road informed the inscription of whiteness as being beyond the category of race, and how American identity has been preternaturally linked to the rewards of personal freedom and democracy that car ownership ostensibly confers.

Chapter 5 continues the discussion of how the shift in the tenor of city planning during the 1920s reinforced the rise of the auto-dependent, decentered city. It examines the city planning tradition and the abdication of commitment to the ideal of urban public space during the 1920s. It also considers how this abdication influenced the institutionalization of land use and racial zoning concomitant with the enforcement of racially restrictive covenants. The chapter then examines the rise of the planning commission as the final nail in the coffin of citizen participation in municipal and transportation politics. Further, the chapter examines the refinement of national industrial policy dedicated to the promotion of the auto-industrial complex. It also looks at the implications that the consolidation of capital investment for auto infrastructure had for the decentralization of Los Angeles. In exploring this last point, the chapter focuses on how "place competition" between the new suburban commercial districts that sprung up in the wake of the confluence of streetcar/auto development precipitated decentralization.

Chapter 6 looks at the impact of transit racism and housing discrimination upon South Central Los Angeles, which became the hub of black settlement during World War II. Although blacks made considerable gains in defense industry employment, the combined effects of segregation and commercial decentralization set the tenor of spatial apartheid in the city. As the city moved to dismantle the streetcar system during the postwar era, the community became increasingly more transit-dependent, forced to negotiate between a middling, second-class bus system and costly private transit. In addition to these issues, the chapter also examines the trajectory of postwar development in downtown Los Angeles vis-à-vis the effacement of East L.A. communities and Mexican women's activism.

Chapter 7 examines the politics of Los Angeles's postwar bus system and the ontological role the city bus has played in the inscription of black female urban subjects. It traces public and urban planning policy's shift toward rubberized transit and analyzes the implications of this shift for the postwar, black female urban subject and urban communities. Los Angeles's traditional emphasis upon facilitating traffic flow via street and highway development altered the urban subject's spatial and temporal relationship to the city street. By freeing city dwellers from what was often regarded as a subpar streetcar system, the automobile also allowed the driver to avoid contact with the Other. In this regard the automobile succeeded in refining the vision of posturban, decentralized L.A. that the streetcar had enabled.

In conclusion, chapter 8 examines the politics of postwar highway development, assessing the impact of two generations of autocentric public policy upon contemporary mass transit in L.A. Having led the nation in exurban commercial and job development, the increasing drain of living wage employment from the central city has devastated the communities of the working poor. This chapter analyzes the implications of this trend with respect to mobility in communities of color. The growth of Latino communities in neighborhoods that were once predominantly African

American has fundamentally changed the black-white axis of city politics, opening up new vistas for coalition politics between black and Latino communities. With this in mind, it looks at how issues of multimodalism are being raised by multiracial organizations such as the Bus Riders Union, toward a consideration of what implications transit activism might have for redefining public space in the city. The chapter then assesses how emerging issues such as welfare reform have made the stakes for transit-dependent communities in Los Angeles even higher. As the city becomes more deeply mired in the politics of the Red Line subway, the prospect of new highway development threatens to undermine the cohesion of communities of color by displacing even greater numbers of South Los Angeles residents. In this respect, the legacy of the Pacific Electric Railway and autopia has come full circle.

CHAPTER ONE
Dreaming of La Plaza

> The freeway ran out, in a scrap metal yard in San Pedro or on the main street of Palmdale or out somewhere no place at all where the flawless burning concrete just stopped, turned into common road...when that happened she would keep in careful control, portage skillfully back, feel for the first time the heavy weight of the becalmed car beneath her.[1]
>
> —Joan Didion (1970, 17)

Sometimes you could smell the bus as it approached, a mile, five blocks, then an intersection away, biting at your heels, as you spit lightening bolts, hop fire hydrants, bag "No Parking" signs, leap over fat meridians of crosswalk to make the bus stop, landing as the doors flopped open, in a dripping, panting, tongue-lolling, frying-warthog-in-a-skillet hot flash. Riding was a low tech marvel, a wallop of sputtering open windows and greasy poles and roaches thieving in the house of the stop button. The bus driver tamed the treachery of La Brea Boulevard, a second past Rodeo Road, in the southwestern part of L.A., guiding the behemoth's descent past the dark houses of Nod on the hill, ferrying east through the big, fat, yawning six-lane stew of Venice Boulevard, surfing the sleepless ruckus of Crenshaw Boulevard, 10 p.m. on a Sunday; a three-gas-station habit jonesing every corner, row upon row of stucco as far as your eyes drove you. Even then, the vision of the bus was always receding; the reek, the jiggle, the strange encounter of flesh to flesh mimicking the glossolalia of a city subway.

I spent twenty years in Los Angeles watching cars go by through the windows of the city bus; watching crowded bus stops from the rear mirrors of cars, barely seeing their inhabitants; committing bus schedules, on-ramps, and road detours to memory; driving into the blinding sun in the white-knuckle grip of rush hour.

The dialectic of bus and car runs deep through the city's bloodstream. It's a hoary set of conflicts, made all the more onerous by the axiom that the dominance of the automobile in southern California is ineradicable. Ghost music from passing cars punches through the windows of my apartment. The ruckus of cars speeding, braking, lingering, honking, farting, creating a space all its own. The area I live in, Leimert Park, is walkable and green.

Developed in 1928, it is a community of wide center-divider cleaved streets, cryptic marathon alleys, idyllic walkways, and beautiful Spanish, Mediterranean and Americana architecture. The original design of Leimert follows that established by the L.A. Railway. Streetcars ran down Crenshaw and Santa Barbara Boulevards (now King Boulevard), the neighborhood's main thoroughfares. The layout of Leimert Park is significant because it reflects much of the emphasis upon balancing commercial and residential space with auto traffic that characterized Frederick Law Olmsted and Charles Cheney's 1924 "Major Traffic Street Plan." Olmsted and Cheney's plan outlined a system of parkways and green spaces that would have revolutionized public space in L.A. The rejection of the plan was one of the many egregious missteps that enshrined autocentrism in L.A. Nonetheless, the area has retained a somewhat East Coast residential flavor. Across from my apartment a small plaza anchors the street, opening up the intersection in such a way that it's not beholden to through traffic. The plaza design/concept is something that has had limited exposure in L.A. While the city originally sprung up around a plaza downtown, the unlimited access to public space that plazas traditionally offer was fundamentally at odds with the city's increasingly privatized, auto-obsessed design.

The community's main plaza at Vernon and Crenshaw Boulevards was developed according to specifications outlined by the Olmsted Brothers landscape design firm.[2] Newly landscaped as part of a community revitalization effort in the late 1990s, today it serves as a public square for musical events and political rallies.

Like many communities in South L.A., Leimert experienced an exodus of whites during the 1950s and 1960s after race-restrictive covenants were abolished. With the decline of black cultural centers such as Central Avenue in South Central L.A. in the 1960s, Leimert has become the de facto center of "black L.A."

In the whirlwind of Crenshaw traffic, it is difficult to envision trolleys shuttling up and down the street. One of the city's most preeminent motorways, an L.A. Railway line ran up Crenshaw until the late 1950s. In the neighborhood north of Slauson Boulevard, at the beginning of the "Crenshaw District," the street is a six-lane behemoth. Businesses are set back behind concrete islets in a manner that evokes the walker-friendly layout of Main Street U.S.A. The divide between this village-based ideal of street design and the autocentric model of the sprawling boulevard has had an important influence on urban subjects' relationship to the built environment. Writer Jane Jacobs has commented on the intimate rhythms of small, tight-knit streets in places like Lower Manhattan. Here, material relationships influence social relationships, shape our sense of connection to the world, create the bloodlink between place and memory. Woven within the politics of race, gender, class, and sexuality is the everyday "poetics" of movement on city streets and sidewalks. There is perhaps no more compelling physical index of a city's "identity" than the layout of its streets. From the warren of one-way side streets, shopping corridors, and regal plazas of Guadalajara, to the mutant bus/car/train cross-pollination of downtown Brooklyn, streets confer cities with their sense of time.

One of the more cryptic aspects of L.A. is the ghostly quiet of its residential streets. Sitting in a parked car in an L.A. suburban subdivision can be akin to sitting on the moon, the absence of significant pedestrian traffic blanketing the street in a heavy portentous quiet like the silences between a slow drip of water.

In the beginning of my research for this book, I came across a picture taken in the 1950s of a streetcar riding down the middle of the Hollywood Freeway. Up until 1952 a Pacific Electric line ran on this section of the freeway, which is known as the Cahuenga Pass. Driving down the Cahuenga Pass north through a sloping range just beyond the Hollywood Bowl, it is almost impossible to conceive that a rail right-of-way once cut through the middle of the highway. Auto traffic has fully remade the stretch over in its image. The Cahuenga Pass at Sunset Boulevard has all the romance of a film noir scene, the white retaining walls of old Hollywood looming along the side of the road.

After the demise of the Pacific Electric Railway, the median strip of the Cahuenga Pass was taken over and made into car lanes by the Division of Highways.[3] The Pass is a vivid transition point, shuttling away from the drone of Hollywood on the north toward the creeping vacuum of suburban Universal City; proffering, as one coasts down the incline going south, a somber peek at the downtown horizon in all its gilded glory. Wide and canal-like, it funnels traffic in a steady stream of bug-eyed white lights, lanes littered with the remains of freshly dismembered coyotes and possum and rabid dogs who wrangle from foothills thick with condos and car dealerships.

The trolley right-of-way on the Cahuenga Pass was a shadow of what L.A.'s transportation network could have been. As early as the 1940s planners contemplated putting rail on the freeways to relieve what was swiftly becoming a losing situation for rapid transit. Instead, the legacy of rapid rail is more rightfully embodied by Universal City's junction of condos and car dealerships. Unchecked residential and commercial development has pushed the boundaries of the county, making it one of the largest in the country. The specter of such byways as the Cahuenga Pass continues to haunt the city, to influence the "poetics" of space that inform the way it has been imagined.

In his critique *Los Angeles: The Architecture of the Four Ecologies,* design historian Reyner Banham proposes that the geographical text of L.A. is a transportation palimpsest: each successive system of transportation having been sketched onto the outlines of its forebear.[4] From the first transcontinental railroad lines of the 1880s, to the supernatural might of the freeways, the soldering of L.A. with the automobile has become the model of postwar urban development in the United States. Despite the powerful influence rail transit had upon the formation of the city, the automobile's influence upon the very spirit and psyche of L.A. is so indelible that contemporary rail transit has, until very recently, been viewed as an oxymoron.

The fetishization of the automobile in L.A. is the culmination of early mythology of the city as a more egalitarian, less urban city than the "vertical cities" of New York, Boston, and Philadelphia. In wedding the iconography of Main Street U.S.A. with that of a "utopic" society, L.A. eschewed the dense centralization of cities that had matured during the industrial era. In flouting this boundedness, L.A. has been envisioned in the popular imagination as a place whose disaggregated sprawl defies cartographic boundary—the perfect homologue to the American spirit of restless discovery. The freeway system has been critical to mapping the city's racial, demographic, and temporal boundaries. It renders the city both intelligible and unintelligible, influences access to jobs and social services, limits lines of community engagement, and effectively others the "inner city" communities that border it.

The freeway's imprint on the social, economic, and political structure of the city reflects a "geocratic" distribution of power and resources. According to social historian Douglas Rae, spatial mobility is one of the most valuable commodities within a geocratic society. Here, "differential access to place becomes a decisive instrument of the creation and perpetuation of advantage."[5] The United States' shift from public to private transportation resulted in the geocratic inscription of urban self and subjectivity. Rae has observed that this alignment of power arose during the political and social sea change that occurred in the United States between the landmark *Plessy v. Ferguson* Supreme Court ruling in 1896 and that of *Brown v. Board of Education* in 1954.[6] During that period the transition from fixed-path transportation (e.g., trains, walking, trolleys) to variable-path transportation (automobiles) weakened the historic dominance of the central city. Thus, as the auto complex gradually gained sway over the planning and organization of urban space (via the segregation of land use through zoning ordinances and restrictive covenants), the horizontal, posturban development of Los Angeles emerged as a new "prototype" of social and racial inequality.

Within contemporary cultural criticism, as well as countless works of fiction, L.A. has become the linchpin of a peculiarly American discourse of place. Memorialized as Protestant Eden turned noirist nightmare and reluctant postmodern icon by white male writers as wide-ranging as Jean Baudrillard and Philip K. Dick, L.A. occurs as a space of projection—the foremost paradigm of posturban civilization and its discontents, a city whose unholy matrimony with the automobile, combined with its racial "balkanization," has worked a kind of dread seduction upon Euro-Americana.[7]

However, for writers like Wanda Coleman and Bebe Moore Campbell, L.A. is a source of deep ambivalence, a problematic home turf whose fault lines of race, gender, and class both detract from and contribute to its confounding richness. In Campbell's novel *Brothers and Sisters*, set in L.A. after the 1992 uprising, Campbell skillfully parses the everyday politics working people in L.A. must negotiate, homing in on the unexpected emotional connections created across seemingly unbridgeable ethnic and racial divides. In Coleman's short story collection *War of the Eyes*, the hybrid suburban/urban landscapes of working-class black and Latino L.A. provide a pungent backdrop for explorations of desire and longing. Just as the 1965 Watts Rebellion brought Los Angeles African American communities into national focus, the uprising presented yet another glimpse into how the cult of California dreamin' was experienced by communities of color in the post-Vietnam era. For example, in exploring the complex racial politics of this period, Anna Deavere Smith's 1995 performance piece *Twilight Los Angeles* draws from a collage of L.A. voices and communities to create a textured social history of the spatial apartheid, institutional racism, gender hierarchy, and interethnic schisms that precipitated the uprising. Smith's reenactments of the interviews she conducted with area residents during the uprising are the blank spaces within official histories of the event. Portraying everyone from former Los Angeles police chief Daryl Gates to a Korean grocer whose business was burned down during the unrest, Smith's body becomes a canvas for the collective memory of the city.

The city's early identity as an antiurban haven for xenophobic, white Midwestern Protestant settlers has become one of the constituting fictions of American national identity. In reality, L.A. came into being as El Pueblo de Nuestra Senora la Reina de Los Angeles in 1781, founded by "44 settlers...more than half with some African blood."[8] This alternative genealogy of Los Angeles history is the ghostly narrative underlying the city's Anglo Midwestern myth of identity. In his book *Thirdspace*, Edward Soja uses the metaphor of the palimpsest to suggest the revision of the region's multiracial origins during the period when California was part of Mexico.[9] At the center of town was La Plaza, an area located downtown at the junction of Alameda, Aliso, and Los Angeles Streets.[10] For Soja, the palimpsest metaphor disrupts the teleological inscription of the city as a proving ground for the white frontier subject. Nearly one hundred years later in 1871, the city's Chinese community was attacked by mobs of "Hispanophobic" Yankee marauders in what would be considered an "international embarrassment" for the region.[11] After this campaign of "ethnic cleansing," the city began to reinvent itself as a mecca for Anglo American enterprise, and the Plaza was displaced as city center.[12]

In 1881, when the Southern Pacific Railroad made the first link to the east (followed by the Santa Fe Railroad in 1885), the "new urban mythology" of Los Angeles as fount of Arcadian culture was a potent brew for white Midwesterners. The country roiled in the shadow of Reconstruction as the South began its transition from a slave-based economy to Jim Crow apartheid. During the early years of the transcontinental link, L.A. battled fierce competition from other new settlements in the Southwest and Pacific Northwest.[13] Using the same promotional tactics that Midwestern railroads had used to attract newly arrived European immigrants living in the eastern United States to the Midwest, Southern Pacific's publicists portrayed L.A. as a garden of plenty. Banking on Midwestern white America's increasing discontent with the agrarian way of life, the railroad promoters and boosters of the region drew a vivid picture of L.A. as a tranquil refuge from the rigors of farming.[14]

The first seeds of L.A. utopianism, of the city as the embodiment of the "good life," lay in these overtures. By offering the white Midwesterner a reprieve from farming, L.A. represented an opportunity to realize a life that combined all the insularity, community, and homogeneity of Main Street with a decidedly postindustrial and posturban flavor. In essence, "Los Angeles bec[ame] the focus of the final phase of Protestant Americans' historic trek West, the latest journey of a restless Mayflower," avatar of the "first truly (white) American city."[15] Seeking to wipe out all traces of Indian and Mexican cultural influence upon the region, the boom period sojourn of this "Mayflower" was to have profound implications for the delimiting of time and space embodied in the sprawl of L.A. County.

When my grandmother arrived in L.A. in 1951, she was privy to the death of one era and the inauguration of another. L.A.'s train system hung by a thread. In the postwar zeitgeist of unlimited prosperity, owning a car had become an even greater symbol of the divide between the haves and have-nots than it had been in the 1930s and 1940s. In this emergent culture of drive-in movies, diners, drag races, and lovers' lanes, the social mobility that cars seemed to afford was seductive for many. Within this climate the narrative of L.A. assumed the architecture of the drive, the fantasy of infinite space, anticipating the era when the mammoth expanse of the freeways would become the monument to the city's "boomtown" Anglo-frontier heritage. When my grandmother's family settled in Central L.A. near the Los Angeles Coliseum and the University of southern California, the north-south 110 Harbor Freeway corridor had not yet cut its swath through downtown. Both my mother, who was in elementary school at the time, and my grandmother recall riding the streetcars often to work. My grandmother worked a succession of menial jobs, as a factory worker and domestic, before joining the flow of black industrial workers as an assembly-line employee at aircraft manufacturer McDonnell Douglass in the 1970s. Both my grandmother and mother vividly recall the code of segregation in the city, where black and Latino settlement tapered off in the more westerly parts of the city, and it was tacitly understood that certain areas, such as the beach, were reserved for whites.

While whites and people of color were thrown together on streetcars, buses, and roads, separate and unequal remained the rule within the city's neighborhoods. The segregation of blacks and Latinos in Eastern and South Central L.A. was a powerful inspiration for white imagination of racial space. This deep cultural divide allowed white males to envision their relationship to the city, to meditate on the limitations of the American Dream, and the attendant trials of masculinity. Narratives of white urban unrest emerged forcefully within the genre of literary noir.[16] Noir, as Howard Klein notes,

> is essentially a mythos about white male panic—the white knight in a cesspool of urban decay...the hard-boiled story cannot help but operate...as white males building a social imaginary. The booster myths (sunshine, climate, Protestant Eden) generate an emptiness that leads to violence and despair, in the form of urban fables. The crime on the dark streets stands in for the fears about foreigners...it pits the white, usually Protestant, shamus against a world that is purely transient, as if no poor communities exist except as a hangout for crooks and addicts.[17]

Novels such as Raymond Chandler's *High Window* and *Farewell My Lovely* portrayed downtown L.A. as a nether zone of crime and illicitness (vividly represented by areas such as Chinatown, in which whites were allowed to conduct all number of shady enterprises with impunity).[18] Literary visions of a decadent, economically depressed downtown rife with vice, amorality, and urban blight foreshadowed white Protestant abandonment of the inner city for the segregated provincialism of the crabgrass frontier.

The transience and instability of inner cities is a common theme in American culture. The notion of having accessible public space where diverse groups, classes, and cultures meet (often moving against the grain of one other) runs counter to the individualist ideal of Western capitalist consumption and its relentless segregation of space. In the tragic romance of noir, the inner city becomes a medium through which the conflict between the individual and the community is utilized to test and ultimately validate white heroism, the inner city serving as mise-en-scène. Variations on this theme of tragic white romantic heroism can be seen in some of the great and not-so-great noir portrayals of L.A. from *Double Indemnity* to *Grand Canyon*. In each portrayal L.A. remains unintelligible, the city's seduction of behind-the-wheel mastery and liberation fundamentally elusive for the white male protagonist.

The quest to glean some essential truth about L.A. as a city in which the white male subject is cast as avatar, is emblematic of the way Western power-knowledge operates. Power-knowledge, as delineated by philosopher Michel Foucault, refers to the cultural, social, and political construction of knowledge as a crucial elaboration of power. Knowledge, whether it be the axiom that the world is round or the premise that races are biologically distinct from one another "is governed by power relations."[19] Depending on a culture's particular structure of power, authority, and "discipline," certain "knowledges" are privileged while others are marginalized as minoritarian. As an object of knowledge, the inability of L.A. to be read as a coherent text is a function of both its multiculturalism and its spatial layout. Although New York's cultural fabric is similarly diverse, it has a firmer status in the pantheon of American social ideals because it is the spiritual homeland of the bootstrapping assimilated white immigrant. Because L.A.'s immigrant story originates from the geopolitical shifts of the so-called Third World, it cannot be so easily incorporated into this pantheon. Until very recently the white, usually Protestant shamus, negotiating between the world of "sunshine" and noir, has been the official interpreter of the city's dystopia. White critics such as Mike Davis, Reyner Banham, Edward Soja, and Kevin Starr have all contributed to the canon of L.A. as the model of postindustrial American development. Whereas Davis's work remains one of the most trenchant critiques of the "imperialist" power politics of the region, none of these works seriously consider the social and political agency communities of color have drawn upon to shape the symbolic character of the city. In the vision of these writers, communities of color remain objects of investigation, summoned to highlight the inequities of L.A. power politics. Indeed, none of these critiques take into account how communities of color envision the relationship between the built environment and the way they experience the American Dream. In her work *The Power of Place*, Dolores Hayden looks closely at the role public space has played in shaping community identity and racial solidarity. Hayden identifies the paradox whereby both the terroristic *and* the liberating potential of segregated public spaces "make memories cohere in complex ways."[20] "Place-making" enables disenfranchised communities to exercise agency in spaces that are often predicated on either criminalizing these communities and/or making them invisible. Place-making reflects the degree to which space is forged through repression and struggle, ideology and social history, offering rich insight into how cultural identity is performed. Place-making on public transit has been a revolutionary source of civil resistance for segregated communities of color. In his book *Race Rebels*, social historian Robin Kelley characterizes public buses and streetcars during the civil rights era in Montgomery, Alabama, as "moving theaters":

> Theater can have two meanings: as a site of performance and as a site of military conflict. First, dramas of conflict repression and resistance are performed in which passengers witness, or participate in, a wide variety of "skirmishes" that shape their collective memory, illustrate the limitations as well as the possibilities of resistance to domination, and draw more passengers into the performance.[21]

In L.A. that theme is reflected in the activism of the Bus Riders Union (BRU). The multidisciplinary activism of the group has changed the landscape of L.A. transportation politics. In addition to recruiting and organizing new members by going out on city buses, some of the members perform skits that dramatize sociopolitical issues on the bus, tackling issues that touch on everything from disability rights to California's Proposition 187 (which denied benefits to illegal immigrants). According to organizer Barbara Lott-Holland, these strategies have been successful in pulling in reluctant bus riders who might not have otherwise connected with the more grassroots political approach of the group.[22] This form of organizing is a vibrant means of place-making, allowing working-class people to assume ownership over spaces that have historically been marked as Other. Forged in struggle, this place-making dynamic is one that envisions social and political discourse as vital to the experience and imagination of public space—a dream of a "mobile" La Plaza. Here, the struggle for democratic citizenship is linked to the struggle to liberate public space.

Bus riders have spearheaded a grassroots transit movement unprecedented in a city where, if USC urban planning professor James E. Moore II (one of the "Adam Smith" cadre against whom Starr inveighs) is to be believed, "the dream of every bus rider is not to have clean, well-maintained buses, but to own a car."[23] The bus riders' protests have been bolstered by studies (such as that of the libertarian Reason Foundation, a report cowritten by Moore) that have raised questions about the feasibility of the MTA's rail expansion agenda.[24] Drawing upon the spirit of civil rights era activism, the BRU succeeded in foregrounding the way gender, race, and class discrimination contributes to transit dependency, particularly in an era in which the federal government's billion-dollar Highway Trust Fund outlays perennially eclipse funding for education and social welfare. Since 1992 the BRU has protested against the poor conditions on the buses through direct action against MTA mismanagement. Going from bus to bus wearing yellow T-shirts that exhorted riders to "Fight Transit Racism," the union organized disgruntled black and Latino riders into one of the most visible multiracial political coalitions in the city.[25] After watching the MTA lavish millions of federal dollars on a much-reviled subway, the union filed a federal civil rights lawsuit against the organization with the NAACP Legal Defense and Education Fund and other social justice groups. The suit charged the MTA with creating a two-tiered transit system that discriminated against predominantly low-income "minority" bus riders in favor of white-collar rail commuters. Mobilizing communities of color, in 1996 the BRU succeeded in winning a federal consent decree that required the MTA to upgrade bus service and put a cap on fare hikes.[26]

The BRU is an arm of the multiracial Labor/Community Strategy Center, which has mobilized against cases of environmental racism that involved such issues as ambient air pollution in communities of color. The Center has formed partnerships with other grassroots environmental justice groups such as Concerned Citizens of South Central and Mothers of East L.A. Mobilizing around common themes of disenfranchisement across black, Latino, and Asian communities, the BRU is one of the few organizations in Los Angeles that has managed to navigate through the fractious identity politics and language issues that have historically threatened the longevity of multiracial coalitions.[27]

The BRU's organizing strategies reflect the extent to which the bus is a medium where female agency can be forcefully articulated. As one of the most transit-dependent populations in the city, women must constantly negotiate the social proscriptions placed on their mobility and the tenuous freedoms that a nominally accessible public transit system affords them.

Hence, the BRU's vision of La Plaza rejects the segregation and solipsism of freeway culture. During the postwar era, the freeway became the most powerful metaphor for the imperialist sensibility of the white male urban imagination. Whereas white Midwestern Depression-era visions of L.A. revolved around the pastoral bounty of the city, postwar visions of L.A. reflected the city's emergence as a center for defense manufacturing and highway development. southern California became home to the most extensive freeway system in the United States with the passage of the 1956 *Interstate Highway Act*. The refinement of the highway complex enshrined the hierarchy of public and private space, such that in southern California, the cradle of autopia, "the birth of a freeway" became an almost "semi-mythic event."[28] "Driving the freeway," historian David Brodsly opines in his evocative book *L.A. Freeway*, "is absolutely central to the experience of living in L.A. and any anthropologist would head to the nearest onramp, for nowhere would he or she observe such large-scale public activity."[29] In postwar L.A., the overpass/connector ramp became one of the primary vectors of space in the region. By building upon Los Angeles's legacy of land speculation, "the freeway" is at once the most elegant and insidious emblem of the city's drive to transcend the limitations of space and time.[30]

With the introduction of freeways, L.A. ostensibly became a city "without boundaries," as highway developers and homebuilders began staking their claim to some of the remotest regions of the county. Under this regime, the freeway represents the triumph of time over space, knocking through communities indiscriminately in the service of providing the driver twenty-four hour access to the road. Acting as conduit and insulation, the freeway allows the driving subject to avoid meaningful contact with the city by seamlessly ushering her from point to point. Within this economy of movement the city is reduced to signifiers: the signage, traffic jams, center dividers, and ramps of the freeway becoming the most significant symbols of "cultural" and spatial connection for the driving subject. Here, the manic pace of getting to one's designated exit or interchange is the gospel of road perfor-mance. At once suspended in time and propelled forward in time, the driving subject essentially experiences time both through the march of names that flash by on exit signs and the choreography of cars switching lanes.

This dynamic has had particularly important implications for the construction of whiteness in the city. For example, within the mise-en-scène of the highway, the language of speed and access evoked in a 1907 Santa Fe ad depicting a young white girl taking in the sights of California

Seeing California
From a car window is the easy way—and very

pleasant, too.

> A favorite one-day trip is that over the Rite-Shaped Track of the Santa Fe...through the orange groves of southern California.[31]

can be viewed as a metaphor for the delimiting drive of whiteness, the association of whiteness with private space. It is a vision of passage and possibility enabled by the "invisible" interface of attentive black porters and segregated cars. Thus, while the Jim Crow code of the railroads reinforced the inscription of the white body as the prime signifier of private space, the influence of streetcar development solidified the patterns of spatial apartheid that informed transportation politics in contemporary L.A.

Semaphores

For much of the past thirty years, contemporary L.A. has been in violent conflict with its streetcar ancestry. However, this moment in history finds it doubling back again, in deference to the rhythm of the standard gauge, the frequency the streetcars ran on when the first electric trains were patented in 1888. The city is now in the midst of a kind of transportation renaissance. The planning and development of rail in contemporary Los Angeles is the culmination of two decades' worth of efforts to rectify southern California's lag behind other regions (such as Washington, D.C. and the Bay Area in northern California) that had taken advantage of the greater availability of federal funding for rail in the 1960s and 1970s.[32] Whereas San Francisco's Bay Area Rapid Transit System was born of consensus over the role rail should play in the region, Los Angeles's postwar hostility toward rail precluded the city from building the necessary political support to garner federal funding.[33] However, as highway construction declined in the 1970s, "images of modernity in transportation...changed dramatically...rail transit was becoming symbolic of progress and municipal accomplishment."[34] In 1980 the Los Angeles County Transportation Commission (LACTC) sponsored a successful ballot measure (Proposition A) that allotted part of county sales taxes to the development of rapid rail.[35] The success of the measure paved the way for implementation of a four-part transit plan that featured both light and heavy rail lines, express buses, and high-occupancy vehicle lanes on the freeways.

The LACTC's plan began to come to fruition in the 1990s. The city's first light-rail, streetcar line began operation in the early 1990s, running from the Pacific Electric–pioneered city of Long Beach in the south to downtown. Commuter rail was developed to the outermost suburbs of Riverside, San Bernardino, and Orange Counties. While these developments still seem surreal to a bus-bred native of L.A., the introduction of fixed rail into the city was the most unprecedented development of all. The MTA's Red Line Subway project was intended to be the proverbial jewel in the crown of the city's public transit revival. The subway was to confer world-class status upon a city long disdained as a suburban backwater, revitalizing downtown by bringing desperately sought-after white-collar commuters back to work and shop in the central city.[36] Instead, the MTA has been mired in controversy over the system's ever-ballooning budget, political infighting over site selection, and the organization's egregious neglect of city buses. The Red Line now has the dubious distinction of being the most expensive public works project in the West and perhaps the most derided public works project in the country.[37] Policymakers who salivated over the prospect of a subway have seen their ambitions drastically scaled back. A federal investigation of the MTA's alleged misappropriation of funds resulted in funding cutbacks.[38]

The troubled saga of the Red Line is a perverse coda to the reign of the Pacific Electric. In 1905, when electric railways were a burgeoning national industry, Henry Huntington was cornered by a *Los Angeles Record* reporter and questioned on his expansion plans for the Pacific Electric. Having already established his then fledgling railway in southern California Huntington maintained (contrary to the fears of steam railroad officials who saw their business shrinking as a result of electric railway competition) he would not "build to the moon," but settle for the more reasonable goal of southern and northern California.[39] The thundering irony of Huntington's statement is borne out in the P.E.'s offspring, the freeway, whose sway is perhaps the most fierce and elegant testimony to the extent which the railway's real estate machinations have influenced the rhythm of the city. The relic of the Pacific Electric map tells the entire story of urban empire. The map is a fascinating chronicle of both the streetcar and the railroad's influence upon the region. Trolley lines radiate from most of the major streets, stopping on almost every intersection. Interurban service from the P.E. intersects with local service from the Los Angeles Railway, and overlaps with commercial freight and passenger service offered by the Atchison Topeka, Santa Fe, and Southern Pacific railroads.[40] The configuration of the map roughly traces the line of settlement in post–World War I Los Angeles. The downtown, radial focus of the network extends to major southern suburbs such as Long Beach; central suburbs such as

Compton and Watts; northern suburbs such as Pasadena and Glendale; Westside suburbs such as Santa Monica and Venice; Valley suburbs such as San Fernando and Van Nuys; and the furthermost eastern counties of Riverside and San Bernardino. Scattered in between the railway lines and railroad routes are miscellaneous bus (then called motor coach) lines. The map reveals that buses had established an early presence in the region—a harbinger of national trends to come. What is perhaps most striking about the map is its sheer extensiveness, the fact that virtually every pocket of the county was accessible by streetcar. The communities were arguably better connected then they are now in this era of high-tech infrastructure.

Looking at the map of the Los Angeles freeway system, you notice the Pacific Coast Highway (PCH) Route 1 shadows the old coastal route of the P.E. line, overtaking the line at Santa Monica. The PCH stakes out the northern California path that ultimately eluded the Pacific Electric. Sinuous, at times breathtaking, the wholly uneconomical drive that awaits a navigator of Route 1 on any given morning—leaving the clamor of L.A. County and the somnolence of Ventura County for the brooding stretch of coastal cities just past Morro Bay—is a hairpin curve delectation, as it winds through the cliffs of Big Sur, Carmel, and Monterey, and gobbles up a good two hours of a trip that would be better served by the more judicious Highway 101, or the desert-bound Interstate 5.

The journey up Route 1 is but one of the many examples of the way the automobile has rewritten time. Races from southern California to northern California were a popular pastime in the state during the first two decades of the auto's invention. In 1910 it took a Cadillac 30-horsepower stock car approximately sixteen hours to make the five-hundred-mile journey between L.A. and San Francisco, in an expedition which encountered more than its share of delays and detours because of the piecemeal condition of the state's highways.[41] Reviser of spatial relationships historically shaped by fixed-path transit, the car reinvigorated the narrative of the American frontier. Thus "it was as a means to adventure, a symbol of speed, a conqueror of time and space that the automobile made its first...impact on southern California."[42]

As a conquest of time and space, the motorization of the United States precipitated the decline of the central city, foregrounding the profound bias against public space that animates American notions of national identity. The "evolution" of the city of L.A. is perhaps the foremost example of this bias. Though this example has been much reviled within contemporary postindustrial American social discourse, early American ideology on governance and city development foreshadow how sprawl is the corollary to the nation's frontier heritage. Indeed, "the growth of sprawl should not surprise us in a nation that sprawled across the continent, pushing back the wilderness well ahead of transportation technology, well ahead of government, well ahead of planning."[43] The emphasis upon "pushing the boundaries" of space informed early American visions of urban development, setting up a dichotomy between the city and the suburb which reflected the tensions between the Jeffersonian and Hamiltonian models of nationhood.[44] Within the trajectory of American social discourse, the city has been articulated through narratives of Otherness and crisis, narratives based on social Darwinist, essentialist notions of urban racial pathology. The evolution of whiteness in the postindustrial era exemplifies this dynamic. In the wake of the New Deal era, suburbanization and highway development embodied American national identity at its fullest potential. The city was framed as its double/Other. As the ancestral point and proving ground for the European immigrant, the city is part and parcel of a teleological relationship whereby American whiteness is constructed as being beyond race and racial identity. It was through their abandonment of the city that non-Anglo European immigrants gained inclusion into the category of American whiteness. At the turn of the century, when immigration from eastern and southern Europe had reached its peak, street railways were at the vanguard of suburban growth. The street railways forever altered the shape of the American city, foreshadowing the automobile's push to the hinterlands. Streetcar development set the stage for the economic, racial, and demographic shifts that accompanied the interstate era, articulating the psychic landscape of a bootstraps Americana indebted to the medium of the track tie.

CHAPTER TWO
Whiteness and the City

> Where the city is imagined as the nation's sibling and conceived as the white body's double, the concept of otherness becomes a racialized, alien intrusion, a difficult cultural virus...racialization cannot simply be collapsed into the temporality of the post-war experience. In this sense what might be described as the cultural problem of whiteness refers not only to the occlusion of its racialized history, but also where it insinuates and conceals itself discursively as the horizon of universal representation. It is a white mythology which has erased within itself the fabulous scene that produced it, the scene that nevertheless remains active and stirring, inscribed in white ink, an invisible design covered over in the palimpsest.[1]
>
> —Barnor Hesse (1997, 86)

When you make the final descent into L.A. at the end of a flight from the East Coast, it is impossible not to be struck, having fumbled from one pole of the nation to the other, by the city's schizoidness, a sense of grinding closure conveyed in one breath by its faux-Midwestern flatness and undone in the same breath by the ricochet run of the freeways. Approaching the airport at the end of one flight I pressed against the window in hopeful reconnaissance, searching for the spire of a movie theater in Inglewood, a suburb of Los Angeles and the city I grew up in. One of the few movies I vividly recall seeing there was *Blackula*, first run, part of the last wave of 1970s blaxploitation flicks. Flying overhead, I am there in the dark, holding my mother's hand, happily swallowed by the giant screen of the half-empty theater. The theater was converted into a church during the late seventies, and has since been designated a city landmark, even as the Main Street layout of the area that surrounds it suffered a decline in commercial development. With its jutting marquee, and ornate, dome-topped tower, the theater is a beauty, one of the few remaining in southern California that boasts the Art Deco design of the 1920s.

The theater is located on Manchester Avenue, one of the first streets I recall intimately, the first I rode the bus on alone—to school, to work, to the ocean, where the streetcars once ran as far north as Santa Monica, and as far south as Balboa, on the Pacific Coast Highway. My fear of and desire for the city came alive on Manchester, a wide thoroughfare that stretched past the tree-lined streets of my predominantly black middle-class community. Manchester was a time capsule, a summary of all the provincial and metropolitan yearnings of Los Angeles. It was part pedestrian village and auto derby, a four-laned wonder that saw Inglewood go from a white, restrictive covenant town to black Americana.

Circling down, I was somewhere in the crumbling, much-ridiculed downtown, the low occupancy office buildings, the gas stations, strip malls, and twenty-bucks-a-night motels that round out the occasional green space of Manchester. The decline of parts of Manchester and downtown Inglewood reflects the inequity of geocratic alignments of power and access. While it has become standard to speak of the way the automobile compresses time, it is equally important to remember that the flip-side of this geocratic contract of automobility is the expansion of time for bus riders who crowd the streets of downtown. Market Street, the main artery of downtown Inglewood, is a hub for service workers, school aides, students, domestics, and welfare-to-work municipal laborers who often must weave through byzantine bus connections to get to their jobs. It is estimated that 4 to 5 percent of all trips in the United States utilize public transportation. Out of that figure 60 percent of riders are women, and 48 percent are women of color.[2] Wending through the airport terminal to the parking lot after my flight is over, I await the pleasures of the car, the familiar insularity of the drive out Sepulveda Boulevard, newly widened to expressway size to accommodate more lanes by the airport. I navigate the flatness of the street, temporarily in control of my body, fleetingly aware of the illusion of safety that masks the unsafe space that the automobile provides for the black urban subject. Much of the black subject's southern "California dreamin'" has been done behind the wheel. From the modest suburbia of Inglewood, to the more toney enclaves of Baldwin Hills in Southwest L.A., black mobility has been forged in paradox, in the interstice of public/private. Driving L.A. is an enactment of this paradox. Freeways such as the 105 (which runs south of the airport) crisscross over the graves of communities that were uprooted decades before construction ever got under way. These communities were essentially forced to sacrifice their "patch" of the American Dream to make way for white exurban flight. The pleasure, desire, and discontent that autopia inspires in black urban subjects are woven within a system of spatial apartheid that has not only racialized the "inner-city," but retarded the growth of community by exacerbating the schism between the black working poor and the black middle class.

This schism is symptomatic of the black migrant's ambivalence toward the suburban ideal. Writing on the differences between the "black" urban imagination and that of Anglo America, Toni Morrison observes that black subjects "could not share what even the poorest white factory worker or white welfare recipient could feel: that in some way the city belonged to him."[3] For

Morrison, black "affection" for the city lay with the rhythms of its neighborhoods, in the village-like atmosphere that lent black migrants their sense of community. Thus, while Anglo American fear of the city was informed by a reverence for the individualism ostensibly conferred by rural life, the black migrant valued the city's potential for integration.[4] For black city dwellers during the Great Migration era, the rite of urban passage allowed them to experience the individualism that the white immigrant/migrant identified with the agrarian ideal.

The conflict between these two views of the city is reflected in the ways in which transportation technology has historically been conceived as a modernizing agent for the redemption of urban ethnic communities. As I am descending to the Los Angeles airport, driving the city of memory in my car, the ontological seductions of travel temporarily defuse the threat that "the city" does not belong to me. Remembering the dark movie theater, I cross from the streets of my first bus ride into autopia, where the black driver seeks an invisibility denied her by the devaluation of the city street. In Chapter 1 I argued that autopia represents an Arcadian retreat from the collective responsibilities of city life. Socialized to view public space as alien and threatening, citizens orient themselves around the private space of the car, the isolated pod of the nuclear family and the opiate of consumer culture. This is the American way. The resurgence of pedestrian-oriented designer shopping enclaves in Pasadena and Santa Monica notwithstanding, this model has been valorized as the fulfillment of Anglo American identity. As the most influential urban expression of the American conflation of private land ownership with individual liberty, L.A. reflects many key themes in the United States' invention of national identity. These themes include the redemption of the white immigrant, the fetishization of urban otherness (i.e., white suburbia under siege), and the reinvention of the frontier.

The Antiurban Tradition

The United States' investment in the auto industrial complex has had far-reaching implications for the environment, industrial policy, urban design, and racial geography. The auto's monopoly over the landscape of American cities has refigured the way the modern urban subject experiences time and space to such an extent that the train-centered ethos of Manhattan seems like a distant node in an alien galaxy. Circle over the airport of any major city in the country and it is clear that internal combustion strongly influences the language of the American body. At the beginning of the new millennium, there are few spaces forbidden to the car (an area in Yellowstone Park is purported to be the farthest in the country from automobile accessibility). Traveling to Manhattan from Brooklyn in New York, I stalk the subway platform with this knowledge; the L.A. native caught deer-in-the-headlights by the dog train, humid with rush-hour bodies huddled conspiratorially. While ridership on the New York subways has increased because of the implementation of the Metrocard option, the city's passenger advocacy organization, the Straphangers' Campaign, charges that the quality of service is at an all-time low. In many ways, the crawlspace of New York and the lunar sprawl of Los Angeles are parallel universes of the same ideology that argues for the modernizing agency of transportation technology. The subways of New York furthered industrial capital and forged "new" constructs of white subjectivity for European immigrants. L.A.'s autopia was written in the image of postindustrial capital, refining white subjectivity within the landscape of segregation.

Racial upheaval and the geography of the auto regime have come to represent Los Angeles's dystopian legacy for posturban development. These two themes have been sounded again and again as the primary factors responsible for the city's "undoing" since the civil unrest of 1992. The irony of L.A.'s dystopic image is the extent to which this vision conforms to early twentieth-century ideals of posturban development: staunchly antiurban, decentralized and decentered, assimilationist (for its white European immigrant communities), segregated for its older African, Latino, and Asian American communities and newer "third-world" immigrant communities. The struggle for the soul of American cities has been waged on the volatile front of transportation because mass transit has historically reflected the way the United States positions itself as a frontier society—a bulwark against otherness and an antidote to the European ideal of community.[5] This "old antagonistic relationship in our culture between city and country which transposes into the opposition between the individual and the group" has reached its zenith with the racialization of the inner-city.[6]

The genesis of this conflict between city and country can be seen in the opposition between the Jeffersonian ideal and the Hamiltonian ideal of the republic. Whereas Jefferson placed emphasis on the individual landholder's role in forming a public consensus based on agrarian values, Hamilton favored a "city-based republic" governed by market principles.[7] Although Hamilton's federalist view of strong government and urban cohesion has been rejected, his emphasis on the rights of the individual has been wedded with the Jeffersonian notion of the agrarian ideal.[8] As geographer David Harvey notes:

The Jeffersonian land system, with its repetitive mathematical grid that still dominates the landscape of the United States, likewise sought the rational partitioning of space so as to promote the formation of an agrarian democracy.[9]

This rational partitioning of space would come to be one of the defining features of modern American urban planning. Rationalization of space went hand in hand with the Enlightenment notion that history was teleological, "a record of...continuous progress."[10] However, while agrarian space was infinitely civilizable, urban space, with its intimation of otherness and difference, would prove to be more recalcitrant. The tension between the agrarian ideal and the city was expressed in early American ambivalence toward technology. In his work *The Machine in the Garden*, Leo Marx examines the seeming contradiction between the American cathexis upon the agrarian ideal and the march to progress symbolized by modern technology.[11] According to Marx, this contradiction was articulated most evocatively with the coming of the railroad.[12] Although the railroad was initially viewed as a betrayal of the Jeffersonian ideal by such writers as Ralph Waldo Emerson, it was ultimately used as a metaphor for the construction of American national identity during the industrial revolution.[13] As Marx notes, the industrial revolution was characterized as a "railway journey in the direction of nature."[14] Ironically, it wasn't the vitality and dynamism of the city that railroad technology affirmed, but that of the countryside.

The redemptive presence of the machine in the garden has always been the paradox of American antiurbanism. Despite the colossal ecological footprint made by the thousands of miles of concrete that form the connective tissue of communities nationwide, we drive the highway "in the direction of nature" to suburban subdivisions, malls, and resorts redolent with the trappings of a vanquished pastoralism. West Hills Mall, Briarwood, Raintree. In Los Angeles County the signposts of faux pastoralism provide a lexicon for the way we experience the road. Our schizoid, nostalgic relationship to the Jeffersonian vision of home, hearth, and male sovereignty infects all of our dreams of what is possible in the city.

Envisioning Whiteness

Where did the conflation of inner-city with blackness and otherness begin? By now it is common to hear suburbanized communities that are predominantly African American referred to as the inner-city. For example, in a *New York Times* magazine article published in the year 2000 on the entrepreneurial ventures of Magic Johnson, the wealthy enclave of Ladera Heights was referred to as South Central despite being west of La Cienega Boulevard (the unofficial line of demarcation for westside status), a stone's throw from the L.A. Airport and having a number of white homeowners.

American whiteness emerges from this nexus of race and geography. Symbolically, the defining feature of American whiteness, its ontological force, is its capacity to *disappear* as a site of racial difference, to, in essence, go beyond the category and *confines* of race. Throughout this book I use the terms *ontology* and *ontological* in the senses in which these terms are deployed in Heidegger's works on "being" and "temporality." In this context ontology refers to that movement that attempts to divine or determine the substance of being. Heidegger has linked the meaning of being to presence, specifically to the "there is-ness" of a particular phenomenon or thing.[15] In this view subjects can never fully attain pure presence. Subjectivity hinges on suspension—being betwixt and between absence and presence. Being articulates the simultaneity of past and future tense, such that it "is its past in the manner of its being which...actually 'occurs' out of its future."[16] In this respect, the assumed linearity of being (the idea that we progress seamlessly from birth to death), as well as that of self-presence, is an illusion. Because the subject can never be fully present, it always exists in a state of transit. For Heidegger, the enigma of time (or temporality) is at the core of the meaning of being. Considerations of time are intimately bound up with place.[17]

In the United States, where notions of whiteness are inflected through the opposition of the fixed category of blackness, and the dynamic category of the immigrant, race has been inscribed as a temporal category. A space of subjection, danger, and otherness (or, as bell hooks has termed it, the "outer limit of outness"), blackness is conceived as alternately static and dynamic, frozen in time and stylistically mobile, both beyond and within the pale of western civilization.[18] From the colonial period to the present, blackness has been constructed as the ultimate site of difference, symbol of an elusive essence of being that confirmed the humanity and civilized status of the first wave of British colonists in the sixteenth century. Within this view blackness was framed as existing *outside of time*. Stripped of their own histories, African Americans existed as an adjunct to a European history that was written through the lens of racial otherness.[19] Blackness enables whiteness to become visible as a racial category. The dialectical relationship between whiteness and blackness allows whiteness qua whiteness to masquerade as the standard for humanity, normality, and universal moral and cultural values.[20]

It is in this sense that the category of race operates in a manner akin to metaphor. Metaphor disturbs the mimetic relationship between the object of reference and its ostensible meaning. In other words the things or objects that metaphors describe are not complete in their beingness before a metaphor is used to illuminate their meaning. When Carl Sandburg wrote that the "fog comes in on little cat feet," he provided the reader with a means of imagining the fog by using a superficially incongruous symbol. Sandburg's allusion suggests that the unique qualities of fog come into focus through the proxy of the cat's feet. The dislocations of metaphor allow us to construct meaning by forcing a correspondence between one thing and another thing that is wholly different. By calling the beingness of the referent into question and disrupting its claim to self-presence, metaphor is a path of transit that brings to light the spatial and temporal aspects of meaning.[21]

We live in metaphors that spatialize race and racialize space. The terms *ghetto*, *barrio*, *inner-city*, *suburb*, and *outpost* all serve as shorthand for race, marking otherness, providing a context for inclusion and exclusion, and rendering the social practices of certain communities transparent. In my classes when we discuss the way race is inflected through the discourse of space in the United States I frequently ask my students if they've ever heard of the phrase "black suburban." Their perplexed looks speak volumes about the extent to which the ethnic invisibility of Anglo American identity structures public and private space in the United States

Understanding how whiteness came to stand in for humanity is the key to divining how the dialectic of slavery and freedom, plutocracy and democracy, flows within the bloodstream of American culture. The term *white ethnic*, used frequently to designate Irish, Italian, and Jewish whites, somehow becomes oxymoronic when used in reference to Anglo Americans. The ethnicity of Anglo Americans is the paradox lurking within the rhetoric of liberal democracy and first-world citizenship. For Anglo American ethnicity undergirds all of the hallmarks of civilization that ostensibly shape the way we experience what it is to be authentically American.

This theme of white invisibility and the social construction of space is powerfully reflected in the cultural representation of crime. Since the 1990s some of the most sensationally publicized tabloid crimes have all been filtered through the lens of domestic tragedy and redemption. From the young mass murderers at Columbine High School to the so-called American Taliban fighter in the war against Afghanistan, white suburbia is ritually absolved of responsibility for the pathologies of its "troubled" offspring. Some would argue that class is a compelling influence upon how such crimes are viewed in the dominant culture. According to this view white working-class killers are viewed more harshly than those from privileged backgrounds. Yet the tenor of forgiveness and rebuke that informed public perception of highly publicized cases of South Carolina mother Susan Smith and Texas mother of five Pamela

Yates—poor white women who killed their children—highlight how white privilege supercedes class, defanging even the most socially repugnant crime. In the ensuing furor over the murders, both of these women became symbols of beleaguered womanhood—a position that has historically not been available to black women charged with similar crimes.

These examples are not mere testimony to the inveterate racism of the criminal justice system but to the racialization of space. The specter of intractable inner-city criminality influences the way that "white crimes" are framed. This is in part due to the legacy of ethnic invisibility that cleaves to American whiteness. The dialectic of blighted inner-city and imperiled suburb ghosts within the nation's psychological and emotional investment in crime. Here, the fantasy of the criminal Other is just as much a part of the fabric of urban development as highways, sidewalks, and buildings.

Urban cities provide some of the most viscerally potent metaphors for the racialization of space. For blackness and whiteness are locations within which the performance of nationhood and national identity are endlessly staged. The hyper-embodiment of blackness as *the* site of racial difference allows the racial and ethnic specificity of whiteness to go unmarked. As a racial category, blackness is both a prescribed and fixed location in time as well as a voluble source of unharnessed vitality. Conversely, whiteness is ontologically mobile, able to assume guises and identities without the burdens of racial embodiment. In this respect, whiteness dissimulates itself into the greater body of power/knowledge as the universal subject of American social history. Through the edifice of the Other, whiteness transits into the position of racial *in-difference*. Within the history of the American city, this dynamic of transiting has played a large role in the construction of the non-Anglo European immigrant and the figure of the Anglo American at the frontier of national identity.

In her critique *Whiteness and the Literary Imagination*, Toni Morrison argues that "a dark, abiding signing Africanist presence" has informed the metaphoric, poetic, and symbolic aspects of America's literary heritage.[22] In an evocative reading of America's literary imagination, Morrison holds that the conjuring and projection of this "Africanist presence" has been the driving force in "the highly problematic construction of the American as the new white man":

> As a metaphor for transacting the whole process of Americanization, while burying its particular racial ingredients, this Africanist presence may be something the United States cannot do without. Deep within the word "American" is its association with race...Americans did not have a profligate, predatory nobility from which to wrest an identity of national virtue while continuing to covet aristocratic license and luxury. The

> American nation negotiated both its disdain and its envy...through a self-reflexive contemplation of fabricated, mythological Africanism.[23]

This Africanist presence was a space in which the dread, desire, and moral yearnings of the nation were exorcized. The ideal of sovereignty embodied within American nationhood would not have been complete without the dialectic of slavery and freedom. In dedicating the new republic to the ethos of individualism, to the citizen's right to remain free from the purview of the state in matters of commerce and civil liberty, the framers placed this paradox at the very heart of American national identity. The black slave's status as captive/ private property/ward provided a locus from which white citizenship could define and *affirm* itself.[24] The non-personhood of the enslaved black body acted as a signifier of race itself, a signifier of race as excess. In this sense, the enslaved black body, as racial "surplus"/pure presence, was staged in opposition to the racially unmarked, or "unraced," body of the free white worker upon whom the ideal of American citizenship was based.[25]

In the literary imagination of "young America," the Africanist presence was obliquely used to pose all of the burning moral, philosophical, sexual, and existential questions of the late colonial and revolutionary age.[26] The Africanist presence was a backdrop upon which the birth pangs of the nation could be projected. In this respect, the figure of the black slave became a "serviceable" point of reference for the articulation of an American whiteness masquerading as the universal standard for human consciousness.[27]

Hence, the paradox of American democracy, the "presence of the unfree within the heart of the democratic experiment," has always been subsumed within the invisibility of whiteness.[28] The specter of the white worker's body, its non-slave status, anchors the ostensibly "race neutral" language of republicanism that informs the spirit of the Constitution.[29] As David Roediger observes in the *The Wages of Whiteness,* the "revolutionary ethic" codified in the Constitution held that blacks were "the antithesis of republican citizens" due to their "slavish dispositions."[30] In this view, "the innate strength and ingenuity of a people protected them from enslavement"; therefore, the black slave was naturally indisposed to the very concept of freedom.[31] In the period after the Revolutionary War, when the new republic grappled with the vestiges of its colonial relationship with the British empire, a seminal brew of racism and republicanism begat the free white worker as cornerstone of American citizenship.[32] The ability of whiteness to transgress boundaries of time and body, to *fix*, as it were, the enslaved black body as the outer limit of "being," defined, validated, and affirmed the white subject's inalienable right to freedom.

"America," then, cannot be envisioned without the resonance of race: race as a mode of transit and fixity, as temporal marker and symbol of passage. The brutal genius and perversity of the United States lies in the fact that the source of its democratic ethos sprung from the violent denial of human and civil rights to Americans of color. In looking at the way turn-of-the-century city planning discourse and sociological narrative influenced the construction of the city as "raced" space, it is critical to recognize how the paradox of American democracy reinforced the passage of the non-Anglo white immigrant from "city dweller" to "citizen."[33] What spatial mechanisms facilitated this rite of passage? How did the descendants of Anglo indentured servants, German menial laborers, and Irish domestics become unraced, transformed into de facto Anglo Americans, who, according to popular American lore, "pulled themselves up by their bootstraps" despite class barriers? Finally, how does this lore inform the cultural geography of L.A., where there are no demographically significant enclaves of western European white "ethnics"?

In the collective memory of American culture, the spatial layout of the working-class white neighborhoods that formed the backbone of bootstraps white immigrant mythology is almost uniformly urban—row houses with bustling sidewalks and congested streets in which the close proximity of families imposed a certain degree of intimacy. This vision of spatiality powerfully informs the evolutionary stereotype that clings to the history of the migration of whites from city to suburb. According to this view the single-family detached home in the suburbs is the most highly evolved form of American living space. However, even in communities where virtually all of the more prosperous relatives of working-class whites have fled to the suburbs, vestiges of the old folkways remain, embedded within the collective memory of formerly white neighborhoods like the south side of Chicago or Flatbush in Brooklyn.

The line of ethnic succession in American neighborhoods is part of the myth of upward mobility that informs our national heritage. Yet, Los Angeles's drive to will itself into becoming a major city bespoke a new form of self-realizing whiteness uniquely suited to the challenges of twenty-first-century manifest destiny and postindustrial capitalism. As Kevin Starr notes, early L.A.

> deliberately fashioned [its] identity in this era as an Anglo American colony on the Pacific Rim. Although the L.A. of today is a polyglot, polycultural world city, its controlling oligarchy in the early twentieth century...considered L.A. the latest and most promising English-speaking city on the planet and placed special emphasis on its Anglo heritage.[34]

As the native-born white American community of L.A. swelled after World War I, land speculation, boosterism, and transportation politics emerged as the driving forces of the region. Development became L.A.'s biggest growth industry. Whereas L.A. was envisioned as the "democratic" alternative to the unruly roil of such urban icons as New York, the city's premium on private space, single-family housing, and racial segregation was a precedent-setting example of the profound hostility to democratic urban living that emerged in the postwar era. As Thomas Angotti observes on the elevation of the American Dream house within city planning:

> Although there is no official national urban policy, national, social, fiscal and infrastructure policies combine to promote this dream. Suburban growth and its counterpart, downtown renewal, are premised on the maintenance and reinforcement of inequalities between central city and suburbs...based on differences of race and class.[35]

The spatial development of L.A. and New York exemplify different aspects of this trajectory. In the case of New York, the city developed a well-maintained and widely used public transportation system to disperse key segments of its population to the suburbs while simultaneously maintaining a strong central business district. In southern California, Los Angeles's public transportation system accelerated suburbanization, which was in turn nourished by the region's cathexis upon the automobile. Suburbanization ultimately sounded the death knell for the city's central business district. The persistence of classic American, central city–oriented urbanism in New York owes much to the radial pattern of the New York city subway, and its reinforcement of the high-rise architecture and densely populated development that marked the city's rise as a financial center.

However, nurtured in the anti-immigrant, rationalist rhetoric of city planners and local government, antiurbanism also figured strongly in "port of entry" New York. This drive for rationality in urban space emerged from "post-Civil War turmoil, when reformers worried how to discipline and regulate the urban masses and how to control and arrange the spatial growth of cities."[36] Flowing from this tradition, antiurbanism had a profound influence on the formation of white identity during the New Deal, World War II, and postwar eras. It was during these periods that the city was framed as "Other," alien to the ideal of the American Dream.

The association of blackness with the moral and social decay of the city was part and parcel of the emergence of the welfare state. Filling in the gaps where the private sphere left off, the state's provision of social services for housing, transportation, education, and health care, influenced mainstream perception of the public sphere as a de facto welfare state.[37] As European immigrants began moving away from the central cities, pulling themselves up by their bootstraps with the aid of New Deal social welfare programs, the image of "the city" was increasingly linked to the specter of racial otherness.[38] Within the constituting fiction of U.S national identity, the city has been figured first as immigrant way station, and finally as "black" outpost.[39]

As the first truly posturban metropolis, Los Angeles was not only conceived in opposition to the idea of the centered city, but was envisioned as the logical destination of an evolving white Anglo-Saxon cultural hegemony. The seemingly pell-mell structure of L.A. expressed the defiance of boundary critical to the articulation of whiteness. The gradual assimilation of inner-city European immigrants in eastern cities such as New York and Boston was in part dependent upon their gaining full access to private space. Joining labor unions, moving from the inner cities to the suburbs, white European immigrants acquired the privileges of white citizenship by capitalizing upon the "racialization" of public and private space.

The "problem" of the unassimilated immigrant figured largely in social reformers' perceptions of the city as intractable. The city and the immigrant were a space of crisis terminally at odds with the United States' vision of liberal democracy. Thus, within the Anglo middle-class lens of the planning establishment, the specter of urban crowding, pollution, and substandard housing was not only a grave indictment of the ills of the industrial era, but an insidious threat to the nation's progress. Here, the language of city planning resounded with themes of chaos, reform, and redemption. The scourge of immigrant culture, embodied by the intractable city, could only be neutralized through the "Americanization" of the immigrant.[40] The association of the very structure of the city with the presumably inherent degeneracy of immigrant culture reverberated throughout urban sociology during the Great Migration period.

Long viewed by urban planners as the source of anomie and low moral values, the central city was often portrayed as a barrier to immigrant assimilation.[41] Planners' anxiety over the corrupting influence of the city was manifest in turn-of-the-century housing policy. Assimilation of immigrants into American society was one of the linchpins of housing reform and city planning.[42] In keeping with the Jeffersonian ideal of antiurbanism, early social reformers extolled the virtues of suburban living. As a compromise between the agrarian and the urban, the suburb would ideally "enable Americans to pursue wealth and retain the amenities and values of rural life."[43] Ironically, up until the development of manufacturing during the late 1800s, the elite lived in the urban core, while the poor and working classes lived on the outskirts of the city.[44]

While the advent of the omnibus and the steam railway facilitated suburban settlement for a small minority of urban dwellers, it was the advent of the electric railway that made the vision of urban dispersal possible.⁴⁵ Indeed, the streetcar was viewed by many planners as a "moral influence" that could alleviate the "evils of urban life."⁴⁶

Thus, the push for better housing for white immigrants in turn-of-the-century planning was furthered by the advent of electric rail. For the turn-of-the-century urban dweller, the extension of streetcar lines into the periphery of the city presented an opportunity to retreat from the overly ethnic trappings of urban life:

> Residents of eastern cities welcomed the almost simultaneous introduction in the 1840s of horse-drawn trolleys and steam railroads, not only for the speed and comfort they added to commuting, but because they encouraged the beginning of residential decentralization on a very modest scale. The city dweller of 1880 may have dreamed vaguely of a small frame house in the suburbs with a garden and white picket fence, but day-to-day reality was his struggle for survival in the inner-city. For the working class urbanite, physical mobility meant escaping from poverty and perhaps other ethnic groups; his horizon often stretched only as far as new neighborhoods a few blocks away.⁴⁷

Broadening the horizons of inner-city dwellers, the streetcar was integral to neutralizing the problem of European immigrants, helping them achieve a level of "Anglo conformity" which would have been inconceivable in the densely populated, ethnically insurgent city.⁴⁸

Moreover, the anticity/antiurban bias of turn-of-the-century city planning reflected deeper anxieties over the sociopolitical dislocations and ostensibly radical tendencies of the immigrant population.⁴⁹ The influence of these anxieties was starkly illustrated by the tenor of pre–World War I housing policy. Housing policy of this period focused on redeeming white immigrants from the presumed ills of tenement living, thereby "bringing the slums and their residents into a constructive, predictable and safe relationship with the rest of society."⁵⁰

The relentlessly assimilationist agenda of early city planning was to find its most powerful agent in the land speculation enterprises of the street railway companies. Privately owned, adhering to the monopolistic precedent that the steam railroads had set during the nineteenth century, the railways were the first true architects of suburban America. Redefining the frontier psychology of a postindustrial United States, the incursions of the railways laid the groundwork for the mammoth federal highway projects that would ironically doom the streetcar industry to extinction. The paradox of the railways—the failure of private enterprise to adequately provide for public service *and* realize a profit within the context of the market economy—highlights the egregiousness of the anti-government rush-to-privatize zeitgeist that infected contemporary political rhetoric before the attacks of September 11. Whereas mass motorization reflected the federal government's careful cultivation of its relationship with the "auto-oil and rubber nexus" (via highway legislation and funding), privately managed public transportation became more and more problematic in the period after the Depression. The streetcars ultimately threatened the decentralization of the new American city, conflicting with the delicate process of the expansion of Anglo American subjectivity.[51] Despite providing extensions to outlying cities, the radial course that most streetcar systems adhered to was ultimately deemed incompatible with the rise of satellite communities that were rapidly usurping the central business district by developing their own commercial centers.[52]

The growth of these satellite communities, and the singular pursuit of suburbanization at the expense of urban renewal, would have far-reaching implications for the trajectory of race and ethnicity in the United States Furthered by federal programs offering affordable home mortgages and subsidies for road and highway improvements, the suburbanization of America reinscribed the dichotomy between public and private space in the United States with a vengeance.

The city was a symbol of the white European immigrant's nineteenth-century past. It became a crucible for white "ethnic" communities traditionally viewed as intransigent to the Anglo American ethos of individualism. In New York City this dynamic was manifested in city planning and transportation policy designed to diffuse the concentration of white immigrant enclaves in downtown communities. Following in the path of electric streetcars, the New York City subway system spearheaded the push to the suburbs. Public transportation in Los Angeles refined the imperial destiny of Anglo American settlers, reinscribing the telos of a surpassing whiteness. Mass transit of New York acted as a transitional, near-redemptive force in the European immigrant's passage from ethnic/racial difference to the unraced category of white citizen.

The theme of chaos, reform, and redemption that runs through early city planning discourse foregrounds the teleological nature of Anglo American visions of the city. These themes mirror the obsession with destiny and transcendence that undergirds American conceptions of nationhood. As a breeding ground for "un-American" values, the social decay of the city was viewed as a scourge upon American domestic expansion. Indeed, one early twentieth-century reformer bombastically opined that the urban core was "destined to become the graveyard of the human race."[53] In this respect, the narrative of early city planning underlined the pitfalls of industrialism while simultaneously holding up the ideal of the preindustrial small town, uncontaminated by the "problem" of class stratification or ethnicity.

Pathological and forbidding, the city was viewed as "an artificial way of life" morally desolated by the blight of tenement housing.[54]

At the turn of the century, the most prominent trends in city planning were the "City Beautiful" movement and the "City Practical" movement.[55] Influenced by the Columbian Exposition in Chicago in 1893 and the World's Fair in St. Louis in 1904, the City Beautiful movement focused on the aestheticization of the city rather than the more pressing needs of housing and social services, promoting instead the erection of public monuments, plazas, and parks.[56] Foreshadowing the displacement of inner-city residents for highways during the interstate era, some of the City Beautiful projects were erected after extensive slum clearance that made no provisions for the displaced.[57] Deemed ineffectual and aristocratic by many planners, who were disturbed by its neglect of the inner-city housing crisis, City Beautiful had little impact on the urban landscape.[58]

The City Practical movement was a response to the limitations of the City Beautiful movement. Whereas the City Beautiful movement took an almost genteel and puritanical approach to the city, extolling the virtues of beautification as a means of uplift for the urban dweller, City Practical set its sights squarely on the market. City Practical advocates proposed a more technocratic approach to city planning, seeking to reinforce the relationship between business, property owners, and municipal government.[59] Although initially more engaged with improving housing conditions than City Beautiful, City Practical became preoccupied with the business community's demand for "efficiency" and "competence" in urban development.[60] Accordingly, City Practical advocates like New York planner George Ford sought to tailor housing policy to the concerns of the business community.[61] Deeply critical of City Beautiful's fixation on "frills and furbelows" in a social climate in which "the hideous slum, reeking with filth and disease" was allowed to thrive, Ford's righteous indignation over urban living conditions wavered in the face of businesses' increasing demand for accountability from city planners.[62] As a result, planning of the pre–World War I period became mired in the discourse of statistics and cost analysis—privileging the needs of landlords and developers.

The ultimate ineffectiveness of these trends in city planning was indicative of the deeper crisis of vision and authority that would continue to haunt the profession. The primacy of the market economy, and the tremendous influence that land speculation had on the growth of the early American city, reinforced the dominance of private developers and landlords. As a result, urban planners' influence was severely limited.[63] Whereas city planning was crucial to the development of the modern European city, in the United States, the prevailing emphasis on the protection of private property and the rights and prerogatives of landlords and corporate landholding interests ensured that American city planning would always be a handmaiden to private enterprise.[64] Emerging from the spirit of reform that fueled the progressive era of late nineteenth and early twentieth century American politics, city planning essentially mediated the demands of private enterprise and local government.[65] Beholden to the dictates of the market, the planning profession in the United States assumed a largely titular role after World War I, sucked into the postwar push for suburbanization.

In his analysis *The Urban Wilderness*, historian Sam Bass Warner links the failure of city planning in the United States to the legacy of seventeenth-century land law.[66] In Warner's view, planning's failure to advocate for affordable housing or livable urban public space can be traced back to the association of private property with civil liberty:

> Despite the best efforts of generations of reformers who have attempted to work without disturbing the basic relationships of private property within our tradition of land law and land management, the American city is the inhumane place it is because we cling to the formulations of the seventeenth century and the myths of a society of small proprietors.[67]

The segregation of public from private space implicit in "the myths of a society of small proprietors" is informed by the association of white citizenship with the inalienable right to private property. The colonists' belief in the sanctity of this right, as embodied in the Revolutionary War, impresses its ancestry upon the very architecture of suburban America. The suburb has become the ur-space of American "civilization," the avatar of white modernity. The turn-of-the-century conflation of non-Anglo whites with a degraded public sphere foreshadowed the association of the postwar city with a telos of race and racial embodiment. Here, the dissimulation of American whiteness in the city was forever interfaced with the fixity of American blackness. Crossing frontiers of body, space, and time, the transiting of non-Anglo white immigrants in the American city is inscribed within the alienation of public from private space.

Thus, the non-Anglo white immigrant's passage from urban scourge to suburban Horatio Alger has a dialectical relationship to the generations-long conveyance of black migrants to the "inner city." Whereas inner-city white immigrant communities were the targets of intense Americanization campaigns, the black Southern migrants that gradually took their place in Northern cities from 1915 to the World War II era were considered to be beyond the pale of American values. In the fever pitch of welfare reform and the anti-affirmation action movement, there is a savage irony to these early twentieth-century Americanization efforts. The ostensible failure of African Americans to seize upon the twin privileges of bourgeois democracy and laissez faire has become the mantra of conservative urban sociology. Invidious comparisons between the abject state of the black community and the relative prosperity of immigrants who "came here with nothing" fuel the myth of bootstraps Americana. When expounding on the downward spiral of the inner-city, the work of contemporary social critics invokes the specter of an irredeemable black inner-city landscape. One of the most influential examples of this tradition was Daniel Patrick Moynihan's 1965 Labor Department study on "The Problem of the Negro Family." Moynihan suggested that black social dysfunction lay within a pathological family structure in which women had usurped traditional male leadership.[68] This thesis, so commonplace in antiwelfare screeds, insidiously ascribes the crisis of the inner-city to black America's failure to prosper from the largesse of the federal government. According to this thesis, the institution of public housing, welfare, and Head Start effectively stymied black acquisition of American values by fostering a vicious cycle of dependency. This argument suggests that there is no more compelling example of the social bankruptcy of the public sphere than the specter of inner-city black poverty.

In this view, black pathology and urban blight are soldered together in a narrative whose perpetual subtext is the trajectory of the white immigrant. Here, the immigrant's crucible of poverty, assimilation, and escape from the inner-city is the true testament of American nationhood. By shedding cultural and ethnic difference, white immigrants attained their "American-ness" (i.e., their whiteness), laid claim to the spoils of bourgeois democracy, and emerged as full citizens. In this sense the material and ontological transiting of the white immigrant was a passage to racial invisibility.

Rites of Passage

While turn-of-the-century L.A. embodied all of the manifest destiny–driven dislocations of Anglo American heritage, turn-of-the-century New York was a premier site for the non-Anglo white immigrant's introduction to the privileges of that heritage. In 1905, the Pacific Electric Railway became a major player in the economy of southern California, with the opening of hotly anticipated lines in Long Beach and Pasadena. Much of the Pacific Electric was built by Mexican immigrants, some of whom were descended from the railroad workers who helped build the Southern Pacific and Santa Fe railroads in the nineteenth century.[69] Other workers were part of a recruitment effort made by the railways during the reign of Porfirio Diaz, which was a particularly tumultuous period in Mexico's political history. Many of these workers were seduced by the promise of double the wages that they made in Mexico.[70] For a ten-hour workday,

Mexican track laborers laid tracks and did landscaping at the stations at a rate of $1.50 to $1.75, far lower than the industry standard.[71] Thus, the railways continued the legacy of the railroads (who had exploited the labor of Chinese immigrants) by exploiting cheap Mexican labor. Mexican railway workers were housed in work camps under atrocious conditions in housing units that they were also required to pay for.[72] The xenophobic climate of the era spurred a chorus of dissent from whites who feared immigrant labor would take jobs away from "native" workers.[73]

Citizen protests about conditions at the camps eventually led the railway to make improvements.[74] Thereafter, true to American form, the company cast itself as redeemer of the laborers' slovenly, immigrant ways. Conveniently editing out the history of squalor in the Pacific Electric's labor camps during the 1920s, a 1927 article in the *Pacific Electric Magazine* saw fit to proclaim that "the big task of the Pacific Electric was to educate these immigrants in cleanliness and right living."[75]

Yet, as per the late twentieth century, where multinationals exploit cheap, "third world" labor (even as the rhetoric of preserving the integrity of the American worker fuels public policy), the use of unskilled Mexican, Chinese, and African American labor by southern California businesses was the engine of growth for the fledgling city. This reality collided with the aggressive anti-urbanism of the white Midwestern transplant community, for whom immigrants and people of color represented all the odious disarray of an urban landscape against which southern California stood as an oasis.[76]

Consistent with other violent ironies of American enterprise and growth, the very firmament of white suburban comfort and the democratic ideal rested upon an available supply of cheap labor—labor which was exiled to an older, urban core that became a tax base for the development of the suburban hinterlands. Thus, the transportation palimpsest of the region was shaped by the labor and segregation of workers who were deemed to be beyond the pale of the region's ethos of the "good life." While Mexican workers dwelled in cramped labor camps with several families to a rental house, white Midwestern migrants were creating the first golden colonies of the single-family dwelling. By 1920, Pasadena, one of the first communities to have a trolley line, boasted a population of 45,354 and gradually grew into the preserve of old money southern California. Similarly, Long Beach, the first city to have a Pacific Electric line in 1901, reached a population of 55,593 by the 1920s and blossomed into one of the most prominent suburbs of the South Bay region of Los Angeles. These communities became the cynosure of the white notion of the "good life," mining the "Main Street, USA" cadences of an "existence that is led, half actually, half imaginatively, in Shelby, Indiana." [77]

While Los Angeles used immigrant railway labor to invent its mythos of white Arcadian plenitude, the opening of the first leg of the New York Subway system in 1904 evoked other narratives of white mobility. With the majority of the island's population living south of Twentieth Street, and the bulk of upper Manhattan largely undeveloped and unpopulated, the advent of the subway system ushered in a new era of embodiment and public space.[78] Echoing P.E. magnate Henry Huntington (who, in 1901, proclaimed the railway "the finest road in the world"), underground railway founder Abraham Hewitt declared that the subway would confirm New York's "imperial destiny as the greatest city in the world."[79] Indeed, soon after the subway opened, Hewitt's design was given the imprimatur of officials of the oldest fixed rail system in the world—riding the rails in this new regime of the underground at speeds of over forty miles per hour a British transit expert pronounced it "more technologically advanced than London's."[80]

Central to this early symbol of the United States' eclipse of its colonial forebear was a narrative of public/private in which the moving of bodies became a means of reconfiguring the "crisis" of the urban immigrant presence. Ruled by the logic of suspension, detour, disconnection, and disappearance, the "new underground" advanced the vision of New York as a boundless metropolis, dispersing inner-city residents to the outer boroughs and thus neutralizing the "problem" of the unassimilated immigrant. Privately owned yet publicly operated, the subway system, as the electric railway had before it, delivered its brand of public service with laissez-faire capitalism.

The institution of the subway illustrates the extent to which capitalist modernization facilitated the non-Anglo European immigrants' transition to unraced status. By contributing to the diffusion of close-knit white ethnic communities south of Twentieth Street in downtown Manhattan, the transit system facilitated white access to a level of class mobility the inner-city could not afford. Indeed, the contrast between the inner-city tenure of European immigrants during the late nineteenth and early twentieth century, and that of black migrants during the postwar years, offers a compelling illustration of the malleability of American whiteness. Free of the endemic job discrimination and segregation that impeded black migrants, European immigrants were able to achieve upward mobility and enjoy the "fruits" of democratic citizenship denied to native Americans of color. As Sam Bass Warner notes, "The historical process of urbanization (followed by European immigrants) where newcomers advanced through better jobs or accumulation of property was denied to blacks."[81] As a result, black urban areas "were very far from being 'ports of entry,' stopping places for the first years or the first generation, as twentieth century Italian slums had been."[82]

In the New York of the newly minted subway, the formation of the TWU in 1934 provides a compelling example of how trade unionism enabled white European immigrants to gain access to bourgeois democracy. At the height of the American labor movement during the 1930s and 1940s trade unionism was a linchpin for white immigrant class mobility. As an industry that relied heavily on white immigrant and African, Asian, and Latino labor, mass transit was paradigmatic of the demographic shifts the American city would experience as the era of mass suburbanization got underway.

An often unwieldy alliance between Irish immigrants and the Communist Party, the Transport Workers Union (TWU) was the first non-company union in a labor-intensive industry where wages accounted for 68 [ercemt of operational costs and employees worked an average of sixty hours a week. Employer to large numbers of older and more recent Irish immigrants, the New York transit system was a microcosm of early twentieth-century hierarchies among white "ethnic" immigrants, immigrants of color, and African Americans.[83] For example, in the Brooklyn Manhattan Transit (BMT) system, track workers were primarily Italian, while Scots worked largely in skilled signalmen positions, and heavy maintenance work was reserved for West Indians and Irish.[84] Although a somewhat less rigid pattern of representation obtained amongst white employees in the Interborough Rapid Transit (IRT) system, the common denominator for stratification was a nexus of race, language, and class.[85]

Thus, the formation of the TWU within the then independently managed IRT and BMT systems represented a departure from the historically fractious relationship between transit employees and labor unions. The history of the union is a study in the uneasy kinship between the politics of ethnic identity and radical reform. As a symbol of the trajectory of Irish American community identity, the early TWU's struggle to adopt Communist principles of unionization within an "autocratic" corporate-managed industry steadfastly opposed to *legitimate* unionization was a watershed in New York transit history.[86] Noting the differences between the successful unionization of the garment industry during the same period that transit unionism sputtered and failed, Joshua Freeman observes:

> In some industries, like garment...companies were typically small, underfinanced and engaged in vicious market competition. Some employers were willing to make an accommodation with unions in order to rationalize the industry, achieve labor stability...the transit industry, by contrast, was dominated by a few powerful corporations. Their monopoly status, combined with income flows limited by an all-but-fixed fare, focused their concern on keeping down wages. Transit managers believed that company unions, paternal benefit programs...enabled them to do this, and they were willing to marshal their considerable financial and political resources to stop unionization.[87]

Moreover, with its high volume of unskilled positions, the transit industry was a magnet for both newly arrived European immigrants and the recently unemployed. As a result, "the presence of a classic reserve army of labor sometimes literally at the door" was a strong deterrent to a push for higher wages and better working conditions.[88]

Thus, immigrant labor was the backbone of an industry reliant upon a work force that would be "reliable and controllable, even under conditions of intense exploitation."[89] This dynamic demands further analysis vis-à-vis the construction and performance of community within the context of transit politics, as well as the paradox of community and identity that the subway contributed to authoring.

As I have already suggested, the rise of postindustrial modernization brought about less hierarchical, more inclusive constructs of whiteness and white identity that were inscribed through the narrative agency of mass transit. While the TWU's volatile coalition of European immigrants helped transform the transit industry from within, the vision of urban dispersal furthered by the interborough subway commute transformed the coalition's ethnic solidarity and identification from without.[90]

In the view of progressive reformers, "the Lower East Side, Hell's Kitchen (et al.)...amounted to foreign colonies that encouraged newcomers to cling to their native languages, religions and folkways rather than assimilating with American culture."[91] By moving significant numbers of these populations into outlying areas such as Washington Heights and the Bronx, the subway allowed white immigrants to participate in the Main Street USA. mythology that has been so primary to the construction of Anglo American national identity. While the two- and three- family homes of the outer boroughs of New York were a far cry from the grid-of-plenty comforts of the detached, postage stamp–sized gardens and homes of postwar Levittown, they were the first step on the rung of the ladder to suburban redemption.

In this respect, the subway system helped reinforce the perception of New York's outer boroughs as safe havens "embodying the small town ideal: clean...prosperous and conducive to voting, home ownership and acculturation."[92] Here, the effacement of distinct ethnic and cultural practices—within the context of a *defining* concept or identification of ethnic self and identity—contributed to the articulation of white (ethnic) identity as signifier of private space. By encouraging segregation, the subway reinforced the inscription of the public as Other. Yet by providing a model for viable mass transit for over ninety years, the subway has helped keep public space alive in the urban United States In post-subway New York, as in the United States as a whole, the public signifies a blue collar subjectivity resistant to assimilation. Unassimilable, the public is hence evocative of an ethnic identity that stands in high relief to the invisibility of American whiteness qua whiteness. Urban reformers' emphasis upon moving immigrants away from "the center" was thus symbolic of the betwixt- and-between status that immigrant communities occupied vis-à-vis the notion of whiteness as unraced space.[93]

In looking at the "transiting" of the white immigrant in the city, it is critical to underline the role that trade unionism played in conferring white privilege and racial invisibility on white "ethnic" communities. Irish American participation in the TWU is illustrative in this regard. In the same period that the transit system enabled a new model of community and ethnic identity, Irish Americans established a solid niche within the industry during its first fifty years.[94] As Joshua Freeman observes, "Irish community life and Irish culture permeated the industry" such that "even the non-Irish were affected."[95] Primarily hailing from the poorer counties of southern and western Ireland, Irish transit workers relied on a wide network of friends and family within the industry for job openings and advancement.[96] Because the majority of Irish immigrants came from rural areas and were largely unskilled for urban labor, they sought employment in low-paying fields that were shunned by "native born" Anglos such as transit and construction. Further, due to the transit industry's requirement that its workers be fluent in English, the Irish were more heavily represented in transit than were other non-native English-speaking immigrant groups.

The TWU was founded by a small group of former IRA activists and the Communist Party (CP).[97] The workers with IRA ties were involved in an organization called Clan na Gael, an American-based secret society founded in 1867 to provide financial, political, and occasional military assistance to the republican movement in Ireland. More politically progressive than Irish workers who were not involved in the Clan, Clan members tended to subscribe to a philosophy of "left republicanism," which was based upon the struggle for international and "militant industrial unionism" within a free Irish State.[98] It was these views (in marked contrast to the more conservative, Catholic-dominated worldview of the Irish American community in general) that spurred Clan members in the industry to respond to the layoffs and deep cuts in wages that accompanied the Depression with a plan for unionization.[99]

During this period, the CP had begun to focus more actively upon developing party representation among workers in blue-collar industries.[100] The Party's forays into such industries as marine and mass transit were considered crucial to building the proletariat base of membership and organization that had eluded it since its inception—a factor that had become even more acute in the Depression-ravaged 1930s.[101]

In many ways, the formation of the TWU was the linchpin of the New York CP's effort to legitimize its identity as a "revolutionary mass party."[102] When leaders from the CP and Clan transit workers came together in 1934, it was a somewhat singular moment in the Congress of Industrial Organizations' history. The TWU was distinctive because it was an Irish dominated union (a rarity in the 1930s) in the public sector. A "pioneer in public-sector unionism," it encompassed a wide cross section of Irish American political and ideological views, ranging from the pro-Communist sentiment of union leaders such as Mike Quill to the more conservative religious bent of the Irish Catholic rank and file.[103]

As a forerunner of public-sector unionism, the TWU was integral to the movement of mass unionism that redefined workers' relationship to the overall political, social, and economic landscape of American society.[104] However, the performance of mass unionism was also critical in shaping a discourse of wage labor in which class and race were conflated within the space of white agency. The advent of unionization in the years during and after the New Deal inscribed the worker as a social actor, such that

> with this change in worker's status came a redefinition of the very notion of what America was. Until the 1930's the accepted image of the United States was still as the land of the founding fathers, a white, Protestant, middle class nation. By the end of World War II the dominant image had become 'a house for all people', as immortalized in scores of movies and books in which the metaphor for the nation was the platoon consisting of soldiers from every class, regional and ethnic background.[105]

While Freeman's quote suggests that this melting pot theme was, in part, an expression of the rise of the multiethnic coalitions of 1930s era mass unionism, I would argue that the American trade union played a more insidious role—that of making white privilege available to European immigrant communities traditionally excluded from the Protestant constructs of class and race privilege. Indeed, the superficially unlikely alliance between Irish transit workers and the CP (which spanned nearly twenty years) was itself emblematic of how whites achieved political and economic agency through a brand of class struggle based on what W.E.B. Du Bois has labeled the "wages of whiteness."[106]

The advent of racially segregated trade unionism increased the value of this wage for the ethnically disenfranchised worker, compensating for even the most "alienating and exploitative class relationships."[107] While the New Deal may have promoted the notion of worker agency, it did little to alter racist notions of black labor. The legacy of slavery still deeply informed white perceptions of the "sloth" and "animality" of black workers, who were employed to do "cut and cover" work in the subway tunnels, the lowest paid and most hazardous positions in the system. While white workers may have been divided by class, language, and ethnicity, they nonetheless regarded themselves as "equals."[108] Solidarity among white workers was crucial to the postwar whitening of the inner-city European immigrant. As David Roediger explains, "white workers defined themselves by negation—as not black and not Chinese...they considered themselves manly/respectable/Americanized/mature/middle class because they were not allegedly degraded and dissolute people of color."[109]

Despite the aura of revolutionary moment and rhetoric of interracial solidarity that the CP lent to the TWU platform, transit unionism, like the subway itself, became an agent of whitening. The masses of European immigrants for whom the transit industry was the first form of gainful employment in the United States were allowed to move beyond the urban confines of the ethnic enclave. Embracing the legacy of unraced cultural identity "not only enabled the not-yet-white ethnics to live more easily with the white American population, but to live more easily...with the vast changes industrial capitalist America required of them."[110]

Within the history of the TWU, the CP's professed commitment to attacking racial discrimination in labor belied the reality. Largely complicit with white racism within the union, the Party's rhetoric of class solidarity was merely a veneer for securing white ethnic access to upward mobility. As Earl Ofari Hutchinson has observed in his book *Blacks and Reds,* the American Communist Party's failure to adequately address the intersection of race and class oppression undermined its overtures to black workers throughout its troubled history.[111] In many instances homegrown racism (on both the part of party leadership and the rank and file), as well as the classic paternalism and myopia of Marxist ideology vis-à-vis the colonial status of "third world" peoples, precluded a viable relationship between the CP and progressive black workers.

Though the TWU had traditionally made concerted attempts to attract black IRT and BMT workers since its inception, its anemic efforts to force management to hire blacks in positions other than that of porter drew fire from the Urban League and the NAACP.[112] Indeed, the Union's repeated waffling of opportunities to make good on its claim of antiracism prompted the NAACP (in the aftermath of the organization's lone struggle with IRT management to promote blacks from porters to platform men and station agents) to comment that, while it subscribed to "the principles of organized labor...we cannot conscientiously urge unionization...in the face of mistreatment and betrayal by union leaders."[113] The tenor of mutual ambivalence and mistrust that informed relations between the TWU and black organizations was symbolic of the CP's failure to evaluate the role white privilege and white solidarity played in trade unionism. Nowhere was this connection made more evident than in the TWU's drive to ensure seniority rights for (white) workers. A key issue in its negotiations with IRT management, the question of seniority rights emerged even more forcefully for the TWU when the NAACP succeeded in getting six blacks promoted to station agent after a protracted dispute with the transit corporation. Though the corporation's promotion of the six was only won with the tacit understanding that they would have lower seniority than the 250 white workers also hired for these positions, the promotions touched off a firestorm of opposition among white workers in the TWU.[114] Indeed, "for weeks afterward union meetings were punctuated with 'open opposition from the floor' to giving Negroes 'white men's jobs.'"[115] The TWU's concession to white solidarity is an important example of how white subject formation influenced the othering of public space in the American city.

In this regard, the text of bourgeois democracy and modernization was predicated upon the inscription of white ethnic immigrants within an unmarked, privatized space of whiteness. Within this narrative of modernization, the development of the subway furthered the construction of the "new white man," signifier of the unmarked space of identity performed within the binary of public/private. It is here that Abraham Hewitt's vision of New York's imperial destiny takes its place alongside the frontier vision of southern California's Pacific Electric Railway.

CHAPTER THREE

The Northern Drive: Black Women in Transit

> She reported that while in a train station she was perplexed about which rest room she and other black females were supposed to use—the one with the sign 'For Ladies' or the other rest room "For Colored People."[1]
> —Sharon Harley (1978, 91)

> It is there to back and frame you.
> —Toni Morrison, *Jazz* (9)

A snapshot dream of 104th Street in Watts, lapping, dead-ending at the railroad tracks. It is the street where Markham Middle School is located, the school where my mother spent much of her teaching career. Since the early 1990s the Blue Line light-rail system has traveled along these tracks from downtown to Long Beach. When my mother arrived in the city from Little Rock, Arkansas, in 1951 on the Santa Fe Railroad, the right-of-way was used by the Pacific Electric Railway (dubbed the "Red Cars"). The "only stop that is an actual building instead of a platform" on the Blue Line, the Watts junction was formerly a Pacific Electric station, and was built at the turn of the century.[2] Growing up in L.A., my mother always boarded the streetcar at the front, fascinated by the "antenna" dragging the overhead wires. After attending Markham during the 1950s (part of the first graduating class—a group that was about 85 percent black and 15 percent Chicano), she returned to teach English composition and literature, remaining there for thirty-two years.

In the snapshot Markham is a garden school with open patios, rambling hallways, and a phalanx of dour brick classrooms. Its grounds sprawl to the southeast, toward the intergalactic peaks of the Watts Towers, the found object sculpture created by the Italian immigrant artist Simon Rodia from bottle shards, pieces of metal, and other neighborhood flotsam. The train tracks stretch the length of the school in an almost unbroken expanse from north to south. In the 1920s, when the area was home to its own branch of the Klan (and the so-called "cotton curtain" that separated South Central L.A. from the rest of the city that had not yet been raised), the tracks were part of the Southern Pacific and Santa Fe Railroads.

Having taught at the school through the upheaval of the civil rights and Black Power movements, the Watts Rebellion, and the civil unrest of 1992, both my mother and the rooms of the school have borne witness to the progressive miseducation of inner-city students in the wake of the Great Migration. Throughout her tenure at Markham she received numerous offers to become an administrator at schools in predominantly white West L.A. She remained at the school both because of her passionate belief in the students and her commitment to the school's role as a cultural and social force in a community under siege.

Braced against the tracks, the school suggests a vision of open space in a community reputed to have none. The lush foliage around the quad at the entrance, coupled with the near labyrinthine grounds, evokes an expansiveness that is prototypically southern Californian. Near the entry of the school there is an outdoor stage that has harbored both graduates en route to their diplomas and jittery Romeo and Juliets in school productions that my mother directed. Late afternoons, when the school has emptied, its grounds seem peculiarly melancholic, a sad lyricism in the shade of the trees and patios and hallways that I've always had difficulty distinguishing from one another, but that I know my mother knows implicitly, navigating them with her eyes closed, paths of another time.

For my mother and her siblings, riding the Red Cars was mostly reserved for weekends, school held at bay for a moment in those magical two days of chores, boredom, and reverie. On the streetcars, "we could go anywhere, mingle with anybody," my mother remembered. During the mid-1950s my grandmother, who worked periodically as a domestic, bought a car, and weekend trips on the streetcar were replaced with a drive from Watts to downtown shops on Broadway. The ride was a way of taking measure of the city. It hearkened back to the family's days in Little Rock when they would ride the bus to the end of the line and back on Sundays to see the city. These Sunday excursions were novel in that they were the "only time I would see white people," my mother told me, wryly adding, "we knew white people were out there somewhere."

The "out thereness" of white people was one of the paradoxes of Jim Crow. The loving, often nostalgic portrayals of black life that have emerged in many contemporary narratives on southern black community vividly evoke the other side of segregation, in which whiteness was an outer limit of being. In these narratives the ties that bonded blacks were strong and resilient, highlighting a brand of racial kinship that eludes contemporary urban black America. Films such as *Once upon a Time When We Were Colored* and *Down in the Delta* are among some of the more vivid pop culture evocations of a period in which black dignity and community were near-sacred values. In these portrayals the specter of white terror, though real, was never crippling. Whereas many of these portrayals airbrush the patriarchy and heterosexism that undergirded such models of community, they are nonetheless illustrative for what they suggest about the black migrant's ambivalence toward the "possibility machine" of the North.[3]

As a teenager growing up in Los Angeles in the 1960s, Genethia Hudley Hayes had a similar impression of the evocative cultural and political power of public buses and trolleys for segregated black communities. A longtime community activist and current member of the Los Angeles Unified School District Board of Education, Hayes moved to L.A. from the west-side of Chicago in 1958. Relocating with her family to Leimert Park, she was acutely aware of the nuances that informed de facto segregation of public spaces in urban Chicago versus the suburban circumscription that governed public space in L.A.'s promised land. Echoing the sentiments of other migrants who came to L.A. with high expectations, Hayes mused, "We believed that this was the most progressive venue for us...L.A. was akin to Hollywood or Disneyland—no racism, no playing field that couldn't be leveled." Hayes's family settled in a single-family home not far from where I live near Santa Barbara Boulevard (now King Boulevard). Although she had been accustomed to living in mixed communities in Chicago, Leimert Park was an altogether different experience. In 1958 Hayes's family was one of the few black families on the block. One of her most indelible early memories of the neighborhood was the sense of private space that it afforded. The large lawns, vibrant colors, and diverse array of stucco and Spanish-style architecture of the neighborhood houses contributed to the general aura of middle-class well-being that pervaded the community. While Hayes believes that class lines in Chicago's black communities were not as deeply defined, the burgeoning middle-class black presence in Leimert Park was beginning to exhibit the elitism that characterized the city's east-side–west-side schism. Though the easing of restrictive covenants had permitted blacks to move into west-side neighborhoods like Leimert Park during the late 1950s, the divide between more affluent blacks on the west-side and poorer blacks on the eastside was becoming more acute. For Hayes, this "self-imposed classism" was a barrier to achieving deeper community ties. Employment discrimination relegated many college-educated blacks to government jobs in the postal service. Moreover, the pecking order of the postwar black community was becoming more onerous—with blacks from the Deep South being viewed in some instances as less "cultured" than those from the Midwest and the East Coast.

However, public transportation was a mediating influence for L.A.'s diverse black communities. Because most east- and west-side black communities still depended on the bus and streetcar systems for everyday travel, public transit allowed the mingling of different classes, opening up a space for public conversation, and, in some respects, political solidarity. Buses and trolleys enabled blacks to check in with one another, to muckrake on everything from cultural politics to city politics. The welfare of black children traveling alone on buses and trolleys was carefully regarded by older black folk, who saw to it that they had the proper fare, were appropriately respectful to other passengers, and disembarked safely at the right stop. The atmosphere of caring and concern that pervaded the bus and trolley was integral to Hayes's intellectual development as a politically conscious adult:

> In 1958 when you used the bus or the J car there were black people on the bus and it was fun...you knew the old people, people who were going to Murray's for breakfast, people who were going shopping...I didn't see a lot of white people on the bus, it was a black thing...being able to be a listener to grown people's conversation. Even the drivers were black and conscientious. These are the kinds of things that made me know how I felt about being African American.

The world of public transit was a rich source of black cultural capital. It was here that the paradox of segregation and the migrant's dream of the redemptive possibility of California collided. While the streetcar system dwindled down to a few lines in the late 1950s, the double-edged nature of the "possibility machine" of the North was insidiously reflected in the automobile's capacity to deepen social and spatial divisions within black communities. Hayes partly attributes the decline of community to the social disconnection of driving. In her view, driving engendered insularity, and thus hastened the decline in black folks' collective sense of responsibility for one another. Increasingly, as car ownership became one of the main symbols of identity and status in black communities during the 1960s and 1970s, the camaraderie that prevailed on public transportation vanished—as did many of the social spaces, restaurants, and clubs that blacks had frequented along the Crenshaw corridor.

The nostalgia of these vanished spaces of the streetcar era resonates with the vanished spaces of southern lived experience—the ur-text of black community. Living in L.A., immersed in the vibrant flood of dialect and idiom of black community, I'm often surprised by how the cadences of southern black community are very much alive in the way third- and fourth-generation Angelenos (young black folk in their teens, twenties and thirties with no tangible connection to the South) speak. Despite all of the dislocations of interstate travel, and the dominant culture's injunctions against Black English and its attendant cultural "pathologies," the southern tongue is not easily broken. Indeed, the spiritual and cultural impoverishment of the North was often counterpoised with the South's spiritual resonance as the ancestral home of black migrants. Migration-era women's literature and blues narratives have captured this ambivalence. These portrayals focus on the degree to which conflicts with sexuality, domestic abuse, white terrorism, and economic opportunity informed black women's imagining of urban space and mobility.

In Toni Morrison's *Jazz* and Ann Petry's *The Street,* urban imagination is filtered through the psychic divide between rural and urban life. Each novel alludes to the role urban transit played in the way black women negotiated work and the hierarchy of public and private space. A space of conflict and desire, transportation, both metaphoric and "actual," is a primary site for the performance of black female subjectivity.

A tableaux that captures the transports of unfulfilled longing as symbolized by the psychic landscape of turn-of-the-century New York (dubbed "the City"), Toni Morrison's *Jazz* finds the inner lives of black migrants in the language of their neighborhoods, streets, and private spaces. Grounding her portrait in the disjunct, swirling, improvised rhythms of jazz, Morrison's narrative departs from the urban determinism of Migration-era writers such as Petry and Richard Wright. In Morrison's novel the city becomes a character, a metaphor for the postmodern condition of her protagonists, who are betwixt and between their memories of the South, and their envisioning/imagining of the works-in-progress quality that their lives assume in the North. Thus, the elliptical, memory-drenched drive of the story becomes a metonym for the narrative drive of the City. Morrison's City lives inside of her characters. Her language captures the way they inhabit space and the way space inhabits them. It highlights the manner in which the boundary between consciousness and the material/empirical "fact" of public space is contested. Reflecting on the arrival of her protagonists Joe and Violet Trace from Virginia to "the City" in 1906, Morrison writes, "When the train trembled approaching the water surrounding the City, they thought it was like them: nervous at having gotten there at last, but terrified of what was on the other side."[4] The terror of the other side—the degree to which the migration functioned as a Rubicon for black selfhood—was a major theme in expressions of black ambivalence toward the North. For example, the alienating industrial "coldness" of city life in modern Chicago reverberates throughout Richard Wright's autobiography *American Hunger.* Reconsidering his decision to migrate, Wright wondered, "Should I have come here? But going back was impossible. I had fled a known terror, and perhaps I could cope with this unknown terror that lay ahead."[5]

The extent to which migration represented an *ontological* struggle—a struggle for being—for the black migrant was played out in both the public space of mass transit and the city street. Musing on the street's power to transform the migrant's body by rewriting her visual and spatial cues, Toni Morrison's unnamed narrator remarks at the beginning of *Jazz*, "If you pay attention to the street plans all laid out, the City can't hurt you." Indeed, in the City, "a schoolgirl never pauses at a stoplight but looks up and down the street before stepping off the curb...men accommodate themselves to tall buildings and wee porches," and a woman feels "restfulness in kitchen chores when she knows the lamp oil or the staple is just around the corner and not seven miles away; the amazement of throwing open the window and being hypnotized for hours by people on the street below."[6] Jazz riff and ruckus, the musicality, tragedy, and violence of the street is the dominant discourse of Morrison's City, whose

> fascination, permanent and out of control, seizes children, young girls, men of every description, mothers, brides, and barfly women, and if they have their way and get to the City, they feel more like themselves, more like the people they always believed they were. Nothing can pry them away from that; the City is what they want it to be.[7]

Morrison's rendering of the near-hypnotic power of the city street illustrates what Edward Soja has characterized as "an alternative mode of understanding space as a transdisciplinary standpoint or location from which to see and to be seen, to give voice and assert radical subjectivity."[8] The street, as articulated through the "social structure of the sidewalk," is the conduit through which a hundred different convergences, transactions, and encounters blur the boundaries of lived and imagined time in the city.[9]

However, the vitality of the street is equally indebted to the logic of the train, to the sensation of the body enclosed in a streetcar, spreading out to the horizon. It was within the space of the train that the migrant's imagining of the city came alive. The electric railway, bicycle, and walking conferred women with greater "mobility and visibility."[10] Whether it was Violet Trace, coming to the city in an early stream of the migration, or my mother, gazing fiercely from the front of an unsegregated train in the Eisenhower era, the migrant's journey to and within the city transformed her imagining of time and space.

Although the Northern streetcar was the seeming antithesis of the repressive regime of the Jim Crow South, the regimentation of black bodies in Northern public space was no less pernicious. Gone were the partitions and signs marked "white" and "colored," the byzantine rules of boarding and disembarking, the violent confrontations between white conductors, white motormen, and black passengers. The relatively close and seemingly unconscious contact between black and white in the public sphere was a "revelation" for migrants such as

Richard Wright. Riding in a Chicago streetcar in *American Hunger*, Wright observed:

> Another white man sat beside me and buried his face in a newspaper. How could that possibly be? Was he conscious of my blackness?[11]

In the South, the experience of riding in a public conveyance was inextricably linked to blackness, to both the psychic and material economy of racial presence. However, the performance of racial difference assumed a somewhat more oblique quality in the North. Riding on the streetcar, Wright's query into the nature of his embodiment (his failure to be "recognized" for what he was) cuts to the root of the inscription of blackness as the ultimate site of difference. Wright's sense of ambivalence about his newfound "invisibility" effectively highlights how blackness is conflated with the city and public being.

As he walks through the crowded streets of Chicago and interacts with his white coworkers in the diner where he's employed as a dishwasher, Wright is constantly amazed at the seeming insignificance of his blackness. Every instance of casual contact with whites goes unmarked and unremarked. Wright's sense of bafflement over whites' indifference to the fact of his blackness is a signal moment in the black Southern migrant's transition from the terroristic racialization of Jim Crow to the racial embodiment of Northern de facto segregation. For Wright, and many of the migrants who waxed about the North in the *Chicago Defender,* whites' lack of consciousness of their blackness (coupled with the seemingly race-neutral construction of public space in the North), was a confirmation of the democratic promise of migration, a validation of the rights of citizenship they had been brutally denied under Jim Crow.

Although blacks had been in a constant state of migration from the antebellum period to the turn of the century, the most significant phase of mass black migration occurred during the World War I era. This phase coincided with the golden years of the streetcar industry.[12] While the streetcars pushed the frontiers of American cities, African Americans migrated from southern states such as Mississippi, South Carolina, Georgia, and Alabama, spurred in part by the decline of the cotton industry and increasing white terrorism. Rail transit had been a crucible for a generation of black riders since the 1896 *Plessy v. Ferguson* railroad case, which officially enshrined "separate but equal" statutes in the South.[13] In cities throughout the South, black riders boycotted streetcars and railroads, organizing rallies and lobbying state and local government over Jim Crow conveyances.[14] In Norfolk, Virginia, Savannah, Chattanooga, and Nashville, blacks set up their own transit companies. When all else failed "they walked, rode their own vans, wagons and carriages or used the services of black hack-men who reduced their rates for the protestors."[15]

Between 1898 and 1908, Maryland, Virginia, North Carolina, South Carolina (states that experienced some of the heaviest out-migration), and Oklahoma adopted railroad segregation statutes.[16] Black passengers were generally confined to the trains' end berth, which was the dirtiest and most unkempt car.[17] Jim Crow cars were frequently used by white crew members to drink, smoke, and change clothes.[18] Gruelingly long rides were made even less tolerable by cramped seats (sometimes cars were so cramped that there were none) and ramshackle cars "easily smashed to kindling in a wreck."[19] My grandfather, who traveled frequently from his home in Quincy, Missouri, to Chicago during the Great Depression, recalled how travelers would pack their own food, the cars filling with the smell of the chicken dinners that have now become an iconic part of collective memory of the migration:

> Immediately, now that they were out of Delaware and a long way from Maryland there would be no green-as-poison curtain separating the colored people from the rest of the diners.[20]

They watch the countryside drop away, the endless play of small towns, the interminable stops and breakdowns. They awake to a string of new faces, children playing in the aisles amidst crumpled newspapers, the conductor clicking tickets up and down the car. A line of passengers beats down the door of the toilet. The headlights of cars float outside the window as the drivers wait for the train to pass, white beams blazing over the red glare of the semaphore.

Reflecting on the allure of the North, historian Jacqueline Jones maintained, "if the South embodied the explicit evil of the pharaoh's Egypt, the North eventually came to represent an ambiguous kind of promised land for the two million black people who participated in the exodus between 1900 and 1930."[21] Though some of these migrants were semiskilled and skilled laborers, the vast majority of them were either unskilled workers and/or sharecroppers from the tenant farm regime that had succeeded slavery. Cotton had been in high demand for the majority of World War I, yet rising prices, coupled with overall inflation, crippled the industry and left black tenant workers in desperate straits.[22]

The brutality of the tenant farm system, an institution which was every bit as dehumanizing as slavery, has been well documented.[23] Disenfranchised by the literacy and property qualifications levied upon black voters throughout the South, black tenant farmers effectively served as slave labor. Moreover, during World War I when "work or fight" rules were imposed to discourage labor organizing, black women and men were overwhelmingly targeted.[24] After attempts to organize black women workers were rebuffed by the racist American Federation of Labor (AFL), the National Association of Black Club Women (NACW) formed the Women Wage-Earners Association.[25] In 1917 when the Wage-Earners Association led a strike against the American Cigar Company in Norfolk, Virginia, the strikers were arrested and branded "slackers."[26]

The premium placed on black women's work in the South would have far-reaching implications for the construction of femininity and public space in the North. White plantation owners waged campaigns against black women sharecroppers who quit their jobs because of the demands of motherhood and/or domestic work.[27] Black women were often forced to return back to work by owners who accused them of undermining the sharecropping system by withholding their labor. The coercion and marshalling of black female labor under Jim Crow was not only a powerful reminder of the value of black women's work to that particular segment of the U.S. economy, but yet another stark example of how relations of public and private are infinitely gendered and racialized.

That black women were forced to work after attempting to "claim" their "rights" to the private, domestic sphere—i.e., to claim their rights as "normal" women—underscores the fallacy of separating gender from the racial and material conditions of its inscription. The history of black women's work under slavery underscored the inherent contradictions of the gender-based cleavage of private and public. Workers first and foremost, black women were positioned betwixt and between public and private.[28] The "masculinization"[29] of black women under slavery effectively ensured that black women would always be in opposition to Anglo American constructs of the feminine.

Hence, the dialectical construction of the black woman as fallen double to the white feminine ideal has profoundly influenced the way women's work is framed vis-à-vis emergent American notions of femininity. Seeking to escape increasingly unbearable economic and social conditions in the South, black female migrants to the North were doubly in search of their own frontiers of work and self. The stress of combating white brutality, sexual assault, and other forms of abuse in the workplace and on the streets of southern cities prompted many women to view migrating North as a means of regaining agency. As Darlene Clark Hine notes, "The most common, and certainly the most compelling, motive for running, fleeing, migrating was a desire to retain or claim some control over ownership of their own sexual beings and the children they bore."[30] Ahead of the wave of female mass employment that burgeoned during World War II, black female migrants would seize upon the galvanic narratives in the *Chicago Defender*—the bible of black southern unrest, and premier champion of the "Northern Drive," as the migration was dubbed—and take up their challenge.

The voice of the northern transplant, the *Chicago Defender* was a fount of possibility for many prospective migrants. The paper routinely portrayed the migration as a "religious movement."[31] Stories of those who had "crossed over" ignited even the smallest southern towns with "the fever" of migration. In the early phases of the migration the Mississippi Delta region was most strongly affected. The bedrock of the southern cotton economy, as well as black community, the Delta region experienced a near exodus of black families between World War I and World War II.[32] In some instances entire neighborhoods migrated, as "a constant flow of letters containing cash and advice between North and South facilitated the gradual migration of whole clans and even villages."[33] Some communities created migration clubs that helped prospective migrants seek out discount railroad fares.[34] Most migrants headed to Philadelphia, New York, and Boston.[35] Arousing the ire of white landowners and politicians, migrants were routinely threatened with violence when they attempted to leave town. In fact, in some cities the railroad stations refused to sell tickets to blacks who wished to go North.[36] Often, the trains themselves became the scene of terroristic attacks upon migrants in transit.[37] Terrorist propaganda against black migration was so vociferous within white southern communities that eleven states passed laws prohibiting black workers from migrating during the 1880s.[38]

The notion of a law against black migration—in this nation of so-called frontierspeople no less—points to yet another violent paradox of American democracy. Prohibitions on black mobility were a deadly enterprise. Throughout the South "arrested men were brought back and held pending investigation and legal operations to stop the wholesale immigration North."[39]

The harassment of black migrants on northern-bound trains evokes a powerful image with respect to the dynamics of Jim Crow and the key role that the public conveyance played in the construction of public space during World War I. While the railroad was an agent of possibility for white immigrants, for blacks it was a crucible for their struggle for citizenship:

> Why does the Negro leave the South? Indeed? You would feel a large part of this answer if you could be on this train, in this Jim Crow car and share for one night the longing of the people to reach the line that divides Missouri from Arkansas or any other part of "the line" that separates Dixie from the rest of creation.[40]

The legacy of this journey lies in the paramilitarization of public space. Public transportation increasingly represents "the line" that many communities of color, bypassed in the sweep of the interstate, cannot cross. In the post New Deal 1990s the inner city has become a Rubicon of sorts; intractable to the redress of public policy, offering the starkest testimony to the failure of African

Americans to do "as the immigrants did"—that is, make the successful transition from urban to suburban.

After the Harlem Renaissance of the 1920s, Chicago began to eclipse New York as the mecca for northern black culture and community. Despite the violence directed toward black migrants, railroads such as the Illinois Central (dubbed the "most powerful economic actor in Mississippi") offered discount tickets in conjunction with northern employers' efforts to recruit black workers.[41] The first wave of the migration was propelled by northern industries' growing demand for unskilled labor. Restrictions on European immigration and the outbreak of World War I opened up jobs that had previously been off limits to blacks.[42] Black women were employed as waitresses and laborers in food packing plants and the garment industry, only to see these positions disappear after the war ended.[43]

While the existence of a growing black community and greater job opportunities attracted many blacks to Chicago, it was especially popular for black women, who often migrated on their own.[44] While some black female migrants were young, single, and better educated than women who chose not to migrate, others were middle-aged, older, and had been employed as sharecroppers or domestics all their lives. Some women, such as my grandmother, left their families behind to stay with relatives until they could be sent for.[45] It was common for women to make one complete journey, while men often traveled more circuitously, stopping in cities along the way to visit friends and relatives and take odd jobs.[46] Arriving in the cities many women fell victim to the schemes of northern employment agencies that fronted for houses of prostitution. Shut out of the manufacturing trades and clerical occupations that welcomed white women, early black female migrants were overwhelmingly employed as domestics, working for wages which were far less than those of white domestics. They would often be forced to take work as day laborers, gathering at a specific site in the neighborhood where white employers would pick them up for temporary domestic assignments.[47]

Concerned with the exploitation of black female domestic workers, black labor activist Nannie Helen Burroughs formed the National Association of Women Wage Earners in Washington, D.C., in the 1920s.[48] Working to improve conditions for women who were outside of the avowedly racist mainstream of American labor unionization, the organization sought to protect the rights of recent black women migrants by agitating for federal legislation. In 1919, National Association of Colored Women president Mary Church Terrell, a staunch advocate of black women's unionization, had attempted to get explicit recognition of the specific needs of black women workers in the platform of the first meeting of the International Congress of Working Women.[49] Terrell's efforts were bedeviled by the same racism and classism that had historically prevented multiracial coalitions between black and white women. While the congress addressed the need for equal wages, job training, and maternity benefits, its platform privileged the concerns of middle-class women. Indeed, Terrell's emphasis on the necessity of unionization "was low in the priorities of the congress, which was more concerned about the few workers on the higher rungs of the occupational ladder than about the majority of those who were in lower-status jobs and in desperate need of protection."[50]

In Morrison's *Jazz*, the pulse of lower-wage "women's" work drives the City. Days off from work granted women a special reprieve from the burdens of public space. In the city, "schoolteachers, cafe singers, office typists and market-stall women all looked forward to Saturday off."(51) Come Saturday, the city "arranges itself for the weekend: the day before payday, the day after payday, the pre-Sabbath activity, the closed shop and the quiet school hall; barred bank vaults and offices locked in darkness."(51) In noting the significance of certain days of the week, Morrison's narrator evokes the stealth and bittersweet ephemerality of clandestine liaisons that took place between lovers such as Joe Trace and Dorcas, the teenage girl with whom he betrays his wife Violet, a hairdresser. The smoldering triangle that erupts between the three of them is the compass of a narrative in which the imagining of the city takes place in stolen time, in the interstices of work and household chores, at the hairdresser's, on the train, in neighborhood stores. In *Jazz*, the imagining of urban public space and women's work is deeply intertwined. After Joe kills Dorcas, Violet becomes obsessed with the life of the girl, ultimately falling in love with the image she has created of her. The transfiguring power of the City becomes the medium for this obsession. Violet's devouring desire is homologous to the City's capacity to inscribe the self within its illicit spaces. The City "is there to back and frame you," Morrison's narrator muses. It is a signifying presence, an accomplice to Violet's "mad" fit of doubleness, where, her senses deranged, she prepares to go to the funeral of Dorcas with a knife and "last in line at the car stop, noticed a child's cold wrist jutting out of a too-short hand-me-down coat, *that* Violet slammed past a whitewoman into the seat of a trolley four minutes late."(90)

The passion, abandonment, and ecstatic sense of possibility that the City incites nonetheless required black women to observe a certain code of being, one that was always informed by the terroristic presence of whiteness and white masculinity. The regulation of black women's bodies in American cities played a key role in the way public space was defined during the Migration era. In *Jazz*, Dorcas's Aunt Alice schools her on the art of disembodiment, showing her "how to crawl along the walls of buildings, disappear into doorways, cut across corners choked in traffic."(55) Alice's instruction on the ways of being female in the city, of the need to alter one's body to conform to the regime of race and gender on the city street, points to the staging of the urban black woman's body as a site of amorality and crisis.

The presence of large numbers of single black women in the urban North would have a profound effect on the articulation of femininity and public morals. It would also shape a generation of sociological analysis on the trajectory of urban black families.[51] Indeed, "single Black working women were subjected to criticism regarding their presence as unmarried women in the labor market."[52] The emergence of what Hazel Carby has characterized as a "moral panic" in the wake of black female migration to the North led to the pathologization of black women in the social discourse of the era.[53] Citing a turn-of-the-century study by Frances Kellor, general director of the Inter-Municipal Committee on Household Research in New York, Carby critiques the view that the sexual mores of the black female subject were a potential threat to the social continuity of an emergent northern black middle class community in the throes of forging its version of the American Dream.[54] In this study the "policing" of black women's bodies was necessary to counteract their tendency to seek out positions as prostitutes in order to avoid "hard work."[55]

The association of black female immorality with black women's alleged unwillingness to work was a recurring theme in white southern racial discourse. Branded recalcitrant, "lazy," and generally hostile to the very notion of work, black women, it was believed, would not properly mind their place in the domestic order of white patriarchy, and hence represented a threat to prescribed gender relations. This grotesque caricature informed the association of the black female body with the public sphere. Black women were frequently subjected to an exhaustive and often brutal variety of coercive measures to force them to work. Those who chose to work at home were heaped with scorn by whites.[56] The notion of black women "aping" white women's ways by staying home was perceived as a dangerous violation of the social order:

> By socially prescribed definition, black women could never become ladies...the term itself had predictable racial and class conditions. White Ladies remained cloistered at home, fulfilling their marriage vows of motherhood and genteel domesticity. But black housewives appeared "most lazy"; they stayed "out of the fields doing nothing."[57]

This contradiction between the role of the cloistered white lady and the toiling black woman (who was nothing without either a hoe, pick, or broom in her hand or a white child in her arms) was strongly reflected in the conception of public space in the Jim Crow South. In addition to being viewed as beasts of burden, and thus a parody of "true" femininity, black women were impugned for their "lack of deference" to white people in general and white women in particular.[58] For white southerners the specter of outspoken, insufficiently submissive black women was particularly subversive. Indeed, "the call for white men to protect their ladies from 'insolent' black girls revealed a growing preoccupation with the 'virtue' of white women as a pretext for the persecution of blacks of both sexes."[59] As Jacqueline Jones notes, outraged white men expressed the need to "take a horsewhip" to recalcitrant black women—a further reminder that the penalties for failing to observe established boundaries for public contact had potentially fatal consequences for black women as well as men.[60] This notion that white women needed to be protected from the encroachments of both black men and women reinforces bell hooks's contention that the masculinization of black women has profoundly influenced the construction of gender in the United States. Hence, the stereotype of the lazy, sexually available, insolent black woman transferred to northern territory quite well. Long before the racist grotesquerie of the morally suspect, promiscuous black welfare mother was summoned upon the national stage, the image of the sexually insatiable, preternaturally fertile black wench was used to uphold the moral certitude of slavery and to legitimize the traffic in black bodies. The ritual and institutional rape of black women by white men under slavery was in large part justified as a deterrent to the defilement of white women, "allowing slaveholders to vent their lust harmlessly upon slave women" and thus "protect(ing) the purity of white women."[61]

The violent myth of black female concupiscence was also a function of black women's status as workers first and women incidentally. Undergirding the wench/workhorse stereotype of black femininity is the specter of the black woman as public servant/service. Black women simultaneously "serviced" the sexual needs of "civilized" white men, unburdening white women of their sexual obligations while serving the needs of the white household, further relieving white women of the need to work. Black women's historical status as pure labor excluded them from being considered "proper" mothers and hence "real" women.[62] Ostensibly estranged from the ideals of family, motherhood, and domesticity, black women had a definitive relationship to the public sphere. Whereas the primary value of white femininity rested upon the preservation of the proprietary right of white patriarchy—e.g., the private "share" accrued to white women's domestic and reproductive labors—the primary value of black femininity accrued in the services they conferred to the daily commerce of the tenant farming system and the white household.

The impact apartheid, sexual terrorism, and domestic subjugation had upon southern black women was powerfully evoked in the work of women blues singers. The blues was a space in which black women sought to gain agency over their bodies and their sexuality. Blues narrative allowed black women to critique the vagaries of male-female relationships within the context of the upheaval of migration.[63] As Hazel Carby notes, "the music and song of the women Blues singers embodied the social relations and contradictions of black displacement: of rural migration and urban flux. Not only were they a part of the community that was the subject of their song but they were also a product of the rural-to-urban movement."[64] Indeed, as with the testimonials of the *Chicago Defender*, the Blues songs of rural black women became the mouthpiece for the southern migrant's ambivalence toward migration. For example, Clara Smith's 1924 song "Freight Train Blues" laments her lover's departure to the North, musing, "I hate to hear that engine blow...everytime I hear it blowin' I feel like ridin' too."[65] The psychic and emotional crisis of mobility was a persistent theme in many of these commentaries. While songs such as "Freight Train Blues" focused on the despair of being left behind by a lover, other songs such as Smith's "Chicago Bound Blues" ("had the blues for Chicago and I just can't be satisfied") conveyed the protagonist's exhilaration and triumph at forging her own path.[66] Hence, "what the women blues singers were able to articulate were the possibilities of movement for the women who 'have ramblin on their minds'...for they had made it—the power of movement was theirs."[67]

However, as Carby points out in her reading of "Railroad Blues," a song which was written in response to "Chicago Bound Blues," the blues singer's ambivalence toward migration sounded a cautionary note to women caught between the all-too-illusory promises of freedom in the North and nostalgia for southern black community.[68] Riding the train to the city, the landscape of black feminine serviceability had changed little. Black women were regularly assaulted by streetcar conductors in retaliation for their protests over conditions on the trains. In addition, the degradation of black women was a "normal" part of the mechanisms of public space; the presence of white women within the public sphere in general, and on public transit in particular, was still regarded suspiciously. According to Virginia Scharff,

> public transit became a setting for confusion and struggle over proper relations between the sexes. As whites of different classes mingled on the cars (African Americans of both sexes were expected to sit in the back...), no one was quite certain whether men ought to practice chivalry and offer their seats to women of all classes on crowded cars.[69]

While Scharff narrowly posits public transit as a space in which conflicts of class and gender were primarily played out among whites, the deeper issue is how the public conveyance reflected and exemplified highly racialized constructs of femininity and masculinity. Scharff's parenthetical rendering of the African American presence on public transit reveals the degree to which the use of the term "woman" (implicitly signifying "white woman" in this instance) is highly problematic when deployed in discourse on the construction of gender in public space. Clearly, the issue of "chivalry" would hardly be a decisive factor in determining how black female passengers were regimented on public conveyances. Scharff holds that bourgeois femininity was constantly in danger of being compromised on the streetcar. However, it was contact with the Other, not white women's mere entry into public (read, male) space, that was most directly threatening to not only white middle-class women's claim to bourgeois respectability, but to their role as premier icon of white patriarchal right. Significantly, the issue of class also "drops out" of Scharff's analysis. When she shifts to an assessment of the way white women were impacted by the mass production of the automobile, her analysis focuses exclusively on the experiences of middle-class women. White middle-class women were specifically targeted by automakers such as Ford. Ford portrayed its cars as a means of lightening the domestic load of the overburdened white housewife.

Insofar as black women were serviceable for the reproductive, productive, and symbolic (vis-à-vis the notion of moral panic) continuity of the white family, they effectively validated white women's status as "space" in need of protection, defense, and cultural fortification. In essence, the performance of white femininity on the public streetcar—a degraded context in which the white middle class woman was ever in turmoil about how to "preserve her temper, her reputation, her constitution, and her gown, and still manage to get around town"—was made possible by the *vector* of black female abjection.[70]

The subway train is a site of multiple ontological discourse in Ann Petry's novel *The Street*, a pungent depiction of the struggles of a young black working woman in New York City. Going home to Harlem at 125th Street, Petry's protagonist Lutie Johnson merges with the tumble of the crowd "making room for themselves where no room had existed before."(27) As the train begins "gather(ing) speed for the long run to 125th Street," the run allows for an unbroken moment of reflection. "Train time" is key to an urban beingness where

> the passengers settled down into small private worlds, thus creating the illusion of space between them and their fellow passengers. The worlds were built up behind newspapers and magazines, behind closed eyes or while staring at the varicolored show cards that bordered the coaches.(27)

Petry's description refers to the A express train from 59th Street Columbus Circle, a technological wonder that squashes sixty-six streets into five minutes flat. In the interlude of this miniaturized play of sixty-six streets, the passengers create spaces in the "in-between" time of hurtling through the darkness. Thus, the "railtime" of the subway is a fissure in the sociocultural construction of time.[71] According to Wolfgang Schivelbusch, the railroad "in realizing Newton's mechanics negates precisely all that characterized eotechnical traffic...does not appear embedded in the space of the landscape the way coach and highway are; (but)...seems to strike its way through it."[72] By dislocating the rider from the landscape, the subway causes the body of the rider to become a vector of speed—a desiring machine written in the in-between of station to station. Weary from the ordeal of looking for an apartment at the opening of the novel, Lutie stands in the aisle of the subway car, grasps the strap, and "enter(s) a small private world which shut out the people tightly packed around her."(28) The world Lutie enters is one of remembrance. Staring at an ad featuring a white couple in a picture-perfect kitchen, a "miracle of a kitchen," she travels back to the scene of a job she took as a maid in a suburban Connecticut home. The kitchen was

> so like it that it might have been the same kitchen where she had waxed dishes, scrubbed the linoleum floor and waxed it afterward. Then gone to sit on the small porch outside the kitchen, waiting for the floor to dry and wondering how much longer she would have to stay there. At the time it was the only job she could get.(28)

As Lutie rides the subway, the mise-en-scène of this miracle kitchen, its fictive potential for true female self-realization, unfolds through a complex racial hierarchy. Passing neighborhoods she will never know, neighborhoods that are merely figments of her point of departure and destination, Lutie's musings convey the postmodern condition of the black female urban subject in the city. Her subjectivity is just as beholden to these imagined communities and regimes of being as it is to the self-evident "fact" of her identity as a working-class black female. Here, in the conjunction of transit and work, the racial hierarchy of public and private is thrown into relief. Riding the subway is not only a space in which communities converge and conflict, but it is a space of desire, a space in which the black female critique of the association of the private sphere with the white female body is performed. Here, the ostensible "plenitude" of the modern American kitchen is disrupted by the "heterotopia" of mass transit.[73] The ideal of domesticity that emerged with a vengeance during the postwar period would reinforce the geocratic organization of space articulated in the suburban home off of the highway. Suburban development would undermine the primacy of the urban street as one of the defining units of urban subjectivity. While measures such as race-restrictive covenants and blockbusting were used to keep blacks out of decent housing in the urban North, race riots in cities such as Chicago and East St. Louis promoted an environment of racial terror.

The intractability of American spatial apartheid rests on this legacy. Moreover, while the white immigrant's trajectory became the premier metaphor for the inscription of American national identity, the black migrant's trajectory became the most overdetermined metaphor for the crisis of the modern American city. Rounding out this narrative was the figure of the gender-disrupting black woman. The black female urban subject became an enduring social icon within the narrative of crisis that defined urban life after the "vindication" of American liberal democracy during World War II. With the dawn of the interstate highway in the postwar era, federal and state public policy was beholden to the development of the horizontal city, a regime based on the single-family home's racial hierarchy of masculine and feminine.

Although public transportation was infinitely racialized and gendered in this equation, it has remained a vital space of urban imagination for black female subjects. In many respects, the Migration-era promise and possibility signified by the urban North remains unfulfilled. Transit is so seductive a space because it stands as a frontier of self and subjectivity. It threatens to both disrupt the boundaries of containment imposed by the automobile and to reinforce them. Nowhere is this dynamic more starkly paradoxical than in the phenomenon that has been dubbed "driving while black."

CHAPTER FOUR
Driving While Black

> We characterize this period as the Auto Age not just because driving machines came into existence...but because some quirks of history and economics made the mass ownership of cars temporarily feasible in America, and in so doing imposed an unprecedented, technologically tyrannical regime on every particular of our daily lives. By the mid-twentieth century, owning a car had become a prerequisite for first-class citizenship.[1]
> —William Kunstler (1997, 58)

> The "geographies of exclusion" which mark so much urban space are not only demographically delineated but...are imaginaries linking the social and the psychic, place "race" at the centre of the cityscape and reproducing...the centrality of the couplet "race" and the nation.[2]
> —Sallie Williams and John Westwood (1997, 9)

> And suddenly there is the drone of the traffic report, the fugitive buzz of another freeway sliding from the reporter's tongue on the radio as the driver cuts from the right lane to the center to the shoulder and right again in the lap-dog daze of an afternoon drive on the North Carolina highway with her windows closed to the world, the air conditioner rattling over the first menace of a siren, the highway blissfully empty, save for two or three other cars that blur by, beyond the pale of the police radar.

In 1996, a radio broadcast captured a police "interrogation" of a black woman who had been stopped on the highway in a town in North Carolina. According to the police report that was issued later, the stop was for a routine traffic violation. The motorist, who was unarmed and alone, was subjected to a brutal, psychotic verbal assault by the interrogating officer, forced out of her car, and commanded to get on the ground. Although the incident received scant attention in the "mainstream" press, it was the subject of outrage and intense criticism among black media. For many blacks, the verbal assault and physical intimidation of the motorist was symptomatic of the siege mentality that governs encounters between black citizens and police on the highways and city streets.

However, what was equally significant was the incident's illustration of how black femininity is staged within the regime of power that auto infrastructure imposes upon the built landscape. This theme is evocatively explored in Colleen McElroy's "Sister Detroit," a 1978 short story that depicts the impact of automobility upon a group of black women friends at the end of the Vietnam War.[3] Set after the Watts rebellion of 1965, and before the civil unrest that subsequently rocked Detroit, the story encapsulates the ambivalent desire that the automobile evoked in the black imagination, in an era in which black communities across the country were reeling from urban blight arising from autocentric public policy. Most of the men in the community depicted in the story have been drafted into the war. The four female protagonists' love and work relationships illustrate the role that the automobile plays in reinforcing gender asymmetry within the community. For Anna Ruth, Autherine, and Nona, the automobile is a conflicted symbol. Throughout the story, the automobile is portrayed as the province of men. In the Detroit black community, it was "the black man's stock portfolio, his rolling real estate, his assets realized."(265) An indispensable part of their quest for masculine identity and social status, the car allowed black men to exercise a certain measure of control, and "what roads the city didn't provide by way of streets, it made convenient with expressways that cut through the length of town." The agency and control that the automobile afforded black men provided them with a means of exercising domination over women in the street and in the home. On the streets, the women of McElroy's story are subjected to the appraising looks and verbal come-ons of men in cars. The public space of the street is depicted as a "male" domain in which women are prohibited from participating in the pleasures that automobility affords. When the women of the story do use the automobile it is only as a means of getting to and from work. For the women, the automobile is a symbol of drudgery and servitude, "merely another way to haul them from the house to a day job— the hook between Miss Ann and the killing floor."(266)

The characterization of the car as interface between working for white women and the "killing floor" of the white home is the counterpart to Lutie Johnson's railtime meditation on the model kitchen in the New York subway. In both of these renderings, domestic space is simultaneously inside and outside of the automobile's conquest of space by time. While the automobile facilitated the journey to white employers' homes, it also reinforced the hierarchy that existed between white and black communities. The knot of expressways that bounded the neighborhood not only cut through town but cut time, thus eliminating engagement with inner-city Detroit:

> Real estate developers in the select sections of the inner city that were being upgraded for white residents called those expressways "The River of Lights." Folks around...(the) neighborhood called them "The Track," and tried turning their backs on the whole business unless they were unlucky enough to have a reason to skip town.(265)

The "trail of cheap motels, used-car lots, and strip joints" that the "River of Lights" left in its wake represents the drive-by culture that feeds on many inner-city neighborhoods. As a result, some of these communities have been transformed into havens for the quick consumption of transient, "expressway" populations. In Vietnam-era Detroit, where "there were no Packards available for the women when the men could barely hang on to a job long enough to support one car," driving lessons for women were an indulgence. (266)

McElroy's story effectively captures the contradictions of an apartheid America in which black women domestics travel long hours on the city bus to support the mobility of white middle-class families in neighborhoods beyond the interstate. Despite the connection the women characters make between the automobile and the "killing floor," it is the automobile that ultimately enflames their desire—its status as a mode of spatial agency and enforcer of racial boundaries becoming the conduit for one character's rage and unrest. After taking her absent husband's car for a drive one day, the character Anna Ruth is pulled over by the police, leading them on a high-speed chase after she has defied their order to stop. Driving through central-city neighborhoods to the interstate, through the "River of Lights" that is both barrier and byway, Anna Ruth's escape plays like an act of reclamation. Throughout the chase, people from the neighborhood cheer her on, blocking the way of the police by pushing junk cars in their path, yelling directions to help her elude them, as "young boys threw rocks, practicing for the riots that were soon to come to the city." (275) When she is finally captured—handcuffed, while lying on a stretcher—she exclaims to one of her friends that she just "'bout made Kansas." (276)

This chapter explores the formation of autocentric public policy and the racialization of urban space in the auto age. While the automobile signified freedom of mobility and unlimited access, these freedoms were double-edged for black motorists. Freedom of mobility was intimately tied up with the specter of black embodiment. The elevation of the car in American twentieth century culture played a big role in the representation of the black body as the preeminent metaphor of urban otherness. The motorization of the United States wedded the romance of the open road with a hierarchy of racial being in time and space that was reflected in the antiurbanism that propelled the growth of southern California. During this period, the black body's status as a space of projection and menace (precipitating white "flight" to suburbia via the mythic highway) was indelibly intertwined with the relentless promotion of the auto and the development of auto-related infrastructure. The mainstreaming of the auto in the 1920s and the association of the auto with the good life demonstrate how the animus between auto and urban rail interests inscribed racial being-in-time.

The issue of black subjectivity and blacks' ambivalent view of the automobile during this period raises the question of how the myth of the open road informed both black narratives of deliverance from the terror of Jim Crow in the South as well as the promise of migration to the North. Indeed, how did the advent of the auto influence black perceptions of self during the early migration period? Moreover, how have both the oppressive and liberating aspects of the shift from public to private transportation continued to inform contemporary notions/inscriptions of black self? And finally, how has this legacy influenced the positioning of blacks vis-à-vis the privatization of transit in L.A, and the framing of the highway as the linchpin of national subjectivity?

In many respects, the Great Migration period would be the swan song of the streetcar's unquestioned leadership in urban rapid transit. Concomitantly, the end of World War I saw a fundamental shift in the landscape of social policy and city planning. The sweeping vision of urban renaissance proposed during the City Beautiful movement was supplanted by the vision of the suburban frontier.[4] This rejection had far-reaching implications for transportation policy. The mainstreaming of the auto not only reflected a shift in the industrial and economic focus of the United States but portended a major change in the way the visual and spatial economy of the city was formed. By superficially investing the individual with control over the very play of the horizon, the auto "changed perception...producing more blur and faster shifts in the field of vision," thus reducing the urban subject's experience of time.[5] It was during this period that the federal government began to articulate highway policy. The formation of the federal highway movement, and the creation of subsidies for highway infrastructure, would become the engine of urban postwar development as the auto filled in the margins of urban space, picking up where the streetcars left off, inaugurating the modern suburb. By granting access to the hinterlands, the streetcars fulfilled the frontier vision of the American Dream, conferring "first-class citizenship" to new generations of European immigrants who would leave the inner city en masse at the behest of suburban highway development. It is in this sense that the emergence of the "auto-oil-rubber nexus" in the 1920s compellingly illustrated the mythology of boundary-lessness that links the frontier of race with the romance of the frontier of the highway.

In its 1993 tome *Car Trouble*, the World Resources Institute presents a volley of statistics on the disastrous consequences autocentric public policy has had on the United States. According to the Institute, 2 percent of American land is devoted to roads and other auto-related infrastructure such as parking lots.[6] The interstate highway system, dubbed "the eighth wonder of the world," is thus one of the crowning achievements of a nation that currently spends five times more on highway construction and repair than on mass transit.[7] The root cause of the downsizing of mass transit has been the subject of countless critiques in the postwar era. Arguably the most infamous of these is that of antitrust lawyer Bradford Snell, who posited his GM-Standard Oil conspiracy theory of the American streetcar's demise to the United States Senate Antitrust Committee in 1974.[8] However, the decline of mass transit in the United States was part and parcel of a more comprehensive shift in industrial policy, rather than one act of corporate collusion. Tracing this shift to the disillusionment of World War I, James Kunstler maintains that the communitarian vision of the City Beautiful movement was displaced in favor of the "cynicism" of individual entitlement:

> The City Beautiful movement...represented an important shift in the broad popular consensus about what city life meant. And that consensus furnished the political support for action to make our cities better than they had been. For twenty-five years America indulged in the great public building spree of the City Beautiful movement...these efforts coincided with the heyday of the electric streetcar, a device that liberated the poor and middle-classes from the insularity of their own neighborhoods, giving them access to all parts of the city, and particularly to its symbolic and economic heart: downtown. It was a time of the American city's greatest centrality.[9]

This "brief, anomalous period between 1893 and 1918" was a time of tremendous upheaval in the United States Immigration had been sharply curtailed. As a result, urban car manufacturers such as the Ford Motor Company tapped the services of the "new" labor pool of southern blacks eager to join the migration.

Henry Ford's introduction of the assembly line in the 1920s set "the stage...for the wholesale abandonment of the cities."[10] Ford's standardization of assembly-line mechanization and production "was coined as a model for twentieth-century industrialization."[11] With the advent of the assembly line, Ford and GM began cranking out models that even the masses could afford, causing car ownership to swell from 468,000 in 1910 to over 8 million in 1920.[12] In 1914, Ford also made the canny move of paying his workers an historic five-dollar-a-day wage during a severe economic decline. Raising productivity and "stabilizing" the workforce, the size of the wage increase was an insidious attempt to discourage workers from unionizing.[13] The increase was framed as a "family wage," predicated on the notion that men should be the sole breadwinners of the family.[14]

While the pay increases and low automobile prices of the Ford Motor Company actively furthered the patriarchal model of capitalist production, they also fueled the fire of American manifest destiny. In 1908, Ford declared that the automobile "will be so low in price that no man making a good salary will be unable to own one—and enjoy with his family the blessings of hours of pleasure in God's great open spaces."[15] With the mass production of the auto, these open spaces were exploited for the full range of consumer delectation, as taxpayer strips, parking areas, motels, and roadside advertising cropped up, offering motorists heretofore unavailable amenities.[16]

The automobile's emergence at the end of World War I and the beginning of the Great Depression made the 1920s a period of intense economic and cultural ferment. Its increasing popularity spurred the government to allocate funding and introduce legislation for better roads. Thereafter, the government forged a partnership with the auto and petroleum industries that would have sweeping implications for the tenor of United States economic growth and the direction of urban development. It was a partnership that would reinforce Americans' deepest hostilities toward the city, as street railways began to falter, and straphangers across the nation expressed their frustration with the abysmal service of their neighborhood trolleys. This 1928 salvo was a typical example:

> We now hear that street-cars are obsolete and ought to be chased from the streets. This is what we have been saying all along. Wake up, citizens, and throttle this octopus![17]

Crowded, inconvenient, glacially slow or recklessly fast (depending upon whose point of view one solicited) street railways were widely regarded as the most blatant symbols of the street railway companies' corporate excess and exploitation in American cities.[18] Incompatible with the California ideal of private space, the intimate hurly-burly of the streetcar evoked, according to some of the propaganda of the day, a primal urban past that had never been part of the canon of Los Angeles lore. As early as 1912, city papers such as the *Los Angeles Record* were vivid in their distaste for the streetcars:

> Inside the air was a pestilence; it was heavy with disease and the emanations from many bodies...anyone leaving this working mass, anyone coming into it...it was in a Los Angeles street car on the 9th day of December, in the year of grace 1912; also on any other day you are of a mind to board a city street car between the hours of 5 and 7 in the afternoon.[19]

The "working mass" the *Record* refers to embodies all the trappings of urban disarray that would resound in the *Los Angeles Times*'s caveats about the proposed development of elevated train lines downtown a decade later.[20]

The grand old American marriage of street franchises and real estate subdivisions had succeeded in opening up every obscure hamlet to the wonders of rapid transit. As a result, "electric cars were regarded as the brand of civic progress, and town boosters everywhere...could be seen outdoors in their nightshirts measuring off trolley tracks by moonlight."[21] However, by the end of

World War I, the streetcar industry had begun to experience a rise in operating expenses, widespread labor strikes, and a small but growing decline in ridership.[22] Many smaller companies that had begun to proliferate in the hinterlands of the country went under, while larger, more stable ones battled back receiverships.[23] Faced with growing unrest from a disgruntled ridership, railway magnates clucked reassuringly to their stockholders and began evoking industry-commissioned studies pooh-poohing the auto's impact. In Los Angeles, the *Pacific Electric Magazine* issued its own broadsides against the auto and bus phenomena, pointing to the hazards posed by bus traffic on crowded streets and the growing number of in-auto accidents.[24]

The traffic issue was a fierce bone of contention and window onto the trajectory of urban transit in the post-Depression era. As early as the teens some big-city traction companies had begun using buses to supplement their trolley lines, a practice that was the subject of intense controversy within the industry.[25] In response to the charge that buses could adequately substitute for streetcars, a 1926 article in the *Pacific Electric Magazine* thundered,

> There has been a lot of misinformation circulated as to the abandonment of the use of streetcars and the substitution therefor[e] of the more modern bus system...does the bus result in economy in rate of fare, street space per passenger carried, and save any time—compared with street cars...the answer is emphatically no![26]

As challenges mounted to the streetcars' dominance over downtown and suburban transportation, such spirited defenses became more and more common. Seeking to discredit speculation about its imminent demise, the industry savaged the auto, dismissed it as a flash in the pan, and extolled the virtues of the five-cent fare. After the results of a traffic survey conducted in Cleveland and Boston reconfirmed the streetcar's sway over urban transportation, the *Pacific Electric Magazine* declared, "the folks who have been weeping for years about the passing of the electric railway may dry their tears."[27] Even so, the industry's chest-pounding attempts at damage control did little to calm widespread public dissatisfaction with the quality of service on trolleys; nor did it dispel the growing belief among industry watchers that the street railway was rapidly succumbing to its own excesses.

Hence, the incursions of the automobile into suburban America could not be stopped by the fulminations of the railways, which were quickly losing public trust in 1920s Los Angeles. In sunny, temperate L.A., the automobile was increasingly becoming the conveyance of choice for a population steeped in the antiurban promise of the good life and the "garden city." Indeed, "using a private car, in addition to being modern and stylish, was also a way the working man could strike a blow against monopoly capitalism, which was personified by the owners of the transit systems...while Henry Huntington was portrayed as a villain, Henry Ford was seen as a savior."[28] Driving through freeway-strapped L.A., the irony of this sentiment resonates deeply. In the perverse landscape of the city, each layer of concrete has been etched by a national economy that helped transform the auto industry into the archenemy of the "working man." However, in 1920s Los Angeles antimonopoly sentiment culminated in a progressive backlash against the street railway companies, many of which were owned by public utilities deeply embroiled in the machine politics of city government.[29] Calls for regulation and reform of public utilities led to the formation of regulatory agencies ostensibly designed to eliminate corporate influence upon city politics.[30] Nonetheless, the power of these agencies was ultimately limited.[31] As Scott Bottles observes, "The middle-class progressives who staffed the regulatory bodies felt uneasy about attacking the property rights of private capital...these progressives fully accepted the legitimacy of the capitalist system...the utilities therefore often found that they could either control, influence, or co-opt the newly established commissions."[32]

The progressive struggle to make street railways more accountable to the public is a compelling example of pre–New Deal urban politics before the interests and aims of private capital and government were fully synchronized. In Los Angeles, a city whose layout was defined by the symbiosis of private capital/ public service, progressive reform efforts (unsurprisingly enough) failed to improve transit service.[33] The influence of private capital upon municipal organization and development was far too powerful a force in city planning for public transit to ever truly serve the needs of the public. The consequences of this axis of power in city planning was portentously illustrated by the controversy over the proposal to build elevated trains in downtown L.A.

Union Station

The shift in power from electoral to regulatory oversight of public transportation was foreshadowed by the political struggle that ensued over the city's proposal to construct a central downtown terminus. Originally intended as a means of consolidating rail service in the region, the Union Station proposal was met with intense opposition from the railroads, who feared that a central terminal would open the region up to competitors.[34] The battle over Union Station was a litmus test for the city's investment in autopia. It represented a critical juncture in the city's identity as a metropolis envisioned as the antithesis to the "crumbling" urban legacy of the industrial city. Just as the auto had been used as a form of protest over the profligacy and perceived undemocratic practices of the streetcar companies, the decision to forgo the development of a new downtown elevated rail network was a seminal moment in L.A. planning. Located on the margins of downtown on Los Angeles Street, Union Station appears an unlikely catalyst for the cementing of the city's claim to autopia.[35] The interior of the station is a study in the collision of the auto world with the city's delphic rail history and its nascent relationship with modern rapid rail. Union Station is the terminus for MetroLink, a commuter rail system, and the Red Line, the MTA's billion-dollar rail enterprise. In many respects, the Union Station conflict doomed modernized rapid rail in the postwar era to failure, paving the way for the debacle of the Red Line in the 1990s.[36]

The call to develop a central terminal emerged during a period when the traffic situation in downtown L.A. was causing a firestorm in city politics. In 1924, two years before the proposal was placed before Los Angeles voters, the landscape architecture team of Frederick Law Olmsted Jr., Harland Bartholomew, and Charles Cheney was appointed to develop a street traffic plan for the city. Dubbed "A Major Street Traffic Plan for Los Angeles," the plan critiqued the system of narrow streets that hindered traffic flow in the city and recommended the development of parkways, subways, and elevateds to combat congestion.[37] Central to the plan was the notion that an integrated system of streets and highways would be more environmentally and aesthetically attuned to the city's communities. The commission's recommendation of elevated trains was echoed in a report released one year later by Kelker-De Leuw, a Chicago engineering firm that had been commissioned by the city to develop a rapid transit plan.[38] The Kelker-De Leuw report was inauspiciously released when the Union Station proposal was put on the table.[39] The report concluded that continued railway expansion would best serve the city. Elevated tracks would hence be the most effective means of "segregating" competing forms of street traffic.[40] Bucking the trend of auto-fascination, the report recommended that the entire county support the proposed elevated system by issuing municipal bonds and allocating tax revenue for its funding.[41] However, because it recommended municipal, countywide support of rapid transit, the Kelker-De Leuw report was viewed with suspicion by suburban communities who balked at the prospect of a tax increase for a system perceived as benefiting the interests of the Central Business District (CBD).[42]

At the height of the city's ambivalence over elevated trains, the Southern Pacific, Santa Fe, and Union Pacific Railroads proposed building elevated lines downtown as a compromise to the Union Station plan.[43] The debate over building a central terminal versus erecting elevated lines encapsulated all of the city's historic hostility toward urban modes of development.[44] Whereas the Kelker-De Leuw proposal had elicited mere debate, the railroads' elevated proposal provoked vigorous opposition from such city institutions as the *L.A.*

Times.⁴⁵ The Union Station issue unequivocally demonstrated that "Los Angeles in the 1920s was in many respects a de facto dictatorship of the *Times* and the Merchants and Manufacturers Association."⁴⁶ In framing its opposition to the proposal, the *Times* prophesied that the development of elevateds downtown would bring all of the turmoil and blight of urban New York, Chicago, Boston, and Philadelphia to L.A.⁴⁷ In a story on elevateds in Chicago, the *Times* portrayed the trains as hazardous, a "curse to any community in which they have been erected."⁴⁸ Moreover, the *Times* claimed, elevated railways had lowered property values in New York. Property values were an issue near and dear to the paper's heart because the Chandler family (the paper's owner and publisher) had extensive real estate holdings near the proposed station site.

For the *Times*, the Union Station issue represented an opportunity to consolidate what was still a powerful, yet slowly eroding, downtown base of capital and commercial enterprise. While the paper had successfully encouraged corporations across the country to locate plants in Los Angeles, resulting in thousands of new jobs, the increasing commercial growth of the suburbs presented a challenge to downtown dominance.⁴⁹ According to Mike Davis, the shift in dominance from downtown to the suburbs was not only a by-product of the rapid motorization of the city but a consequence of the erosion of downtown's real estate "syndicate system."⁵⁰ Hence, "[j]ust as the city became more decentralized, so too did control over its major profit-making activity, the subdivision of the suburban. The fourth-generation elite—now self-consciously defined as a 'Downtown Establishment'—would struggle in vain for the next forty years to 're-center' growth around their enormous fixed investments in the CBD."⁵¹ By opposing the railroads' elevated proposal, the *Times* only strengthened the hand of suburban communities, hastening the CBD's decline.

The *Times*'s vested interest in maintaining the downtown real estate empire was blasted by other L.A. newspapers. The liberal *Los Angeles Record* decried the Union Station plan as "the pet project of Harry Chandler and his big real estate speculating friends."⁵² However, while most newspapers supported the elevateds—citing congestion caused by street tracks as an obstacle to downtown growth—suburban groups were generally opposed to the plan because of its downtown bias.⁵³ Indeed, though downtown institutions such as the Los Angeles Chamber of Commerce firmly supported the elevateds, other downtown property owners—concurring with the *Times*'s portrayal of the plan as a threat to property values—joined to form a group dubbed the Taxpayers' Anti-Elevated Association. The formation of the Anti-Elevated Association was a turning point in the fight against the elevateds. In essence,

> [w]hat had begun as a controversy over steam railroad access suddenly became a large fight over urban mass transportation...engulf(ing) the Kelker-De Leuw plan, rendering

the latter useless. The divisive nature of the issue would leave Los Angeles residents incapable of improving public transit for years to come.[54]

When the Union Station proposal was put before the voters in 1926 as Proposition 8, it came on the heels of a blitz of *L.A. Times* articles savaging elevated rail across the nation.[55] The *Times* articles kayoed the already dubious cause of elevated rail, successfully turning the tide of voters who had supported the railroads' proposal. When voters finally approved the proposition the paper lauded the victory as a "stinging rebuke to the railroads' alternative plan."[56]

The failure of the railroads' elevated proposal was in many regards the first resounding move toward solidifying L.A.'s status as private space citadel.[57] Poised between the Great Depression and the New Deal period, Los Angeles was already facing the sort of sea-change in the traditional urban axis of power and industry that most large metropolitan areas would undergo decades later. In this respect, controversy over the proposal was rightly regarded as a struggle over the direction of the entire region. Driving the streets of contemporary downtown L.A. where Union Station stands venerable and isolated in the crosshairs of the freeway, it is impossible to fathom the metamorphosis the construction of an elevated rail system would have wrought upon the area. In many ways, the failure of the plan exemplified how the anemic political will and dwindling political consciousness for rapid rail would serve the devaluation of public space in the postindustrial United States While the *L.A. Times* successfully played on public distrust of railroad monopolies, casting the Union Station issue as a case of the railroads' historic greed versus the people's right to choose, the public's blind pursuit of better streets made it beholden to an even more formidable purveyor of monopoly power: the auto industry.[58] By rejecting the railroads' proposal, the people of L.A. betrayed the legacy of public transportation in the region.[59] Having imbibed the notion that autos were the gateway to democracy and suburbia, the "public" bore just as much responsibility for the troubled future of rapid rail in the city as did such standard bearers of corporate interest such as the *L.A. Times*. Thereafter,

> [t]he City Council refused to consider the Kelker-De Leuw study...and it was soon forgotten. Without a strong consensus favoring public action the city's denizens did little to save mass transit in L.A., even as they worked feverishly to complete the Major Traffic Street Plan.[60]

The failure of the Kelker-De Leuw and elevated proposals haunts downtown as the road not taken. It resonates as a profound irony, given that the country as a whole would not be completely swept up in the embrace of the auto industry until the 1930s. Shortly after the rejection of these proposals, the L.A.

City Club Committee deemed that the development of a "self-supporting" rapid transit system was untenable, recommending that "Los Angeles should reject the centralized city structure of eastern cities in favor of a 'harmoniously developed community of local centers and garden cities.'"[61] The critique of the old urban industrial center at the core of L.A.'s perception of itself as the apotheosis of the American "good life" of private space, single-family homeownership, and individual rights was henceforth fully "ratified."

Highway Politics and the Gutting of Public Transit

After the dust from Proposition 8 settled, the city was still faced with worsening congestion. A formidable gauntlet of cars, streetcar rights-of-way, and makeshift parking made driving from point A to point B onerous for many. Black-and-white newsreels from the period reveal downtown L.A. to be an iconic maze of urban traffic, cars darting maniacally into the paths of streetcars, pedestrians striding warily into the fray with their packages. Indeed, "[t]he individual had precipitated the traffic crisis by taking to his automobile in protest. By the 1920s this individualistic act had given way to a collective effort to ameliorate the nation's urban transportation system. What emerged from these programs was the public's willingness to tax itself in order to subsidize auto transit."[62] The corollary to this willingness was the public's failure to push for the municipalization of L.A.'s ailing streetcar system. In the minds of many transit historians, this unwillingness doomed the system to failure as a public enterprise.

The defeat of the elevateds in Los Angeles established a dangerous precedent wherein "when rail was failing, straphangers did not fight for public funds to improve service but rather fought against the owners. [And] when motorcars faltered, drivers and the auto industry fought for more aid for the automobile."[63] The traditional public-private schism that had always dogged the Pacific Electric's management of the streetcar system would prove to be its undoing.[64] In a 1924 address to the American Railway Association, Pacific Electric president Paul Shoup outlined the danger this schism posed to the livelihood of the railway industry. Calling for "public protection" for electric railways, Shoup lamented "unregulated competition" from motor bus service along trolley routes.[65] The buses, he claimed, enjoyed an unfair advantage over the railways because they did not have to pay taxes for use of publicly subsidized roads.[66] Moreover, Shoup noted,

> The operators of the private automobile...look upon the motor bus as something of an interloper. They feel that the highway was created for citizens generally and not for

common carrier purposes. It may be that in time private rights-of-way will have to be created for the motorbus operators.[67]

Shoup's remarks anticipate critiques of the fiscal burdens the auto-industrial complex would impose upon the public. By derailing citizens' rights to adequate public transportation, the auto complex would ultimately make automobile ownership compulsory in most cities. Furthermore, although the notion of requiring bus systems to pay for the use of highways seems absurd in a contemporary context, the cautionary note Shoup sounds is prophetic. The economy of highway enterprise has effectively mandated that the public spend in excess of $6,000 a year for maintenance of a vehicle.[68] In this respect, car ownership confers citizenship upon urban subjects in the posturban city, granting them the "inalienable" right to use public rights-of-way to secure private space in time.

Thus, while Los Angeles stood poised to implement the recommendations of the Major Street Traffic Plan, the cause of rapid transit entered an uncertain era, marked by abortive attempts to modernize the existing system. Whereas the New York City subway system benefited early on from a strong foundation of support from municipal government, the issue of municipalization in L.A. was colored by the city's increasing ambivalence toward downtown.

As more and more straphangers gnashed their teeth over abysmal service and fare hikes, 1920s America roiled with the seductions of the auto. For many city dwellers the auto provided a safe haven from the inconvenience and indignity of riding the trolleys, an industry "not yet fifty years old" when it began to stagnate.[69] Though most drivers were still forced to navigate erratically paved roads[70] before the passage of the *Federal Aid Road Act* in 1921, auto travel bespoke all the allure of American individualism. Indeed, the formation of federal policy on highway building reinforced Henry Ford's evocation of the open road as metaphor for free enterprise. In 1923, as part of a vanguard struggle to secure federal subsidies for the highway movement, Federal Bureau of Public Roads chief Thomas MacDonald extolled the virtues of the open road in a national radio broadcast.[71] MacDonald's tireless efforts at garnering public support for highway subsidies allied the cause of free roads for the individual motorist with the nation's view of itself as a democratic society. Stumping for highways in the broadcast, MacDonald proclaimed "radio is free as air; and the open road is symbolic of freedom...no corporation controls them...and the only restrictions on their use are those imposed for the public good."[72] The implication that roads were for the "public good," whereas public transportation (debt-ridden and monopolistic) was for private conveyance, would cast a long shadow over transportation policy, resulting in the sorry mess that Amtrak is today.[73] Thus, MacDonald's comment, "you can judge a civilization by the condition of its roads...We know that the English-speaking people made the fundamental inventions that annihilated space," evocatively allied road building and Anglo American nationhood with the conquest of time over space.[74]

As more Americans began climbing behind the wheel and incorporating auto travel into their everyday journeys, a pivotal alliance between Washington and Detroit was being forged.[75] Under the aegis of MacDonald and his Highway Education Board, the highway movement was gradually weaving together a network of auto-industry executives, government bureaucrats, and politicians. The alliance of government and private industry for the promotion of auto infrastructure would sound the death knell for railroad interests.[76] The auto's seductive appeal to American individualism, the relative cheapness of oil supplies, and the incredible marshalling of resources for auto production and motorways single-handedly transformed the course of national growth. The United States' early embrace of the auto was downright profligate in comparison with that of European nations (with the exception of Germany, which made an early investment in auto technology during Hitler's regime). Contemporary Europeans depend more on public transportation, bicycling, and walking than do Americans—a legacy with implications for everything from our expanding waistlines to our abominable air quality. The United States' slavish devotion to internal combustion transformed the "auto-oil-rubber nexus" into one of the foremost engines of state and federal policy.[77] Macdonald's tenure with the highway bureau inaugurated an era in which government bureaucrats and highway engineers worked closely together to ensure the subsidy of the auto industry. As a result, "the railroads could only watch in awe as Washington and Detroit developed a symbiosis so strong that where one left off and the other began had blurred."[78] Indeed, from World War I on, former auto executives were appointed to everything from Secretary of Defense (GM's Charles Wilson under Eisenhower) to Secretary of Commerce (the Hudson Motor Company's Roy Chapin under Herbert Hoover).[79]

One result of this legacy has been the United States' overinvestment in highways. In the 1930s, when debt-saddled rail companies began going under by the hundreds, and fledgling motor companies folded from overproduction and decreased demand due to the Depression, the highway industry flourished.[80] During this period, the automobile became an even "more entrenched" part of the urban landscape, due, in part, to the lack of "coherent opposition" against it.[81] As Stephen Goddard notes, "while opposed to handouts, President Hoover had justified massive highway spending as a jobs program and pumped a record $175 million into the highway pipeline. By mid-1932, more than a half-million men were at work shoveling dirt and rolling asphalt."[82] After generations of such auto-friendly policy, the auto industry has become one of the biggest recipients of federal welfare. Deemed the great avatar of personal democracy, cars became the beneficiary of massive corporate welfare while rail was the nation's underfunded stepchild.[83] Consequently, the auto industry's influence upon national economic policy has preserved and upheld the right of free and open roads as the one indispensable feature of the eternally contentious relationship between the federal government and the states.

The federal government's early commitment to road construction would effectively undermine public works begun under the New Deal.[84] In James Kunstler's view, Americans were complicit in establishing this disastrous mandate for the auto establishment. Americans, having been

> given the choice between civilizing their cities through public works, and using the car to escape the demands of civility, chose the car. All the money that had gone into the great public building projects of the City Beautiful prior to World War I was afterward channeled into refitting the city to accommodate cars, and building highways in and between cities, to enable the construction of new automobile suburbs outside the city.[85]

While I agree with Kunstler's view of American complicity, the abandonment of the urban public sphere was not merely a matter of privileging the suburban frontier over the city through the agency of the automobile. It was a fulfillment of American self, further endorsement of the nation's particular vision of racial subjectivity.

Race on the Road

As the streetcar industry declined and racial conflict in the inner cities soared, postindustrial, posturban whiteness began to take shape more fully. The "wages of whiteness" cultivated by the TWU and other racially polarized unions would be redeemed on the open road to Anglo American identity. Unlike American-born people of color and immigrants of color, white immigrants had always enjoyed the privileges of naturalized citizenship. The end of Reconstruction, and the repudiation of all federal pretense of redressing the apartheid legacy of slavery, helped refine the collective identity of working-class whites. Time and again, economically disenfranchised white workers, both native-born and immigrant, accented their whiteness so as to gain greater economic and social advantage. This strategy effectively derailed interracial class solidarity, insofar as "the definition of the working-class" came to be articulated in racial terms as "white."[86]

Race mediated the tension between the vision of the suburban frontier/good life and the vision of the city as Other. Early national support for highway infrastructure gave white subjects a powerful medium in which to both perform and confirm their first-class citizenship. The symbolic promise of the open road became a medium in which white subjects were, in contrast to black subjects, "not history-less but historical...not a blind accident of evolution, but a progressive fulfillment of destiny."[87] The Fordian vision of mass car ownership exploited the iconography of dynamism and progress that animates American whiteness, reinforcing its historical opposition to the dark otherness of the city. Thus, America's early induction into the Auto Age re-centered the "manor-in-the-woods" as the premier expression of white democratic privilege. It reinvigorated the white subject's striving to attain the ideal of frontier living, in retreat from the burden of social and communal engagement imposed by life in the city. Indeed, "automobile travel offers...the power to substitute elective movement for loyalty and submission, to exclude one's threatening inferiors from the habitus of personal life, to thwart the will of any merely local political majority and to create polities in which the vital material stakes are mooted by the absence of those who would seek redistribution."[88] The auto boom of the 1920s ensured that the good life would henceforth be within reach of even the most dispossessed white person. For it was during this period that the notion of the open highway was most strongly linked to an American sense of nationhood: the modern highway as a fulfillment of whites' democratic inheritance as Americans. In this scheme the highway signified all the "hard-won" rights and privileges for which generations of white immigrants had "sacrificed." Barnor Hesse has characterized the idea of nation as based on a "retrospective illusion" informed by a narrative of white succession. In this model present and future generations of whites are framed as the "culmination" of the "process of destiny."[89] The modern highway, then, symbolized the future, the "progressive fulfillment of destiny" that defines American whiteness.[90]

While 1920s white America's intoxication with the automobile was shot through with the legacy of imperial conquest, southern blacks also had a deep investment in the transformative power of the automobile. For blacks who had protested Jim Crow on street railways and railroads, automobiles were a means of liberation from the dehumanization of public transit in particular and public space in general. In scores of boycotts, rallies, and lawsuits from the 1890s to the turn of the century, blacks challenged the landmark *Plessy v. Ferguson* decision that officially legalized the doctrine of "separate but equal" in the South.[91] By the early 1900s Jim Crow had become so entrenched in the fabric of southern life that blacks began to concentrate less on its abolition than on improving the quality of travel on segregated trains and buses.[92] To that end, blacks filed numerous lawsuits seeking to make good on the Interstate Commerce Commission's proviso that amenities on railroad trains should be the same for both races.[93] However, as historian Catherine Barnes notes, although blacks were sometimes able to win concessions from the courts, interstate and intrastate travel in the South remained separate and unequal.[94]

Thus, the 1910s and 1920s represented a turning point in blacks' struggle against segregated transit in the South. The formation of the NAACP in 1910 initially promised to provide an official legal challenge to Jim Crow transit. However, as the organization grew, issues such as lynching and voting rights eclipsed its concern with transit discrimination.[95] The mass production of the automobile afforded those few blacks that were able to buy cars a reprieve from the injustice of Jim Crow transit.[96] According to Barnes, "for years, one of the proudest claims of blacks who could afford an auto was that they had never ridden on a segregated streetcar or bus."[97] For many blacks, the auto was a symbol of freedom and control over their bodies, especially over the terms of their embodiment in public space. Contrary to the "freedom of choice" that the automobile afforded the white consumer, black drivers used the auto as a means of resistance to a regime of racial marking which inscribed them as the very *essence* of racial difference. Within this economy, blackness is established as pure presence, the space of projection through which white citizenship is negotiated.[98] Blackness becomes a fixed site of racial-being-in-time: static, bordered, legible, constantly posing the threat of corruption against the backdrop of white transparency.

A brief consideration of the legal construction of race is instructive to this discussion. According to Ian Haney Lopez, "within the logic of transparency, the race of non-whites is readily apparent and regularly noted, while the race of whites is consistently overlooked and scarcely ever mentioned."[99] The American legal system's historic inability to devise legal criteria for white identity supports this position.[100] Historically, in cases where the plaintiff argued his/her right to be identified as white, the courts were unable to arrive at a consensus about what "white" was, resorting instead to definitions of what "white" was not.[101] Consequently,

> [t]he courts established not so much the parameters of whiteness as the non-whiteness of Chinese, South Asians, and so on...in this relational system, the prerequisite cases show that whites are those not constructed as non-white. This is the significance of the "one drop of blood" rule of racial descent in the United States...whites exist as a category of people subject to a double negative: they are those who are not non-white.[102]

Thus, as a category defined as a "double negative," whiteness establishes itself as an absence, whose racial beingness can only be brought into view through the threat of contamination, i.e., the one drop of blood that would dynamically mark the white subject as raced, and therefore "different." This regime of transparency and marking is enforced through the inscription of the other within the structures of public space (e.g., the Jim Crow car). In essence, "racism comes to rest on the body, using the visibility of the body as a major signifier...[and] as a site for racial abuse and violence."[103] Here, the transparency of whiteness, its inability to be named, its "unremarkability," establishes it as having no borders, no spatial boundaries other than that which it assigns to the Other.

The inscription of black otherness on the road highlighted the contradictions of the notion of the road as democratic icon and proving ground for white transparency. As Barnes attests, blacks were hardly guaranteed the freedom that private transportation conferred in this new medium of "unlimited" automobility.[104] For black drivers, the auto was both a means of defying the terms of racial presence—e.g., the violent presencing enacted within the context of the Jim Crow car—and an enforcement of the otherness of black subjects. For example, as more and more blacks in the South began to buy automobiles, southern whites initially expected the same deference on the streets that they demanded on public transit. Whites often required blacks to yield the right-of-way.[105] It was only when it became increasingly clear that yielding to whites in traffic and public rights-of-way posed a danger to public safety that official efforts to "Jim Crow" the open road were abandoned.[106]

Freed from the grosser, workaday indignities of riding on Jim Crow buses and trains, black drivers nonetheless experienced the phenomenon of roadside cinema that private transportation afforded the early twentieth-century driver.[107] This ability to "cleave through miles of scenery in a single day, with the power to start, stop, or change the sequence of onrushing images by merely stepping on a pedal and turning a wheel," was key to the sense of magic and desire the auto inspired in the driver.[108] For the first time, the pure sensory pleasure of movement was available to black drivers and riders. This reconfiguration of being-in-space was mitigated by the ever-present threat of violence. Blacks traveling on the open road in their cars were constantly subject to either being harassed or detained by the police or white motorists. The apprehension of black drivers on the highway, the emblem of American progress and democracy, further underscored the reality that the black body was wholly of the public domain. As a new network of rural roads was stitched together by federal aid, black drivers experienced the brunt of the country's push to "civilization" in the form of these kinds of prohibitions on their freedom of movement. However, just as the construction of white citizenship and individual liberty had been predicated upon belief in the inalienable right to private property—i.e., land, slaves, and women of all races—the ideal of the free and open highway could not have existed without the specter of black otherness.

Indeed, while it is impossible to consider Frederick Jackson Turner's mythologizing of the nineteenth-century frontier without the extermination and cultural genocide of Native Americans, it is also impossible to consider the fluid passing of boundaries of space and time on the road without the specter of racial profiling. The barbaric image of the Rodney King beating was only the most egregious example of how the cost of white freedom of movement is calculated for the black motorist. While the viciousness of that act evoked the specter of "Southern-style" justice for many, it is important to note that profiling has always been one of the defining aspects of black mobility in the North.

Although only a small minority of blacks journeyed to California during this period, the seductions of the car were very much a part of their imaginings of the road to the Golden State. For many black men, the purchase of a car signified independence and masculinity. By allowing them more freedom of control over their own bodies, the auto became a medium through which the North's promise of democracy and equality could be tested. Thus, while the systematic public terrorism of Jim Crow prevented them from fully exercising the rights and responsibilities of male authority, the relative absence of these conditions in the North, coupled with the mobility afforded by the automobile, suggested the possibility of redemption of the black American Dream.

Streetcar Suburbs

The L.A. of the late 1910s and 1920s was rapidly becoming more than a gleam in the eye of the land speculator. The formation of the first Pacific Electric lines in 1901 had gradually carved out many of the iconic communities through which suburban Los Angeles would be memorialized in the cultural imagination of the United States "Bedroom" communities such as Hollywood (Pacific Electric branch completed in 1903), Venice, and the San Fernando Valley (1911) blossomed into major cities as a result of their location along the railway lines.[109] Indeed, "the decade of 1900–1910, in which the electric trolley held a virtual monopoly of interurban transport, witnessed the metropolitan area's largest relative increase in population in the twentieth century."[110]

If the confluence of auto and train in Los Angeles augured "the final phase of Protestant Americans' historic trek West," it was also a symbol of the promise that southern California held for black migrants. The city was just beginning to get its teeth in when mass production of the automobile began and accelerated the growth pattern introduced by the streetcars. It is common to hear testimonials from early black migrants about how L.A. differed from their expectations of what a major city would be like. The prevalence of single-family homes with land in even the most poverty-stricken areas of the city marked L.A. as an anomaly with respect to the dense, concrete cloister of the East and Midwest. Driving through Watts, for example, with its prototypical L.A. stucco homes, illustrates how the stereotype of the blighted inner city clings to black and Latino working-class communities regardless of their condition. Although the area still suffers from many of the same social and economic conditions that spurred the 1965 uprising, it is necessary to note the spatial differences and nuances that govern the quality of life for working-class communities of color in L.A. vis-à-vis those in the East or Midwest.

For those who come from cities in which brownstones, tenements, row houses, city squares and greenbelts dominate the built landscape, the absence of "inner city" in inner-city L.A. is striking. Indeed, "most of what we continue to label the inner city of Los Angeles—including the urban ghettos and barrios of South Central and East L.A.—would appear, especially to those familiar with cities in the eastern United States, Europe, and Asia, as characteristically suburban."[111] Driving down massive-laned Venice Boulevard from east to west, for example, yields every imaginable community and cluster of shops, dark bungalows, rambling garden-style apartment complexes, power plants, and radio stations, until the street divides in trolley tracks and jogs off to the coast. According to urban historian Sam Bass Warner, L.A.'s powerful legacy of streetcar expansion and land speculation kept the city free of the "rigid core, sector and ring structure" that traditionally determined patterns of urban blight in older cities.[112] The early acceptance of the auto refined this pattern. Even in the fledgling days of auto production in 1915, L.A. had an astounding 8:1 ratio of people to cars.[113] Moreover, the widespread perception of the auto as an agent of progress and a symbol of democratic choice over a "corrupt," patronage-bloated streetcar system became the ethos of 1920s L.A. Because suburbanization occurred in southern California before it became a major urban center, L.A. lacks most of the features that have commonly defined the industrial city.[114] However, as the 1992 uprising attests, L.A.'s "inner city" nonetheless evinces the very same dynamics of segregation and land-use discrimination—processes that have their roots in the spatial patterns established by streetcar and freeway development. The first tributary of black migrants to L.A. arrived in an atmosphere that was no less hostile than that of the South. Indeed, although thirty free blacks helped found L.A. in 1781, blacks were prevented from entering California until the end of the Civil War.[115] During the 1880s (in a classically American irony) a statewide labor shortage, due in part to the banning of Chinese laborers under the Chinese Exclusion Act, led to the recruitment of southern blacks by cotton growers in Bakersfield, California.[116] As was true throughout the rest of the nation during this period, blacks were prohibited from owning land under the *State Homestead Act*.[117] Prohibition of land ownership by people of color presaged later municipal zoning policies that effectively barred people of color from moving into the early suburban communities of southern California.[118] Complementing such policies was the vast swath that the Pacific Electric and Los Angeles Railways cut through the fledgling city at the turn of the century. The ultimate emblem of the Anglo American citizen's guarantee of the "inalienable" right to land and liberty, the streetcar system would not only further the white Midwestern migrant's pursuit of the good life in Arcadia, but would help establish Los Angeles's own peculiarly suburbanized version of the urban "inner city."

The trolley tracks that split Venice Boulevard are one of the many artifacts that succinctly articulate Pacific Electric magnate Henry Huntington's strategy for manufacturing a more legible Los Angeles. Huntington designated a site for subdivision, determined the best route for interurban service, and began laying tracks.[119] As a result, L.A.'s railway system was a "series of radiations from the city's center, lengthened from one real estate tract to another without the slightest consideration of the city's symmetrical and economic development."[120] The absence of municipal or regional planning oversight in these decisions has cast a long shadow on the development of the region. The railway's disregard for the organization of the city, combined with an influx of automobile traffic, made traveling downtown a virtual nightmare.[121] In an effort to combat the effects of shrinking ridership and masses of downtown drivers unwilling to adhere to trolley rights-of-way, city officials and the Pacific Electric and Los Angeles Railways proposed a ban on downtown parking in 1919.[122] Predictably outraged, drivers raised a hue and cry about the absence of parking and poorly maintained streets. Some of the most vocal opponents of the parking ban were middle-class white female drivers. According to Virginia Scharff, women drivers criticized the "rough" conditions of the streetcars, decrying overcrowding, slow service, and the rude behavior of streetcar crews.[123] As Scharff points out, the automobile had become a valuable asset for facilitating women's daily chores and shopping. Indeed, women's objections to the ban prompted a broader critique of the gender and class disparities that pitted streetcar riders against motorists.[124] The increasing numbers of female shoppers driving downtown incited the wrath of male workers, who exhorted women to yield space to "tired laborers."[125] The conflict became so heated that when the parking ban was approved, the headline from the *L.A. Record* screamed "No Parking Law Plays Havoc with Leisure-Loving Habits of Milady Autoist."[126]

The clash between white middle-class women and streetcar patrons illustrated how women "found themselves increasingly responsible for producing transportation," as autos became more widely available to the middle-class.[127] Moreover, it also revealed the degree to which the automobile was an ambiguous agent. By simultaneously conferring freedom upon those women who were able to afford to buy cars while curtailing freedom of access for those who depended upon the trolleys, it could be argued that the auto gendered public space in multiple ways. Although motorists of each gender came under fire in the "no parking" debate, men's objections to the presence of white women downtown were clearly informed by the same patriarchal anxieties over white women's presence in commercial districts, the streetcar, and the city sidewalk. These same objections inscribed black women in particular and working-class women of color in general within the public sphere, reinforcing the race and class privilege that allowed white women access to the private space of the automobile. Ford's price cuts notwithstanding, it is important to note that the automobile was still widely considered a leisure item at the time of the ban. Most families did not have cars during this period, and the streetcar was as much a lifeline for working-class families whose female members held jobs as cars were for middle-class white women who did not have to work outside the home. White women's protests of the parking ban attested to the automobile's emergence as a symbol of freedom, convenience, and safety for many women. However, the regime of automobility that emerged in southern California after the Depression foregrounded the degree to which the regimentation of the mass-transit passenger was predicated on the same racial hierarchy that marked and reproduced white femininity as private space.

By 1924 ridership had fallen to an all-time low in the city. The Pacific Electric was embroiled in charges of having bribed the City Council.[128] Repeated proposals to municipalize the system were rejected by taxpayers as being too costly as well as imprudent, given the financial mess the railways were in.[129] After enjoying a brief resurgence during World War II, because of rubber and gasoline shortages which reduced auto use and boosted ridership, most urban streetcar companies were forced to begin converting rail service to bus service.[130] Debt-ridden and underpatronized, most companies found they could no longer compete with the massive federal and state outlays being channeled into highway development and supporting industries such as concrete. Thereafter buses became the prevailing mode of mass transportation in most major cities. In 1953 the Pacific Electric sold its passenger operations to the Metropolitan Coach Lines, facilitating the substitution of bus service on all its rail lines.[131] A year before in 1952, the California state legislature had created the Los Angeles Metropolitan Transit Authority (L.A.M.T.A.), which in turn became the southern California Rapid Transit District in 1964, the managing agency for the new bus system created from the ashes of the Pacific Electric. Although there are competing theories about whether the conversion of passenger operations on big-city streetcar lines was engineered by collaboration between National City Lines (a holding company in which General Motors and Standard had a substantial interest), General Motors, and Standard Oil, the evidence vis-à-vis Los Angeles in particular, and the nation in general, suggests a more complex reading.[132] A constellation of factors, such as policy changes favoring auto infrastructure initiated during the post–World War I era, shifts in capital investment, labor conflicts, and the decentralization of the postwar central business district, contributed to the demise of urban mass rail. Most critical, as Pacific Electric historian Spencer Crump has noted, was "the slowness of the public and public officials to grasp the fact that the role of providing transportation could not be filled by private enterprise."[133] This contradiction has been the bane of public transportation in the United States, which has historically lagged behind other "developed" nations such as Britain and Japan in mass-transit infrastructure.[134] In his elegy to the Pacific Electric, Crump further notes that "if a state authority had been created as late as 1945 to utilize public funds to maintain the red car right-of-ways and purchase modern equipment millions of dollars spent on freeway construction might have been saved."[135]

Crump's wistful assessment aside, the reality was that Los Angeles became the "test site" for the United States' consolidation of its burgeoning auto-industrial complex when a referendum against mass transit emerged from the traffic imbroglio of the 1920s. While historians Scott Bottles and David Brodsly would have us believe that the traffic incidents were symptomatic of the public's desire for greater democracy, these conflicts were in reality a classic twentieth-century reaction to the price of true democracy. The yoking of mass car ownership with the democratic ideal of American citizenship during the New Deal era signaled the final retreat from engagement with improving the public sphere and public space.

Whenever I return to Los Angeles after a several-months-long absence I find yet another right-of-way commandeered by private industry, yet another leg of the old interurban track paved over, another part of the palimpsest blurred. The Atlantis-like quality of the streetcar was evoked in a popular 1980s Hollywood film titled *Who Framed Roger Rabbit?* which blended live actors and cartoon characters to portray a parallel universe L.A., dubbed "Toontown." Set in 1947, the film revolves around an auto-crazed mogul's (appropriately monikered Judge Doom, head of "Cloverleaf Industries") plan to dismantle Toontown's vaunted trolley system, and thus transform it into one long freeway on-ramp. When I saw the film at age nineteen for the first time, the references to the trolley system barely registered in my consciousness. The very notion of a functional mass rail system in L.A. seemed appropriately fantastic for a cartoon movie. The drama played out in the film evokes the familiar GM–Standard Oil–National City Lines conspiracy theme. This theme has either been discredited outright or has elicited heavy criticism from leading transportation scholars in the region.[136] As I suggested earlier, no one factor can account for the untimely demise of the Pacific Electric and Los Angeles Railways. However, the vision that *Rabbit* proposes is compelling in its evocation of the passion and deep sense of place that the streetcar system aroused within Angelenos. In the film, this passion is vividly represented by the character of Eddie Valiant, a scrappy detective played by the British actor Bob Hoskyns. Throughout the film, Valiant attempts to foil Doom's scheme, narrowly escaping death in one scene where he challenges the latter, commenting that "no one will drive the freeway when they can take the Red Car for a nickel."[137] The film's righteous rendering of good (the streetcars) versus evil (the auto) is yet another postwar lament on the schizoid language that rends the soul of L.A., the engine from which all other relationships—demographic, cultural, racial, political—often seem to emerge. In the parallel universe of *Roger Rabbit*, the streetcar (even at the late date of 1947, in the filmmakers' revisionist nod to the nightmare of the almost 1:1 ratio of cars to people in 1980s L.A.) is still somehow very much a factor in the vision of the good-life that the city represented:

> Valiant had answered a kid who had asked him if he had a car that people in Los Angeles did not need a car because they had the best public transportation system in the world. Doom shot back that he—Cloverleaf Industries—had bought the Red Cars in order to dismantle the system. People would *have* to drive on the freeway; there would no longer be an alternative.[138]

It is not too romantic to say that when the last streetcar shuttled into oblivion on April 6, 1961, that a certain vision of the American city died as well. Exploitative, corrupt, promiscuously disrespectful of the logic of American cities, the streetcar system was a perversely American institution. At the interstices of public welfare and private profit, the streetcars paradoxically enabled and disallowed a vision of the city that had more democratic possibility than will ever be afforded by exercising the "right" to turn a key in a car ignition. L.A.'s unwillingness to municipalize the system validated the autocentric bias of state and regional funding and set the stage for the introduction of the *Collier-Burns Act of 1947*, which provided statewide fiscal outlays for freeway construction.

The prohibition upon black mobility and access underlying the white subjects' romance of the road would deeply influence spatial relationships in post–Red Car L.A. As L.A. drove into autopia, the racial economy of the open road manifested itself in the freeway ramp, the lingua franca of the city's neighborhoods. The freeway became the spatial index of the city's racial economy, acting, in the words of Joan Didion, as "the only secular communion Los Angeles has."[139] These relationships have been vividly illustrated by the two most explosive episodes of social unrest in Los Angeles's history: the Watts Rebellion of 1965 and the civil uprising that followed the acquittal of Rodney King's assailants in 1992. Both of these events exemplified the extent to which the city's transit legacy has shaped the racial economy of the postwar era. Whereas the Watts Rebellion highlighted how unequal access to mass transportation reinforced racial and economic stratification in the city, the Rodney King beating and its aftereffects crystallized how the violence of black embodiment informs the gilded narrative of the good life and the black-gold suburb.

CHAPTER FIVE
Little Patch of Green

Not a year has passed since 1900 in which the West has escaped rediscovery.[1]
—Carey McWilliams (1931, 423)

What pleases the nostalgist is not just the relic, but his own recognition of it...less the memory of what actually was than of what was once thought possible.[2]
—David Lowenthal (1985, 8)

Is it not possible...that things we have felt with great intensity have an existence independent of our minds; are in fact still in existence? And if so, will it not be possible, in time, that some device will be invented by which we can tap them? I shall fit a plug into the wall; and listen to the past.[3]
—Virginia Woolf (from Lowenthal, 74)

The houses rush out to greet me as I run. They are somber and big-windowed, with porches that go on forever, that wind from driveway to driveway, stealing the shade of the palm trees, bringing their owners out with church fans and folding chairs to watch the procession of runners coming from downtown. As I run the L.A. Marathon down Exposition Boulevard, people line the street that the train tracks cut like scissors as far as I can see. I have always driven this stretch of the street, ramming through it to the freeway, or rolling coolly by at 35 miles per hour, prowling for cheap gas, keeping an eye out for school kids who zig-zag over the weed-ridden tracks. Running it is different. Running is to feel the full-throttle horizontality of the city in the swing of your arms, the low slant of the rooftops in conversation with the sky, the reflective cadence that the train tracks impose upon the street, as it branches off into Rodeo Road, near my family's home.

I can never remember seeing a train run down this part of Exposition, though I recall stopping many times where the street intersects with La Brea Boulevard several miles to the west, waiting as the gate swings down, listening to the car engines drawl impatiently.

In his book *Histories of Forgetting*, Howard Klein characterizes places in the built landscape that have been erased as "phantom limbs" that can be found only through the traces or "trail" they leave.[4] Klein connects the recovery of this trail with the paradox of forgetting. Forgetting and memory are intimately bound together; for it is only through forgetting that memory can be restored. Exposition Boulevard is one example of the paradox of memory and forgetting. During the late 1940s the street was the southern boundary for black settlement. Much of the entire area south of Exposition was bounded by race-restrictive covenants that prohibited blacks from buying homes there. The street is bifurcated by railroad tracks that were once used by a Pacific Electric Railway route called the Santa Monica Air Line. The line stopped running on October 26, 1953, five years after restrictive covenants had been lifted. Half-industrial, half-residential, the eastern end of the street boasts classic 1930s bungalow homes that have stood in silent witness to the changing face of traffic infrastructure—from train, to car, railroad track to road. During World War II, these homes were inhabited by lower middle-class whites, many of which were probably employed by aerospace industry giants such as Lockheed and Douglas Aircraft, or corporations like General Motors or Bethlehem Steel. Beneficiaries of the wartime boom, rising wages secured by segregated unions, and the GI Bill, archetypal southern California white families such as these would see their base threatened by the Supreme Court's banning of restrictive covenants in 1948. By the 1950s they began to fan farther out to West L.A., as well as to the hinterlands of San Fernando Valley, Riverside, and San Bernardino in the familiar pattern of inner-city white flight.[5]

The Supreme Court's ruling against restrictive covenants was merely the culmination of decades of struggle by blacks against the homeowner associations and real estate agents that had hemmed black residents into a small section of what has come to be known as South Central Los Angeles. As Robert Weaver pointed out in the 1948 study *The Negro Ghetto*, race-restrictive covenants were essentially more pernicious than municipal segregation because they allowed private owners to determine the parameters of segregation, thus relieving the city of oversight or jurisdiction over contested areas. As blacks began to integrate once-restricted areas in Los Angeles, crossing the West side boundary of Main Street, for example, as well as moving south of Exposition, the racial boundaries of the city were rewritten. The economic depression of South Central Los Angeles is part of a long legacy of housing covenants, job discrimination, manufacturing blight, and inequitable transportation. The role highway infrastructure has played in the segregation of this community is a complex history of "forgetting." It lies within the history of streets such as Exposition, streets that are not only living documents of the shifting racial boundaries of the city through time, but of the very structure of racial embodiment, as reflected within the built landscape.

Thus, in remembering the boundaries that Exposition and other streets in the city marked, it is possible to re-envision space beyond the erasure of the white social imaginary. I believe Exposition has resonance for the trajectory of black migrants, for it represents one of the many crossroads of segregation and mobility that blacks were forced to negotiate in Los Angeles. Throughout this work, I have sought to foreground how the erasure of public transportation's social legacy contributed to the regime of racial hierarchy and segregation that characterizes the posturban city. I have tried to make a connection between this erasure and the fetishization of private space, private transportation, and the formation of postwar white subjectivity. The enormous influx of wartime black migration to L.A. occurred during a period when the streetcar system was undergoing a sea change; moving from wartime revitalization to postwar nadir. The nation's deepening investment in motorization transformed the landscape of racial embodiment in the American city. While the black community's coming of age during this period reflected the socioeconomic crisis in jobs, services, and housing that plagued black communities across the country, Los Angeles's status as forerunner for the auto-dependent trajectory of American urban development made it a premier example of racial embodiment during the Cold War era. As access to jobs and social services were increasingly limited by declining transportation services, the transition between trolley and car further etched the ontology of white "mobility" and black "fixity" into the landscape of the city.

Riding through the palimpsest from the legacy of the migration, a legacy born of buried spurs, razed stations, and boundaries of racial embodiment, the trajectory of black Los Angeles is intertwined with the history of segregation in the city. In this chapter I provide an overview of some of the mechanisms of spatial segregation. I focus on the institutionalization of segregating municipal regulations such as deed restrictions, restrictive covenants, and zoning laws during World War II and the postwar era. I look at how these trends in city planning contributed to decentralization and inner-city blight. The theme of nostalgia and the decline of the streetcar system vis-à-vis the social and spatial isolation of the black community in South Central are critical concerns here. Hence, I begin to outline the damage that L.A. antiurbanism has wrought upon the postwar black community, and how visions of the city, particularly that of downtown, have reinforced the cliche of urban crisis and dystopia that clings to Los Angeles. The degree to which African Americans have been able to achieve some modicum of the suburban "American Dream" within the context of crushing racial inequality and hyper-segregation is one of the many contradictions of life in the city. In many respects, the trajectory of streetcar-era black L.A. was symbolic of the "dialectic of extremes, of utopian dreams and dystopian nightmares, of paradigmatic successes and exemplary failures, (that) has always characterized the history and geography of L.A."[6] Insofar as one of the stories of Los Angeles reflects the confluence of the Jeffersonian "manor in the woods" ideal with that of autopia, the socioeconomic isolation of South Central communities is integral to the telos of the American dream.

Early invasion of rail tracks by car traffic during the streetcar era was a major aspect of the system's decline.[7] After appropriations for highway infrastructure were granted in 1916, road construction, coupled with motorists who raced to beat the trolleys by driving onto their rights-of-way, increased trolley travel time and caused frequent accidents.[8] As these conflicts intensified, property owners began to demand that private rights-of-way be abolished so that streets could be widened to accommodate cars.[9]

The gradual conversion of Los Angeles's streets into paved motorways exclusively for automobiles was the last stand for rail. Thereafter, the region would come into its full inheritance of "automotive values" in which "the car ends nowhere...[and] goes everywhere in all directions all the time."[10] While automotive values have long been at the root of American national identity, the aura of "being without boundaries" that the car confers upon drivers has been the most American of seductions—against which the trolley never stood a chance. Now, in an era when the MTA's ambitious plans for the Red Line have been derailed by corrupt patronage politics and massive cost overruns, the paving of tracks on a street that was an important line of demarcation for the racial geography of postwar L.A. is part of the overlay of the palimpsest.[11]

The paved tracks of the Santa Monica Air Line at Exposition and La Brea Boulevard perform this history. They are part of a palimpsest in which "many of the rails and ties, some placed in service as long as eighty years ago, lie buried but a few inches under the asphalt cover of the city streets, or exposed, weathering in the sun and soil."[12] The crossing of the two streets is an interstice between past and future, where Exposition was once the line of demarcation for postwar black L.A. (and to a lesser extent Latinos and Asians), and La Brea Boulevard has become a line of demarcation for contemporary white L.A., streaking by on the Santa Monica freeway. In some respects, the motorization of the city has muted memory of the ways in which these racial boundaries informed and continue to inform the landscape of the city.[13] In trying to make some meaning of space that is distinct from that of the white social imaginary, it is necessary to mark these places as paths along the way of the Migration. As blacks successfully battled restrictive covenants during the 1930s and 1940s (culminating in the Supreme Court's outlawing of restrictive covenants in 1948), these boundaries expanded, opening more westerly communities. The boulevard extends past the University of southern California (USC) to the east, going west toward the coast through Santa Monica, taking often desolate turns through the backyards of houses, factories, and vacant lots. Aside from the trio of gas stations at every other intersection, the residential stretch of Exposition heading toward USC seems largely unchanged from its postwar appearance, its flat, wide-open lanes moderating the slow cadence of vehicle traffic that flows past. In 1991, leading transit advocate Nicholas Patsaouras (for whom the MTA headquarters at Union Station is named) recommended that the Exposition right-of-way be developed as a busway—an idea that was not surprisingly met with indifference by city officials.[14] In 2002, the MTA has begun the preliminary phase of exploration for a light-rail line on Exposition while struggling against the tide of federal funding conflicts and considerable homeowner opposition from residents along the right-of-way. The Exposition line has been touted as the latest magic bullet for relieving traffic congestion. If the line were to be developed, it would be the first to cut through the predominantly white middle- class neighborhoods of West L.A. in addition to more working-class areas of South L.A.—a departure from the usual trend in which rail development in the city primarily disrupted working-class neighborhoods.

Nostalgia

The influence of housing segregation on the southern California Dream is just as primary to the region's identity as the sagas of water, transportation, and racial conquest that are privileged in popular narratives on the formation of Los Angeles. The era of the restrictive covenant sped white Angelenos to the crabgrass frontier while black, Asian, and Latino Angelenos increasingly found themselves locked out of most available housing in the region. Sam Martin, a former typesetter and current member of the L.A. Bus Riders Union, whose parents migrated to L.A. from New Orleans when he was a toddler, remembers Exposition's significance as a boundary line for blacks. Martin would commute from South Los Angeles into downtown at all times of the day and night, often venturing to the more westerly communities of Carthay Circle and Hollywood Circle. Soft-spoken, deliberate, and unsparing in his analysis of the present crisis of the transit system, Martin believes that the current fascination with the old streetcar system is misplaced "nostalgia." He recalled the heavy traffic of downtown L.A. during the 1940s and 1950s when streetcars and cars went head to head for space. In his view, the elimination of trolleys from downtown was "progress," a simple acknowledgment of the incompatibility of the trolleys with the changing face of the region. However, as we spoke, Martin's dismissal reflected a great deal of ambivalence, betraying not a little longing for the trolleys. Indeed, his reflections echoed that of other people who had grown up in the city during this period, their memories revealing an entirely different way of thinking about time and embodiment in traveling the city.

In the 1996 documentary film *Taken for a Ride*, the Los Angeles streetcar system is portrayed as victim of the infamous General Motors conspiracy I alluded to in chapter 4. In making a case for GM's duplicity, the film shows the streetcar system in all its glory, providing wistful testimony from residents who regularly rode the trolleys before their demise. Charlotte Bullock, a longtime L.A. resident, mused about taking daily trips on the J car, which ran east and west down Jefferson Boulevard, until "somebody had the bright idea to get rid of the tracks and get rid of all the trolleys [and] that's when all the headaches started."[15] Looking at the footage of the film, at the elegance of the red cars with their parloresque interiors and big windows, I wondered about my own enfoldment in a collective memory of when L.A. was a "real city." In my desire to will a public transit-scape L.A., to fantasize the rift valleys of this Atlantis, I have often had to remind myself that the streetcars were no panacea for the region and that they helped contribute to the sprawl of the city. Even so, driving across Exposition Boulevard I am once again captive to the urge to look on the horizon and see a train approaching on streets that always seemed to have been "written" by auto traffic. This kind of nostalgia is akin to delirium. Reeling between the irretrievability of the past and the recuperative force of imagining, I watch the video of the streetcars again and again, the play of familiar streets transfigured by the trains that hurtle past on the verge of extinction, the film and my memory forming a jumpcut. It is not just the successive overlay of new transit systems upon the built landscape of the city that contributes to the palimpsest but the overlay of memory, an overlay that disturbs the past, refuses its claim of integrity. According to Maurice Merleau-Ponty:

> To remember is not to restore under the gaze of consciousness a tableau of the self-subsistent past; it is to ensconce oneself in the horizon of the past and to unfold little by little the perspectives contained there until the experiences bounded by that horizon are, as it were, lived anew in their temporal place.[16]

The literary metaphors ("unfold little by little") that Merleau-Ponty uses underscore the fact that memory is a process of inscription, where the horizons of past and present are endlessly blurred. The intimate connection between memory and place makes remembering a form of transport, time travel that transmutes the actual period in which the event, sentiment, moment, taste, sound, smell we seek to recover occurs. This remembering, this grappling with what Howard Klein has dubbed the "what once was-ness of the built environment," is a form of writing, of memorializing the "trace" of everything that is superficially absent, say, from the buildings we inhabit, and the bridges we drive across, but that nonetheless contributes to their cultural and geographic resonance.[17]

In the estimation of some writers, nostalgia is symptomatic of anxiety over the present, and can more accurately be characterized as longing for an event or a past that the subject never personally experienced.[18] In this respect, nostalgia is a means of being present in a time that one has never "actually" seen, and as such is a kind of transport. In his work on perception, Merleau-Ponty held that "if I attempt to imagine some place in the world which I have never seen, the very fact that I should imagine it makes me present at that place."[19] Here, "[t]o imagine is always to make something absent appear in the present, to give a magical quasi-presence to an object that is not there."[20]

In her article on the community of blacks that lived on the East-side during the Migration period up until the Watts Rebellion, Erin Aubry voices the longing and cultural ambivalence of a post-Vietnam generation disconnected from the richness of segregated black community.[21] Chronicling her father's relationship with the community, and his fraternal ties with a group of men who grew up in the area and dubbed themselves the "East side Boys," Aubry captures the spatial memory of a community "disappeared":

> Block by block, year by year, blacks expanded their boundaries southward along Central...in 1936, Central was just beginning to hit its stride as a hub of black business and a mecca for jazz...segregation was still virulent, ubiquitous, but its heavy hand had also compressed the brightest hopes and aspirations of black people into a potent square of time and space made all the stronger because of the strictures placed on it.[22]

As landmarks of black community and restrictive covenant-era solidarity, the memorization of streets like Central Avenue reveal the degree to which the southern heritage of remembrance and nostalgia has left its imprint on the northern black imagination. Here, the segregationist legacy of boundaries such as Exposition Boulevard suggests not only a narrative of prohibition, but a revisioning of time and space. In Aubry's reflections on her interviews with the East side Boys, these spaces become "Other," at once invested with the force and "passion" of the Boys' remembrance, and deformed by the devastation that underdevelopment, westward migration, crime, and poverty have wrought upon South Central L.A.

The simultaneous possibility and impossibility of recovering the past is manifested in the drive, the map of the street transfigured into units of memory. On the Santa Monica Air Line, it took forty minutes to get from the subway terminal downtown on Sixth and Main all the way out to Ocean Park in Santa Monica. Blacks could only enjoy the beach during certain hours. I imagine the swimmers staggering from the train into the sun with their towels folded to their chests, eating their lunches at the side of the road, watching the waves jump higher and higher as they wait.

It has been widely argued that the automobile has not only destroyed meaningful experience with and attachment to place in the city but has played a big role in effacing its history.[23] Despite its vaunted futurity, its transmogrification in the wake of every new strip mall and condo development, the city's impermanence is enfolded within a powerful nostalgia. Nostalgia stalks the city. Before the "riots," before the smog, before the freeways, there was Arcadia and orange groves and an unlimited supply of real estate, mainstream thinking goes. Thus, in this respect, reminiscence is the very engine of the city's fabrication, and is entangled within the very charting of the rail-motorway palimpsest.[24] An almost incongruous nostalgia for the trolleys bumps up against the city's amnesia about their influence. While the physical traces of the streetcar system are embedded within the built landscape of the city, the myths surrounding the system's demise have also left an indelible psychic mark upon the city. The downsizing of public transportation in Los Angeles was precipitated by the climate of political hostility toward mass transit that emerged during the 1920s. Thus, it is ironic, that the streetcar system is often framed as being part of L.A.'s myth as a livable, "utopian" enclave for white middle America. In this narrative, the streetcar is a key element of the white social imaginary for it is a symbol of the era "before" the city's decline into racial unrest and dystopia.

The streetcar system is the freeway's alter ego, the double to the automotive values that it so gothically embodies. Unspoken, but ever-present, it has achieved an "identity" as one of those "symbolic and historic...unvisited, hearsay settings" whose "survival...conveys a sense of security and continuity."[25] At the antipodes of the current transit crisis, the streetcar system is one of the region's reigning paradoxes, the historical byway that begat the chaos of suburban sprawl and was ultimately undone by it. The paradox of the streetcar system is thus utterly in keeping with the unlikely transformation of a desert outpost with no native industry into one of the most important cultural and economic centers in the country.

Thus, driving over the newly paved crossing along Exposition Boulevard becomes a rite of memorization. It is a rite that is both personal and collective—a remembrance of all the racial boundary crossings that those tracks have seen, culminating in the development of the Santa Monica Freeway during the 1950s, shortly after the passage of the *Interstate Highway Act of 1956*. I think it's important to distinguish this remembrance from the well of contemporary American nostalgia that generally valorizes the "family values innocence" of the Eisenhower period, when conservative notions of home, family, and tradition ostensibly prevailed. The era embodied the very antiurban, xenophobic ideology that hastened the twilight of the streetcar and the rise of the automobile. Nostalgia in the American imagination is typically imbricated within this "blindness" to white supremacy and patriarchy. Indeed, this brand of nostalgia assumes that the unraced, ungendered "American" subject can be magically catapulted back to a more innocent period uncomplicated by the specter of women and men of color competing in the workplace, living in suburban neighborhoods, and shopping at the same stores as whites. By eliminating contact between diverse groups of people, the elimination of streetcars promoted the drive for separatism that undergirds this brand of nostalgia.[26] The geocratic alignment of power and place embodied within the hyper-suburban regime of the automobile is both the ideal and the scourge of American nostalgia. While the automobile "liberated" the American subject from onerous encounters with the Other, the toll that auto dependence has taken upon the environment and urban development has been almost universally reviled as cheapening the quality of American standards of living.[27] This paradox continues to haunt American notions of nation, cityhood, and subjectivity. In addition, as more and more people of color and immigrants ride the highways to the crabgrass frontier, it has forced more complex readings of how a multiracial middle class negotiates the psychological divide between inner city, inner-city suburb, and exurb in the post–civil rights era.[28]

In a city that reflects the disjunction of having had one of the most extensive streetcar systems in the world, then having been sculpted to the tune of the internal combustion engine, time is a key element of its mythologization. In his critique of Nietzsche's *Thus Spoke Zarathustra*, Martin Heidegger grapples with the inscrutability of time with respect to the "now," terming it the "transcendental present," in which time flows from a linear frame of past, present, and future.[29] According to Heidegger, the notion of a transcendental present allows the subject to achieve self-identity, or presence, the crux of being in time. Without the fiction of a transcendental present the boundaries between past, present, and future would be inconceivable. In Los Angeles, this fiction of a transcendental present becomes eerily affirmed in the very transience of the landscape. A drive through the city after a four or five months' absence will invariably yield a string of new housing or commercial developments that have sprung up like weeds. While the feverish pursuit of land development has been a key part of the city's legacy, the devouring of space that characterizes the expansion of L.A. County has often made the experience of time in the city a function of the drive. Here, the "handy" signposts of identity and memory are constantly under revision.

This revision has been manifested most indelibly in the rewriting of the city's East side-West side boundaries during the postwar period. On the brink of developing the most extensive highway system in the country, postwar Los Angeles would be a volatile proving ground for the emerging black community. In Los Angeles, the much-coveted patch of green/"green patch" at the core of American national identity became a reality for more African Americans than ever before.[30] For the most part, blacks enjoyed greater employment opportunities. Black appreciation for the city and ambivalence toward the rural found its expression in an unprecedented rate of home ownership.[31] Thus, L.A. embodied a different take on the African American dream of the Promised Land. For some black migrants who forged a path to the region during the postwar period, the openness of the landscape, coupled with the ubiquity of the car, suggested the possibility of upward mobility. L.A.'s early development of a comprehensive freeway network represented a new twist upon the racialization of space established by the metropolises of the east and Midwest. By dividing communities, reshaping urban space to fit the demands of street traffic, and acting as a path of transit for white suburbanites, the highway inflicted some of the most monumental changes on the urban landscape in history. Whereas the streetcar foregrounded the otherness of the inner city yet enabled (by virtue of its focus on downtown) some modicum of urban communitas, the highway consolidated the othering of the inner city. It was within the mise-en-scène of the interstate highway that the valorization of white suburbia and the surpassing drive of whiteness came full circle with national industrial and economic policy.

Migration

Black Los Angeles burgeoned in the twilight of the streetcar era. Having imbibed decades of California hype (some real, some imagined), blacks migrated to Los Angeles in record numbers.[32] Arriving via car and the Santa Fe Railroad, migrants from Texas, Louisiana, the Midwest and the Deep South flooded L.A., inspired by the same mantra of jobs and opportunity that had fueled the first Great Migration a full generation earlier.

It was during this period that Los Angeles began to develop into a national hub of aerospace manufacturing and transportation, flourishing with the prosperity of aerospace giants such as Hughes Aircraft, Douglas Aircraft, and Lockheed. During World War II, California had the highest wages in the country and southern California quickly established itself as one of the foremost defense and manufacturing centers.[33] As Gerald Horne notes, "The war transformed the West from a raw-materials colony for the East to a metropole in its own right."[34] In 1942 the Roosevelt administration increased military production in Los Angeles, San Diego, and San Francisco.[35] During that same year the Southern Pacific Railroad imported scores of workers from the South.[36] Black migration reached record highs when the passage of Executive Order 9066 ordering the relocation and internment of the west coast Japanese community heightened the already-fraught climate of racial terrorism in the city.[37]

The city's industrial maturation, with its heavy dependence upon the reserves of unskilled labor provided by black and Mexican workers, went hand in hand with this oppressiveness. Moreover, the rise of the aerospace industry in the suburban outposts of the city—draining jobs and resources from the "inner-city"—would prove to be problematic for transportation-strapped black and Latino communities.[38]

By 1950 the Pacific Electric and Los Angeles Railways were shadows of their former selves, most lines having either been converted to bus service or completely phased out, their rights-of-way plundered to make more room for auto traffic. The downtown traffic conflicts of the 1920s and 1930s bore heavily upon the fate of the streetcar system, as the auto increasingly became the mode of choice throughout the city. In addition to a massive decline in ridership, and mounting overhead, streetcar lines suffered from "invasions" of cars on their rights-of-way.[39] A 1949 planning report issued by the Haynes Foundation of Los Angeles decried the impact that grade crossings were having on vehicular traffic.[40] The report advocated a grade separation program that would "conquer and organize space."[41] As Spencer Crump notes, "when the last Big Red Car made the final run over the Long Beach line in 1961, there were forty grade crossings on the route 1902 had seen arrow-straight and virtually uninterrupted by roads so that the trolleys could achieve speed."[42] With suburban drivers allowed to run rampant in their new model Buicks, De Sotos, and Edsels, the city reeled from the random flow of automobile traffic.[43] In 1937 the Automobile Club issued a landmark survey of Los Angeles traffic that assessed the randomness of traffic patterns and promptly advocated the development of a freeway system to relieve auto congestion. The report played a seminal role in the articulation of planning perspectives on Los Angeles freeways, and spawned a number of committees and surveys on the issue. The most prominent of these was *A Transit Program for the Los Angeles Metropolitan Region* conducted by the Citizens Transportation Survey Committee in 1938.[44] Spearheaded by Lloyd Aldrich, a former Los Angeles city engineer, the group's report recommended the adoption of "multimodalism"; the integration of rail with the new freeway system.[45] Aldrich "grasped the essential element of transportation for a modern metropolis: the time required to complete a journey is more important than the distance traveled."[46] Though the Aldrich plan was never implemented because of a lack of funding, it was one of the last planning proposals to foreground the synergy between public and private transit, the suburbs, and downtown. Indeed, the multimodal plan was "noteworthy" for its day because it acknowledged the debt that the automobile owed to rail.[47] Moreover, it advised a more aesthetically integrated approach to highway design, one that took the potential impact freeways would have on the structure of communities into consideration.[48]

The Good Life and National Identity during Wartime

The gross segregation of the highway era was forged during this transitional period between the hyper-nationalism of World War II and the red hysteria of the postwar era. As the city stood poised on the brink of complete motorization, black Southern and Midwestern migrants touched down in a sunny California dominated by abominable housing conditions, worsening transportation, and white Protestant xenophobia—combustible elements that would boil over into the unrest of 1965. Commenting on the climate of white L.A. in 1965, Edward Soja observes that

> [w]ith a substantial dose of irony, Los Angeles in 1965 could be described quite figuratively as "the first American City." An almost crusade-like mentality pervaded this white, often antipapist, and racially proud Christian majority, supremely confident in its successful inhabitation and preservation of an earthly and preternaturally American paradise.[49]

The marriage of white Midwestern conservatism and white Southern culture set the tenor in limiting black economic and physical mobility.[50] This dynamic etched deeper lines into the transportation palimpsest, feeding the mania for space that characterized the region. In the 1950s the state of California took the lead in spearheading highway development in L.A., after the state legislature conferred itself with the responsibility of highway construction, thus "preempting the authority of the Los Angeles Bureau of Engineering and making the freeways the domain of state engineers and planners."[51] Working as a real estate agent in predominantly black areas (primarily near the Western Boulevard exit of what is now the Santa Monica Freeway) during the 1960s, my grandfather recalls that the neighborhoods demolished by freeway construction were considered elite by the standards of the period. Many of the residents who settled in the area had done so after restrictive covenants had been lifted, only to see their version of the "good life" destroyed by the advance guard of the state's highway welfare program.

The region's "nonhierarchical," horizontal layout made the ghettoization of black communities more pernicious than that of older metropolitan areas.[52] Although L.A.'s version of de facto segregation was of a different stripe than that of Jim Crow, southern California offered the black migrant a greater wealth of professional opportunity, and the promise of a higher standard of living than most had ever been able to attain.[53] The perceived potential for economic security boosted the overall allure of Los Angeles. Consequently, when the war ended, and white soldiers returned to take jobs that had been filled by blacks and Latinos, blacks continued to come to the area.[54]

When this new generation of migrants came to southern California, they were on the cusp of postmodern Los Angeles, in which the apotheosis of the suburban city would reflect a postwar zeitgeist of economic exuberance and cultural angst. Having shed most of the trappings of the traditional modernist, industrial city, postwar L.A. became a space of projection for national anxiety over land, immigration, cultural identity, and racial subjectivity. The city's early assimilation of the automobile made it a barometer for the historical reconciliation of the Jeffersonian pastoral ideal and capitalism's insatiable drive to progress. As Richard Weinstein notes, L.A. "responded to the persistent yearning in the American character for a redemptive contact with nature represented by the West, an escape from the failures of the industrial metropolis, and changes in the notion of the good life, family, and personal destiny."[55] Fresh from its "victory" over fascism in Western Europe and Japan, the United States's zeitgeist was one of self-satisfaction. The city would be a beacon for the unambiguous restoration of patriarchy and white supremacy during the Eisenhower era.

The return of United States soldiers from the war not only restored traditional gender roles in the home and workplace but also ushered in a new era of first- world military might, one in which southern California figured prominently.[56] The region's booming defense economy, coupled with the psychology of frontierism that informed California notions of space, was a perfect complement to the national frenzy for security that enveloped the nation during the postwar era. The jingoism and anticommunist hysteria that culminated in the House Un-American Committee hearings of the 1940s and 1950s defined the political tenor and "moral compass" of the nation for the next few decades. The United States' fetishistic hysteria over the threat of communist infiltration of the western hemisphere during the Cold War crisply accented the brew of Midwestern provincialism and red-blooded American racism that fueled the region.[57] Moreover, the development of the United

States's military- industrial complex in sunny Los Angeles would both solidify the nation's Cold War stance as anticommunist bulwark and help establish southern California as a "hero" in the nation's concentration on military buildup. In this regard, L.A. became a "stand-in for capitalism in general."[58] As Mike Davis opines, "the ultimate world-significance—and oddity—of Los Angeles is that it has come to play the double role of utopia *and* dystopia for advanced capitalism."[59] The consolidation of the defense industry in "Lotusland" was one of the many ironies of the region. For example, the city's harboring of reactionary white Midwestern conservatism and the social progressivism of such organizations as the Garveyite Universal Negro Improvement Association and the American Communist Party invested it with an almost schizoid duality that made it a bellwether for the nation's political future.[60]

This duality was often noted by the postwar black migrant community—forced to navigate the divide between the way race and space were manifested in the North vis-à-vis the Jim Crow South on a daily basis. Larry Aubry, a retired human relations consultant who came to Los Angeles with his family from New Orleans in 1943, observed that L.A.'s "avant-garde" trappings always masked a deeper and more pernicious strain of institutional racism and xenophobia than that of the South.[61] While California's relative openness stoked optimism and not a small degree of romanticism among blacks about the possibilities of advancement, the unadulterated paramilitarism of the city's white communities prevented blacks from harboring any serious illusions about the prospect of being allowed to live the "Good Life."[62] Although the Great Migration had been driven by the spirit of discovery and optimism, the migration to the West was tempered by a soberness born of three decades of evidence that settlement in the North had not significantly eroded institutional barriers to African American citizenship.

The climate of anticommunist hysteria and "Ozzie and Harriet" patriarchy that inaugurated the 1940s and 1950s would be fully articulated in the city's decentralization. Los Angeles, long the national trendsetter for decentralization, would be followed by New York, Chicago, and Boston as each city paid homage to the new model of hyper-segregated, racially zoned communities that have come to define the soul of American cityhood. Under the aegis of the newly formed Federal Housing Authority, suburban housing development became a national priority in the 1930s and 1940s. It was in housing settlements such as that of Levittown, New York, that the suburban ideal of the good life, private space, and the postwar redemption of white masculinity would be immortalized in the tract home subdivision.

Built in 1947, Levittown was intended as a haven for returning World War II veterans and their families.[63] Its founder, William Levitt, a Jew who steadfastly adhered to the FHA's policy of prohibiting racially mixed housing, defended his enforcement of restrictive housing covenants with the obligatory claim that "if we sell one house to a Negro family, then 90 or 95 percent of our white customers will not buy into the community. This is their attitude, not ours."[64] As a retreat from the messiness of urban community, Levittown offered its denizens a vision of private space that was uncomplicated by shared spaces such as parks or social service centers.[65] One of the first settlements to capitalize off of the auto, Levittown set a standard for the regimentation and sanitization of private space whereby suburbia became a refuge from both the encroachments of the urban center and the complications of racial difference. As the vanguard of American sprawl, the homogeneous houses and tightly contained lots of Levittown were perfect examples of how the auto suburb contributes to the specter of an embattled whiteness, cloaked within the ideal of individual liberty. The fiction of suburban containment performed in this early version of a gated community depended upon the staging of whiteness as a space in danger of contamination. Here, "utopian aspirations are always played out against dystopian visions and myths about the potential dangers posed by the threat of urban disintegration; by the 'other,' the urban stranger against whose intrusion the suburban community is set."[66]

A 1997 *New York Times* article on the racist legacy of Levittown's fiftieth anniversary cites the example of Eugene Burnett. Burnett, an African American soldier, "was among thousands of military veterans who lined up for their green patch of the American dream here after World War II," only to be rejected by Levittown's management. Reflecting upon the experience, Burnett said "he still stings from 'the feeling of rejection on that long ride back to Harlem.'"[67] Burnett's reflection has a strong metaphoric resonance. For this ride back to Harlem starkly illustrates the material and ontological valences between the path of transit available to the African-American postwar subject and the Euro-American postwar subject. This narrative of urban exodus and suburban redemption is representative of two different interchanges on the highway: the first leading to the myth of bootstraps white postwar prosperity, the second leading to the decline of the post–Great Migration inner city. "Left behind" in the race to suburban redemption, black subjects and the city have thus been eternally yoked in a narrative of "fixity."[68] The seeds of the postwar inner city and its suburban double lie in this ride back to Harlem.[69] The implications that this ride has had for the articulation of black subjectivity in the age of automotive values reverberates through my own crossing of Exposition Boulevard. Driving through the city, one unknowingly passes many "erased" boundaries that mark the city's geography of de facto segregation and racial embodiment. Going north past Exposition under the freeway overpass, turning west on Adams Boulevard, one enters the West Adams area. This once-exclusive enclave of venerable old homes barred to blacks and Latinos during the 1940s and 1950s is now a largely black and Latino community. The city is filled with examples of communities such as these, neighborhoods that bear the traces of black struggle and white suburban redemption—streets that have been carved out by urban rites of passage that are reflected in the disjunct language of the freeways. In the maw of the freeway, entire neighborhoods have become "vector points" on the map of the city, performing the unintelligibility of East side and West side.[70]

Throughout this work, I have argued that the streetcar companies of the 1910s and 1920s were responsible for promoting a pattern of development that profoundly influenced the racialization of space in the city. Looking at the map of Huntington's railway "empire," its tendrils extending as far north as San Fernando, and as far east as Redlands in San Bernardino County—the Pacific Electric's path neatly presaged the suburban shift to eastern counties propelled by highway development. The growth of the city's Asian and Latino populations has given rise to a new generation of suburban communities. This trend has revivified old East Los Angeles communities such as Monterey Park and Montebello, and forged new ones in the eastern counties of San Fernando and Riverside.[71] The auto-driven ascent of these suburbs (as well as the migration of working and middle-class blacks out of L.A. proper) has been accompanied by an unprecedented volume of highway development. Over the past decade the East side has undergone a spate of infrastructure improvements such as the addition of HOV and diamond lanes, the historic completion of the Interstate 105 freeway, which connects the southern part of the city with the airport, and (nearly fifty years after ill-fated streetcar modernization proposals spearheaded by the Rapid Transit Action Group in the 1940s) the installment of rail onto highway medians. The current firestorm over the Red Line and rail funding is transpiring in a climate in which a phenomenal amount of capital is being devoted to a renaissance in road infrastructure.[72]

The cultural and demographic shifts that have accompanied this renaissance threaten to subvert the comforts of white suburbanism. Fifty years after the institution of federal and state subsidies enabling the mass exodus of whites from the inner cities, the development of more sophisticated road/freeway infrastructure is providing the conduit for a second wave of black, Latino, and Asian migration from the "inner city." In pursuit of their green patch of the American dream, exurbanites of color have created new enclaves of retreat, driving in greater numbers through southern California's heritage of restrictive covenants into the "crabgrass frontier" of Riverside, San Bernardino, and points beyond.

Restrictive Covenants and Housing Discrimination

In Los Angeles restrictive covenants were frequently enforced through neighborhood campaigns of racial terror aimed at black residents impertinent enough to seek residence in white areas. These campaigns were conducted by suburban homeowners' associations.[73] During the 1920s whites in Torrance created the Anti-African Association. Throughout the city white communities frequently waged "Keep the Neighborhood White" campaigns (often with the added boon of the Klan) to safeguard their version of the good life.[74] The city had always been a breeding ground for Klan recruitment, with active chapters based in now predominantly black suburbs such as Willowbrook and Compton (the Klan even led a march through downtown L.A. in protest of black residency).

The prohibition of blacks, Asians, and Latinos from white neighborhoods had its most vivid expression in the East side–West side divide so pungently evoked in Chester Himes's story "Lunching at the Ritzmore" and in the testimony of early black migrants.[75] In a 1940 quote from the *California Eagle*, a white homeowner proclaimed, "If we can't enforce restrictive covenants in this area then pretty soon the whole West side will be gone and be worth nothing for people of our class."[76] In a city in which the West side is still associated with the exclusionary practices of white beach cultures (whose worship of and fierce "environmental" devotion to the coast and all its treasures have been woven through a West Coast Jim Crow-ism every bit as tenacious as its Southern counterparts), the politics of the West side evoke a perverse mix of rage and longing in many black Angelenos, most of whom have been discriminated against when shopping there or attempting to rent an apartment or buy a home.

The East side–West side divide has its origins in the use of deed restrictions to limit residential areas to certain kinds of activities, and certain kinds of residences, in order to "ensure social and racial homogeneity."[77] In essence, "...acting as Jim Crow legislation, deed restrictions were also building a 'white wall' around the black community on Central Avenue."[78]

As in many other major metropolitan cities during this period, this "white wall" resulted in apartheid-like conditions in the inner cities. By the 1920s blacks and Asians were effectively barred from 95 percent of all housing. Many of them were confined to older, unincorporated, and underserved areas of the city.[79] The influx of larger numbers of migrants from the 1930s on led to greater segregation. As a result, local Klan activity intensified during the 1940s.

Consequently, available housing for blacks was severely limited. Compounding the problem was the flagrant violation of zoning codes forbidding commercial and industrial development in predominantly residential areas. According to Alonzo Smith,

> [i]t was said that during the Second World War, the enforcement of zoning codes in black areas during the World War II era was "practically nonexistent." Prior to World War II, Los Angeles had an overwhelmingly middle-class black community, but it was during the 1930s and 1940s that the classic characteristics of what is commonly referred to as black "ghetto" life emerged.[80]

Even so, despite deep segregation, the fledgling sprawl of Los Angeles prevented the "ghettoization" of black communities from assuming the often physically oppressive density and heft of that of Eastern urban cities. In Los Angeles, lower-income, predominantly black communities were dubbed "spatial ghettos because the only characteristic in common with the well established ghettos in North Eastern cities was that the inhabitants were African Americans."[81] Whereas the Eastern ghetto was typified by a mass of monolithic high-rises and tenements, the Los Angeles variant was dominated by "owner-occupied" single-family homes.[82] The phenomenon of inner-city "suburban" segregation is one of Los Angeles's most significant contributions to postwar urbanism. In this respect, the high incidence of home ownership among blacks in Los Angeles is a testament to the peculiar trajectory of black pursuit of the American Dream. Drive through the black "strongholds" of Southwest Los Angeles, and the gamut of class designations is staggering. Within a one-mile radius affluent black professionals, lower-income service workers, middle-class families, and the homeless make up an often uneasy mix of postmodern black Los Angeles. Indeed, the "richest and poorest African American communities (have become) more visibly locked together in their inequalities than ever before."[83] Such diversity of class within a relatively small area is the legacy of discriminatory FHA housing policies, practiced in more subtle ways by banks and real estate agencies today. Although the black population inched more and more westward during the post–World War II and Vietnam War eras, the majority of African Americans have essentially remained in five general areas within the Southwest and South Central regions of the city.[84]

As many historians and sociologists have noted, the confinement of blacks to the central city during and after the migration period would prove to be the greatest inhibiting factor to black economic mobility.[85] While restrictive covenants, blockbusting, and redlining all played a large part in the segregation of black residents, the FHA's refusal to grant loans to racially diverse areas institutionalized the inequity between white and black homeowners.[86] Without these loans and other incentives, the mass "white flight" of the postwar era would have been inconceivable. In Los Angeles, the combination of FHA policies and restrictive covenants had an even more insidious effect on the trajectory of suburbanization. Although the Supreme Court outlawed restrictive covenants in 1948,

> Los Angeles led the country in the loss of federal funds for public housing. The local effect of this pyrrhic victory was increasing over-crowding...in the inner city. In the meantime, white working-class and middle-income families, including the war veterans for whom public housing was also intended, took advantage of the suburban boom, departing the scene of the problem.[87]

The significance of the FHA's role in creating the climate for the othering of the "inner city" cannot be overstated.[88] Nationwide, while the white population in the central city declined over 1.3 million by 1960, the black population grew increasingly more urbanized.[89]

The Supreme Court's 1948 ruling against restrictive covenants came during an era when the streetcar was undergoing a grave transition. While wartime shortages of rubber and oil had boosted service and ridership, helping to stave off the seemingly inevitable failure of the system for another ten years, the automobile's influence upon virtually every aspect of the city's development crippled the cause of rail rapid transit. Buses, which had been an adjunct to the streetcar system since the 1920s, were increasingly being used to replace rail service on the Pacific Electric and Los Angeles Railway lines during the late 1930s.[90] According to Martin Wachs, by 1939 bus service made up thirty-five percent of the Pacific Electric's service.[91]

City Planning and the Horizontal City of the Future

Issues of mobility and access became even more acute for the African American community as city planning grew increasingly indebted to suburban development and private transportation. American city planning, always a fundamentally weak enterprise within the American political economy, suffered a sea change during the Depression era. Planners, embracing decentralization as the best path for "urban" development, began to turn away from their promotion of "core-city oriented systems."[92] As chapter 4 illustrated, the 1920s were a turning point for American city planning because they marked the era of the downtown traffic imbroglio. As downtown congestion became a major issue within metropolitan areas nationwide, and the problems of the streetcar companies mounted, support for public transportation initiatives such as subways and elevateds dwindled.[93]

The integration of the auto into the landscape of the city intensified the problematic relationship between planners and the business establishment. In Los Angeles, the conflict over Union Station underscored city planning's lack of autonomy from the prevailing whims of capital investment and city government.[94] Thus, "at the height of the local real estate boom in 1924, L.A. planner Gordon Whitnall...informed the National Conference of City Planners that western planners had learned from the mistakes made in older eastern cities and would guide their eastern colleagues in planning the horizontal city of the future."[95] The creation of this "horizontal city of the future" was the planners' only mandate in a society that was deeply suspicious of, and more often resistant to, the very notion of municipally authorized urban planning. By promoting highway development, planners merely cottoned to the individualistic ideological and cultural bias of American social thought. As Mark Foster notes, it was many planners' deeply held belief that the "auto would lead them to the 'Promised Land'" of antiurbanism.[96] This Promised Land was rendered hermetic and homogeneous by the automobile, and hence more suitable for the nuclear family's consumption and retreat.[97] Having failed to gain a toehold in the interstice of municipal government and development politics, the city planning tradition had become terminally afflicted with turn-of-the-century social reformers' penchant for viewing urban space as a space of crisis—intractable and beyond redemption. As Foster explains, "core-city problems were becoming increasingly time-consuming and complex, and solutions seemed beyond grasp. Rebuilding central districts, the glittering vision of turn-of-the-century city beautifiers, seemed a romantic dream to many planners by the 1920s."[98]

The death of the "romantic dream" of City Beautiful during the late 1920s gave rise to two key traditions in urban planning. The first was the emergence of the planning commission. The second, and most racially insidious and demographically influential, was the institutionalization of zoning laws. The birth of the planning commission and the institutionalization of zoning helped solidify the model of the decentered, auto-dependent, racially segregated antiurban city. As James Kunstler argues,

> [b]y the 1920s the stage was set for the wholesale abandonment of the cities. The adoption of a view that led ultimately to the extreme separation of uses and the perversities of contemporary zoning laws, and the establishment of the anti-city known as suburbia. It was a view of the *city as a place fit only for work and vice*, and of the suburb as the exclusive realm of the home—and a particular kind of home at that: *the*

> little cabin in the woods...a recapitulation of the frontier experience, a way to avoid the burdens of civility.[99]

As early as 1923, L.A. established a Regional Planning Commission "dominated by members who favored a dispersed, low-density community in conscious reaction to eastern cities."[100] Composed of land developers, real estate agents, and bankers, the commission was even then primarily concerned with street and highway development, foreshadowing the fractiousness that characterized the Union Station battle in 1926. Indeed, "by the late 1920s local planners and traffic engineers generally believed that the future was in rubberized...transit, and they devoted most of their attention to major street and regional highway development."[101] Ultimately, instead of making a contribution to the trajectory of the urban landscape, planning merely facilitated the massive segregation of land use and concomitant preservation of private space during the superhighway era.[102]

The creation of tendentious, highway-friendly planning commissions that were unaccountable to the public and above the fray of electoral politics went hand in hand with the adoption of zoning laws. First implemented in New York in 1916, zoning was originally designed to separate land-use functions. After zoning's constitutionality was established in 1926, segregation of land use became the rule of urban planning. Mixed-use districts were divided to meet landowners' demands.[103] By segregating residential space from retail and manufacturing activity, land-use zoning essentially undermined the cohesiveness of the central city. Segregated space was deemed more compatible with the longer distances served by the automobile.[104] Whereas the tenor and rhythm of the central city had been based on the close proximity of retail stores and services to one another, zoning disrupted the traditional stop-and-go of pedestrian and streetcar traffic, supplanting it with the relentless rush of the automobile.[105]

This new regime of movement, coupled with the establishment of "homogeneous" land use in the form of zoning, would ultimately reinforce racially restrictive covenants.[106] During the 1920s the combined wallop of racially restrictive covenants and zoning prevented people of color from purchasing land.[107] Further, more and more whites capitalized on the G.I. Bill and low-cost FHA mortgage loans to move to the suburbs during the postwar era. Zoning excluded people of color from suburbia by pricing them out of the market.[108] Thus zoning and racially restrictive covenants effectively confined people of color to the central city where mixed use was prevalent.[109]

This shift in the orientation of city planning was consonant with that of national industrial policy. As United States postwar industrial policy increasingly promoted auto, oil, and rubber monopolies of production:

> Corporations, whose dominance was threatened by public opposition during the populist era before World War I, divided the interests of transportation consumers and workers and simultaneously removed the transportation issue from electoral politics...this built-in unresponsive-ness to transit demand limited the mobility of public transportation [and] as local corporate power and employment became linked to the auto-oil-rubber growth industries, planning shifted toward highway construction.[110]

Glenn Yago underscores the degree to which the articulation of national industrial policy vis-à-vis the auto-oil-rubber nexus effectively eliminated citizen participation in urban transportation politics. The corporate dominance of the Big Three—GM, Chrysler, and Ford—has remained undimmed in the last forty years since United States highway policy first began to take shape. During this period "these paragons of the variable path" have emerged as "vital parts of any national political coalition."[111] Consequently, after World War II, the role of municipal government in transportation politics was greatly diminished as "corporate interests and highway technocrats...formed the highway lobby that has dominated transportation policy ever since."[112]

Decentralization

Zoning, the curtailing of citizen participation in transportation politics, and the consolidation of an autocentric national industrial policy yoked posturban segregation with the decline of public transportation in Los Angeles. Concomitant with these forces was the ongoing competition between downtown and the suburbs for jobs, capital investment, and white "exiles" from the city. Each struggled mightily to claim its right to the moral and cultural compass of Los Angeles. Moreover, as the influence of downtown waned, the once-vaunted CBD would become the region that time forgot, characterized by the uneasy coexistence of shining palaces of corporate development such as the Bonaventure Hotel and the Bank of America building with the five-and-dimes and hoary movie palaces of low-rent Broadway.

In his 1991 article on the "transformation" of the Pacific Electric, Sy Adler argues convincingly that "place competition" precipitated the dismantlement of the streetcar system.[113] In contrast to San Francisco, where CBD and suburban interests were "more closely aligned," the historic conflict between downtown and suburban L.A. was far more irreconcilable.[114] While highway and auto subsidies were institutionalized on a federal level with the passage of the *Interstate Highway Act* in 1956, place competition between downtown and suburban commercial coalitions helped hasten the decline of public transit within the city, solidifying the region's dependence upon freeway development.[115] According to Adler,

> [t]he basic feature of the metropolitan development process in the USA is competition to maintain and attract capital investment...place-based coalitions of industry, political and technical activists form to defend and advance their territorial interests...coalitions based in CBDs attempt to deploy neo-colonial, radial transport facilities...in order to connect downtowns with growing peripheral areas. They support infrastructure designed to facilitate travel between centre and periphery, rather than within or between peripheral areas...in opposition to downtown coalitions, suburban office-commercial coalitions attempt to deploy transport facilities that will enable them to establish their independence and that will permit autonomous local economic growth.[116]

Adler maintains that it was this movement of "intrametropolitan competition" that culminated in the dismantlement of Los Angeles's streetcar system.[117] In this respect, "the transportation technology that had first allowed the decentralization and expansion of cities ultimately inhibited that expansion.[118] One of the most enduring ironies in the history of the American city is that the shift of capital investment from downtown into the suburbs was partly a consequence of the kind of decentralized settlement encouraged by streetcar expansion. Moreover, the advent of truck transport for manufacturing would also have a major impact on industrial development.[119] Truck transport enabled warehouses to shift operations from downtown to outlying areas, thus weakening the historic concentration of manufacturing in the CBD, as well as depriving the railroads of their hold on industrial transport.[120] As a result of this shift, "between 1948 and 1963 employment in the twenty-five largest American metropolitan areas grew fastest outside the central city," effectively making the CBD the slowest growing area in the city.[121] Indeed, during the 1930s, most new arrivals to the L.A. area settled in outlying communities. Thus, as more and more suburban areas developed their own industrial and retail centers, motorists, freed from the radial route of streetcar transportation, could now choose to shop in their own neighborhoods.[122]

However, the cause of rapid rail continued to be a deep concern for CBD policymakers. The shelving of Aldrich's 1939 multimodal plan cast a long shadow on another more ambitious proposal for public transit in the region. In 1948, the Rapid Transit Action Group (RTAG), an offshoot of the Metropolitan Traffic and Transit Committee of the Los Angeles Chamber of Commerce, proposed the development of a more extensive fixed rail system in conjunction with highways.[123] Taking into consideration the region's growing diversity and expanding population, the group proposed a network of rail lines that would run in the median of the freeways, anchored by a subway terminal that would supplement that of the Pacific Electric on Hill Street. The group's 1948 publication features vivid illustrations of the proposed rail lines, with freeway train stations eerily similar to those constructed on the Green Line that currently runs on the 105 Freeway from the Los Angeles International Airport. The vision of the city that the publication advances reflects a furious partisanship for rapid rail, based on the prescient notion that automobility would make greater Los Angeles unnavigable and ultimately unlivable. The front of the publication exhorts:

> Autos and buses can't move Los Angeles' four million people *now*. Crawling traffic will come to a shuddering chaotic halt when we have six million people, plus.[124]

The RTAG plan put a new spin on the theme of the good life, identifying rapid rail as the best means of preserving the American dream of single family home ownership ("rail rapid transit will make it possible for us to live where we like and work where we please").[125] This vision was informed by a racial underside. The publication uses the image of a smiling man holding a train as the icon for a timeline illustrating the population growth Boston, Chicago, Philadelphia, and New York had achieved when these cities developed rapid rail. By contrast, the figure of a barefoot, sombrero-wearing "Mexican" man taking a siesta under a palm tree is used to symbolize the lack of progress Los Angeles has made despite its population of two million residents. In this reading, the specter of Los Angeles, "asleep" in the era of rapid rail, is analogous to the Other stranded in his passage to modernity.

RTAG's argument for rapid rail foreshadowed the MTA's defense of the Red Line.[126] Where the MTA has sought to portray the Red Line as the means of Los Angeles' redemption as an urban center in the next millennium, RTAG championed rapid rail as a means of tempering the socially and municipally disruptive consequences of the highway onslaught. In each model, modern transportation technology becomes a means of managing intractable diversity.

When the proposal was put to the Los Angeles City Council for a vote it was defeated by the same coalition of suburban interests that had opposed the elevateds in 1926.[127] The proposed rail system's radial orientation translated into a downtown "bias" for the suburban constituency, which included communities such as Long Beach, Santa Monica, and Pasadena.[128] Moreover, RTAG's recommendation of the creation of a transit district smacked of "socialism" for some property owners in the nearby Wilshire District, who argued against public control of transit on the grounds that it had "always been a private industry."[129]

Ironically, the rejection of the RTAG proposal prompted the downtown-led L.A. Chamber of Commerce to devote more energy to ensuring that freeways would be radially oriented. As a result, "downtown is the clear focus of a set of radials that, given its small share of regional employment, provide it with a surprising accessibility advantage in comparison with other centers of economic activity throughout the region."[130] The legacy of the Aldrich and RTAG defeats was the development of an invasive freeway system that undermined the structural continuity of neighborhoods, in some instances requiring massive resident displacement.[131] Where suburban leadership condemned public subsidy and oversight of transit, it saw nothing wrong with the institutionalization of public welfare for the highway establishment. In many ways, the quashing of these alternative rail visions of the 1940s was the nail in the coffin of postwar transit. The subsequent reign of the freeway made the 1920s screeds of the railway officials against the automobile (i.e., that the "masses would always require public transportation") seem almost surreal.[132] By this time both the Los Angeles Railway (LARY) and the Pacific Electric had started substituting buses on their routes to cover operating deficits.[133]

The shift in production from the central city to the suburbs would dramatically restructure the axis of industrial power and influence within Los Angeles in particular and the American city in general. Whereas the central city had once been the fulcrum for jobs, commerce, and capital investment, the rise of white strongholds such as Glendale, Long Beach, Torrance, and the San Fernando Valley as centers of production and consumption further consolidated inner-city segregation.[134] The exodus of business and job opportunities out of predominantly black and Latino areas such as South Central L.A. had a devastating effect upon those communities' abilities to attract capital investment and receive adequate social services. These factors had profound implications for black mobility.[135]

Thus, mobility—both economic and transit-oriented—emerged as a major issue for South Central as the postwar era transformed it into the spiritual and cultural home of early black Los Angeles. As the city hastened toward the freeway era, restrictive covenants, deed restrictions, and land-use segregation entrenched the East side/West side/South side axis of Los Angeles.

CHAPTER SIX
Station to Station

> Those who were fortunate to find transportation outside the Watts area found that their employment options improved. Many found transportation through the formation of carpools. One participant who worked as an auto mechanic...bought old cars from the junkyard and restored them for use in carpools.[1]
>
> —Keith Collins (1980, 58)

All the buses stop on Broadway, or so it seems, amid the march of flashing lights from the electronic goods stores, the ten-cent watches and chain-link jewelry from the low-rent hawkers booths, the ptomaine palaces that stench out into the late afternoon air, competing with the wave of exhaust fumes. If you miss one line you can take another, or wait in the bustle, bedazzled by the sheer cornucopia of stock—the Foothill transit, the L.A. Department of Transportation shuttle, the Gardena coach, the obscure little paratransit jitneys that wheeze past on ten-cent fares. Several miles to the east of Broadway lies the community of Boyle Heights, the "first neighborhood outside of the center of the city."[2] Inaugurated as a "streetcar suburb" during the railway era, Boyle Heights is a hub of the Eastside Mexican American community. The neighborhood is bounded by the Santa Ana and Pomona freeways, which form an oppressive grid over its streets.[3]

Many of the community's residents shop, work, and recreate on Broadway, which shuttled a Los Angeles Railway line (the local counterpart to the PE interurban system) during its heyday in the wartime era. On weekday afternoons Broadway jumps with homeless men and women, passengers waiting at bus stops for the next local, and women with strollers, holding the hands of small children, checking out the wares of the stores from the corners of their eyes. During the 1930s and 1940s Boyle Heights fostered a generation of community and labor activism from Mexican women who worked in a food processing cannery at the California Sanitary Canning Company. On August 31, 1939, the women staged an historic strike at the plant to protest pay discrimination and hostile working conditions.[4] Traditionally placed in seasonal, piecework positions (the women had the task of washing, grading, and cutting the cannery's fruit products), women were paid for their production level, while men were paid an hourly wage.[5] According to Vicki Ruiz, the strike was the culmination of years of organizing among the workers in Boyle Heights. The women formed a close-knit "female work culture" (that also extended to Jewish women who lived in Boyle Heights during that period), born of the day-to-day choreography of getting in line, handling the fruit, dealing with the anti-Spanish language prejudice of the foremen, and riding the streetcar to and from work.[6] The food processing local was formed under the auspices of the United Cannery, Agricultural, Packing, and Allied Workers of America Union, a Congress of Industrial Organizations (CIO) affiliate that actively recruited black and Latino workers throughout the World War II period.[7]

A forerunner to grassroots Eastside Chicana activism during the post-Vietnam era, the union's activities established a strong heritage of Latina resistance in public space. Going out into the streets to picket grocers who failed to comply with requests not to stock the cannery's products, the women successfully mobilized community support for the action.[8] When the strike was settled, the local received a nominal increase in pay (which was still based on piecework) but also garnered day care benefits and a closed shop.

The food processing workers' struggle for dignity and equal compensation in the workplace established a legacy for redefining the political identity and agency of a community used as a "dumping" ground in the wake of downtown's economic decline. In the post-Vietnam era, groups such as Mothers of East L.A. used the power of family, kin, and local ties to battle back the State of California Department of Corrections' 1986 proposal to build a prison in Boyle Heights.[9] By forging justice coalitions in the public sphere, the Mothers of East L.A. not only problematized the domesticated, machismo-whipped Latina, but linked this exercise of female agency to the idea of community action.

These images of working women are nowhere to be seen in discursive analyses of the spatial economy of downtown. The engine of work that drives downtown—the women who prepare food at the downtown library, clean up the tourist hotel bathrooms, sweep up after me in the train station terminal—belie the elegies that have been issued for Broadway's demise. As one reads the history of the food processing workers, a dynamic narrative of the neighborhoods that lie east of downtown suggests itself. Mike Davis has observed that downtown development "viewed property values in the old Broadway core as irreversibly eroded by the area's centrality to public transport, and especially by its use by Black and Mexican poor."[10] To the extent that downtown has been inscribed as a conflicted, degenerate figure within L.A.'s fantasy of self—held hostage to its technological decline (in the case of the streetcar/car battle) and racial hybridity, only to be partly redeemed by its commercial ascent—it is an overdetermined space, a space of projection for narratives of postmodern anomie. Over the past decade, East Los Angeles communities have battled against freeway construction, prison construction, police brutality, and toxic waste disposal. They have taken up the public space and environmental racism issues that affect black communities in Southwest and South Central, often joining forces with African American groups such as the Concerned Citizens of South Central.[11] The conflicted relationship between black and Latino communities have manifested itself in issues of class, jobs, language access, and ucation. Conflicts between the two communities come in the midst of a dwindling black presence and burgeoning Latino immigrant population. Thus while older, established Mexican communities such as East L.A. have become home to a new generation of Latin and Central American immigrants, former bastions of black community such as South Central have also become increasingly more Latino.

In the drive past East Los Angeles on the I10 San Bernardino freeway, the next leg of the black Migration unfolds. The freeway has had a dual role in articulating postwar black subjectivity, functioning as both a means of othering black communities and as a space of desire for black motorists. As a byway for migrant communities and as a barrier to mobility within the "inner city," the freeway has intensified the legacy of restrictive covenants, while opening up the desert frontier of San Bernardino and Riverside County (part of the so-called Inland Empire) to a new crop of black, Latino, and Asian exurbanites.[12]

Just as the real estate rich–Westside symbolizes the legacy of white middle American manifest destiny, the eastern leg of the 10 is symbolic of another chapter in that legacy's charting. After downtown, the Santa Monica freeway becomes the San Bernardino freeway, traversing the San Bernardino and Riverside Counties. This quarter of the region encompasses some of the flattest, most relentless stretches of suburban and exurban desolation in the Southern California freeway system. Homes in the two counties are hotly sought after by working-class and middle-income people of color weary of what many perceive to be the increasing unlivability of the city of Los Angeles. As some of the first outposts for white flight, these towns offered the Midwesterner all the monochromatic comforts of home with none of the agrarian angst. It is somewhat ironic that these once middle American bastions have "fallen" to globalization before Los Angeles's Westside. The far-flung oil suburbs of these communities would be nourished by the "middle-class grit" of black Angelenos from the second generation of migrants—the suburban refugees whose families flowed in from the Northern Drive.

This chapter focuses on the "underdevelopment" of South Central, with special emphasis on how transit racism and restrictive covenants confined the black population to Watts and a few smaller communities to the west. Housing shortages, overcrowding, and simmering tensions between older residents and newcomers to South Central contributed to the general tenor of unrest in the community. Discrimination against blacks by the Los Angeles Railway limited black job opportunities in the transit sector and resulted in service cutbacks to South Central. The imposition of gasoline rationing, coupled with increasingly mediocre streetcar service, made mobility particularly difficult for inner-city workers forced to work graveyard shifts as domestics and defense laborers. Faced with these conditions, black Angelenos were increasingly disconnected from the city, thus amplifying their ambivalent relationship to the automobile. The decline of streetcar service was cemented with the landmark *Collier Burns Act of 1947*, which established state subsidies for highway development. *Collier Burns*, and the 1956 *Interstate Highway Act*, would officially put California in "the business of highway building."

Downtown/Last Rites

> If you have ever been to the beautiful city of Los Angeles, you will know that Pershing Square, a palm-shaded spot in the center of downtown, is the mecca of motley...here, a short walk from "Skid Row"...haven for men of all races, all creeds...and all stages of deterioration, drifters and hopheads and tbs' and beggars...fraternizing with the tired business men from nearby offices...with the strutting Filipinos, the sharp-cat Mexican youths in their ultra drapes, with the colored guys from out South Central way...along the Hill Street side buses going west line up one behind the other to take you out Wilshire, to Beverly Hills, to Hollywood, to Santa Monica...to the Valley; and the red cars and the yellow cars fill the street with clatter and clang.[13]

The intersection of Hill Street and Sixth Street in downtown Los Angeles is a melancholic collision of old L.A. with new L.A. On the northwest corner of Hill Street, the staircase to the Red Line subway station, named after Pershing Square, leads underground, while on the southwest corner of Hill Street, the old Pacific Electric subway terminal building stands, an obscure archway heading off the facade of a largely forgotten monument to a bygone era. Boarded up and desolate, the building stands midway between the sleek, corporate splendor of Bunker Hill and the old downtown bustle of Grand Central Market, which is filled with mostly Latino-owned stores and vendors. The subway building opened in 1925 and closed in 1955, when the Metropolitan Coach Lines (the Pacific Electric's successor) ended rail service.[14] During World War II the terminal averaged 754 trains a day.[15] The proximity of the two terminals to one another is part reproach to those who would bemoan the "ahistorical" nature of Los Angeles and part confirmation of the amnesiac blight that abounds in popular musings on the city. A block away, Pershing Square is now haven to the third and fourth generation of urban indigency captured in Chester Himes's tableaux above. When I walked through the square one afternoon, it was dominated by homeless men of all races. Spurred by Reagan-era policies, the rise of homelessness in the city was intensified during the 1990s by L.A. County's axing of social services. Rounding out these cutbacks was the gutting of the 1995 *Housing Appropriations Bill* under the Clinton administration. The square is one of the few of its kind in L.A., and over the past century and a half its fortunes have shifted wildly. Once one of the byways for eighteenth-century Spanish expeditions through Los Angeles (most famously that of Felipe de Neve, one of the founders of the city in 1781), the area surrounding the square was originally called El Camino Viejo up until its dedication as a "Public Square or Plaza, for the use and benefit of the Citizens in common of said City" in 1866.[16] This early emphasis on the square's use by the public was a key part of its original design, which was overseen by public parks advocates.[17] The stipulation that the park be designated a "Public Place forever for the enjoyment of the Community in general" underscores the irony of the square's present layout, which reflects the city's attempts to discourage use of the square by the homeless.[18]

Retaining the concrete austerity from when it was turned into a parking lot in the 1960s, the square has a design that is consistent with the paramilitarization of downtown space that Mike Davis has termed "Fortress L.A."[19] Rather than integrating with the mood and tenor of the street—similar to say downtown New Haven, Connecticut's centrally located green, or Washington Square Park in lower Manhattan—Pershing Square is almost an affront to the street. The walls of the square give it the feel of a gated complex, while the scarcity of trees, foliage, and grass all but guarantee that most visits there, particularly on a hot summer day, will be brief. Since the 1970s, police sweeps and patrols of the square have become a common means of enforcing the continuum of private space that extends from the Biltmore Hotel throughout the tony corridor of Bunker Hill. The police state ethos that informs the layout of the square is duly reflected in its "aesthetic" structures, multicolored configurations that rise monolithically out of the concrete sprawl.

The square's spare design and lack of green space or benches for public use are symptomatic of municipal rationalization of public space.[20] As Christine Boyer has shown, this drive for rationality, for "closure" and totality, is the legacy of the Enlightenment drive for order that has so influenced modernist planning.[21] In Pershing Square, the grounds are cut off from the street, such that one is clearly not meant to linger or enjoy the park as a space that is both independent of and integrated with the street. The Square is hence an extension of the street's asphalt monomania. As I walked through it one afternoon, the absence of greenery and the oppressiveness of its concrete architecture made me acutely aware of how the city's othering of the pedestrian and the hypervisibility of the female body reinforce each other. Lolling on the few green patches arrayed around the concrete or on benches jutting from the low walls, each occupant seemed to take note of my presence. Moreover, despite the flow of automobile traffic outside on the street, I felt a mounting sense of isolation, an irrational sense of portent that I have rarely experienced on the most deserted street in New York City.

When walking in Los Angeles, one unconsciously adapts to the rhythms of the automobile, the body a mere addendum to the yellow line in the center of the road, hardwired to the terse cadence of stop and go, buildings reduced to abstraction. When it is after rush hour, after the clamor of school buses and delivery trucks has subsided, one becomes aware of the incredible silence of the city; silence that comes from the houses, or the cars that wait as one crosses the street; silence that looms even in the midst of the thickest downtown crowd.

Pershing Square, the old Pacific Electric subway building, and the new Red Line subway station form a continuum in Los Angeles history. They implicitly comment on the transmutations of time and space that automobility has wrought upon the city. While accounts of the PE station evoke its urban bustle and rhythm—the flow of passengers making transfers, buying the morning paper at newsstands, stopping at the station diner for the ritual cup of coffee (an Owl Drug Store occupies the ground floor in pictures of the building)—the largely empty Red Line station is a monument to the city's hubris.[22] The PE station was a medium of social connection, embodying all of the workaday dynamism that has been stripped from most urban public space in contemporary Los Angeles. The Red Line station, on the other hand, is merely one of the more egregious examples of how political patronage translates into wasteful public works. Entering the station the rider is greeted by a yawning concourse plastered with ads, ticket machines, and precious few patrons. Ironically, the sprawling layout of the station anticipates the kind of dense throng of urban ridership that presently only exists on the city's bus system.[23]

The austerity of Pershing Square is a hybrid of these two examples. As a concession to public space, the city's not so magnanimous gesture of communitas, the Square confirms the containment emphasis of downtown development. It provides the homeless with "somewhere to go," while simultaneously ensuring that they will not sully the onward rush of progress in surrounding Bunker Hill. As the cynosure of downtown corporate urban renewal, Bunker Hill embodies "the gleaming modernist rendering" of a wave of civic boosterism that has driven downtown development.[24]

The oldest urban section in Los Angeles, Bunker Hill occupies a special place in the lore of the city, its fortunes mirroring downtown's rise and fall, its spatial layout staged as space under siege and in need of redemption. In their article "Lost Streets of Bunker Hill," Anastasia Loukaitou-Sideris and Gail Sansbury evoke the area's vitality as an urban space during the 1930s and 1940s:

> The streets of Bunker Hill were an *integrated* and *diverse* landscape. While predominantly residential, these streets hosted a variety of uses and housing, supporting services, schools, playgrounds, hotels, restaurants, and small neighborhood retail establishments...for the elderly population, this proximity to services created a highly desirable residential environment. Years before planners would reinvent the "mixed-use" concept, the overlay of activities in the streets of Bunker Hill contributed to their vibrancy and liveliness.[25]

Although the area was considered an elite enclave (renowned for its stately "carpenter Gothic" and "Queen Anne–Victorian" architecture), the population of the neighborhood diversified during the 1930s, as wealthier residents moved west to more affluent neighborhoods such as Beverly Hills, Hollywood, and West Adams.[26] Thereafter, tenement housing was constructed on the hill. Many of its larger homes were either converted into rooming houses for single men or adapted for commercial use.[27] During the 1950s the area was condemned as "blighted" and was quickly targeted by Los Angeles's Community Redevelopment Agency (CRA) for renewal.[28]

For the poor, "renewal" took the form of displacement, as thousands of residents were forcibly removed from their homes. The streetcar and automobile follies of a generation before reverberated through the CRA's imperial policies toward working-class downtown citizens, many of whom were pushed further east to the crumbling Skid Row district. While downtown had ceased to be a prime spot for most white consumers, it continued to remain popular among Latino, Asian, and black shoppers in neighboring eastern and central communities. Many of these patrons came by bus or streetcar to take advantage of moderate to cheaply priced goods in the garment and jewelry districts and first-run Spanish and English language movies on Broadway.

As a junior high school student I remember taking fifty million buses downtown to go eat at Clifton's, one of the old-style "fly-in-my-soup" self-service cafeterias of the streetcar era. I recall going to the crustily beautiful, red plush Orpheum Theatre to see L.A. jazz legends Ornette Coleman, Billy Higgins, and Charlie Haden jam on a stage out of nineteenth-century burlesque. Then, as now, downtown was an enigma in the ease with which it veered from the air-brushed splendor of Little Tokyo, to the dead, driveby drone of the garment district (with its litany of plastic-wrapped clothes swinging in the wind), and the gaudy crush of Broadway. It was where all the buses dammed up into one great big pit, where food carts and open air carnicerias and zinc-topped lunch counters with hamburger specials ruled forever in the walking flood of wanderers and shoppers.

From the 1960s to the present, the area west of Broadway was sold to offshore capital.[29] Yet, before its fortunes were "reversed" by the onslaught of Canadian- and East Asian–financed postmodernist development, Bunker Hill was the focus of what Howard Klein has characterized as the "downtown myth."[30] As the area lost its allure and social cache for upper middle-class white Angelenos during the 1940s, it became the haven for white drifters and indigent men. Bunker Hill was fantasized in the novels of Raymond Chandler and John Fante as an area "lost" to time.[31] The decline of the area became associated with a moral decay signified by "marginal" districts such as Chinatown or the Mexican barrios in which "the seedier aspects of tourism" could be isolated.[32] The designation of communities of color as districts in which illicit consumption was sanctioned (by the "chaos" of the racial Other) was integral to the downtown myth. Here,

> [t]he downtown myth also stands for the segregated nature of the city as indeed any tourist town tends to be segregated carefully, through commercial zoning, housing covenants, careful promotion and the way police patrons operate from one area to the next.[33]

Chronicling the racial ontology that informed World War II–era Los Angeles, the work of Chester Himes pungently captured the city's own special brand of auto-driven segregation. While white critics (Klein, Davis, et al.) rhapsodize about the cultural anomie and disintegration depicted in Nathaniel West's work, Himes's work draws from a deeper well of schizoid displacement, identifying the nausea of a hyperembodied blackness literally etched into the boundaries of the city. In Himes's story "Lunching at the Ritzmore," Pershing Square becomes the scene for a ribald debunking of the bogus vision of Los Angeles liberalism. At the beginning of the story, a white student and a white drifter meet and ponder the question of whether discrimination against "Negroes" continues to exist. Challenging the white student to a bet after he argues that Negroes aren't the victims of discrimination, the drifter asks a passing black mechanic to settle their contest by getting him to order a meal at the restaurant of his choice. The three march down Hill Street and proceed to attract the "flotsam" of Pershing Square, who mistakenly believe that the group is en route to a free meal. Discussing their choice of restaurant, the mechanic says "These guys are used to seeing colored people down here. All of the domestic workers who work out in Hollywood and Beverly and all out there get off the U car and come down here and catch their buses. It ain't like if it was somewhere on the West Side where they ain't used to seeing them."(p. 19) His critique of the axis of power between the more culturally diverse East side and the predominantly white West side reflects the degree to which downtown still wielded a big commercial influence upon the city in that volatile period. Moreover, Himes's portrayal illustrates the degree to which black employment was tied to downtown, a phenomenon that would be upended in the postwar struggle between industrial core and postindustrial satellite.

South Central

Himes's 1945 novel *If He Hollers Let Him Go* provides a window onto the socioeconomic and psychic displacements of postwar, posturban Los Angeles, deftly illustrating the ghettoizing havoc that decentralization (among other forces) would wreak upon South Central. Part character study, part commentary on the psychological disfigurement of racism, Himes's novel follows the trajectory of Bob Jones, the only black leaderman at a Los Angeles shipyard. Shipyards figured prominently in the South Central black community because they were among the few private industries where blacks were able to break into semiskilled work during wartime. Defense manufacturing jobs became more widely available to blacks after Brotherhood of Sleeping Car Porters' head A. Phillip Randolph threatened to organize a march on Washington in 1941. Randolph's action prompted Franklin Roosevelt to address job discrimination against people of color by issuing Executive Order 8802, establishing the Fair Employment Practices Commission (FEPC) in 1941.[34] The creation of the FEPC, coupled with the severe labor shortage in California, enabled blacks to gain employment in previously all-white industries such as defense, shipping, and auto manufacturing. Before the FEPC, companies led campaigns to recruit out-of-state whites rather than hire blacks living in California.[35]

Throughout the novel, Himes's protagonist Bob Jones drives through the city in his Buick, reflecting on the city's volatile boundaries of class and race:

> At Vernon I turned west to Normandie, driving straight into the sun; north on Normandie to Twenty-eighth Street, then west past Western. This was the West Side. When you asked a Negro where he lived, and he said on the West Side, that was supposed to mean he was better than the Negroes who lived on the South Side. (48)

Himes's work is critical because it focuses on a watershed period in the history of black South Central, as the community struggled to accommodate a wave of new migration in the wake of shrinking postwar job opportunities and rising housing shortages. This wave of new arrivals raised concerns among older, more established migrants, who viewed the new migrants as being backward, "lower class," and generally threatening to their hard-won upward mobility.[36] As early as 1933 (when the black population in Los Angeles was still fairly small), an editorial in the *California Eagle* lamented that "it is not difficult to see that the land-owning and responsible Negro citizens of the South could not go North or West as readily as the less responsible."[37] This elitist representation of new migrants as "the Other" had serious implications for the community's collective identity. Historian Gerald Horne has suggested that interclass animus ultimately doomed substantive political organizing to failure, as "year of arrival consciousness became a substitute for class consciousness."[38]

Thus, from World War II to the postwar era, Watts, "having developed into a black island in an otherwise white sea of southeastern Los Angeles county," saw the westerly push of an emergent black middle class and the continuing disenfranchisement of a black underclass overwhelmingly composed of new migrants.[39] Horne maintains that the black middle classes' heavy emphasis on abolishing restrictive covenants, while unquestionably critical, ultimately displaced the issue of public housing.[40] The absence of concerted political action for public housing reinforced the opposition of city government and private real estate interests. This stance was legitimized by the FHA's longstanding refusal to develop public housing.[41] For example, in both San Francisco and New York, the FHA would not approve insurance for local developers' proposals to construct war housing for blacks.[42] With the FHA's racist imprimatur, banks refused to finance large-scale housing developments in predominantly black areas.[43]

Black mobility was also undermined by the legacy of Watts's incorporation into the city of Los Angeles in 1926.[44] The incorporation of the suburb effectively wedded its political interests with that of the city. As the area's black population grew, this dynamic stifled the development of black political autonomy, limiting the community's ability to mobilize around the issue of public housing.[45] At the height of the housing crisis the neighborhood was thrown a crumb in the form of two housing projects, Jordan Downs and Imperial Courts. Jordan Downs was built before the war ended and Imperial Courts was built after the war ended, and was initially considered "temporary" housing.[46] One of the most infamous examples of the city's failure to develop public housing was the decision to scrap construction of a major public housing complex on the Chavez Ravine site near downtown L.A. and Dodger stadium. The development was aborted because of opposition by the real estate establishment and the FHA's enforcement of restrictive covenant homogeneity clauses.[47] As Raphael Sonenshein notes, "By shutting off housing in other areas,

Los Angeles deprived blacks of their chance to free up new housing for poorer blacks, while building an even stronger middle class."[48] These volatile class and political divisions would rend South Central, reinforcing its isolation from the rest of the city well into the Vietnam era.[49]

The political volatility of the community was exacerbated by economic fallout from the export of jobs and social services to the suburbs. As Los Angeles moved into the highway era, rejecting all but the most modest improvements for the railway system, inadequate transportation turned South Central into an economic outpost. This disparity in access was particularly acute for the workers employed at naval shipyards and as domestics in private homes. As the primary means of employment for blacks, domestic work frequently took them from South Central to the West side homes of white employers.[50] For women, who worked as either live-in or day workers, usually earning $5.00 a day, travel to the West side was typically a communal affair:

> At the end of the day, the domestic workers of a given neighborhood found themselves standing at the same bus stop, wearing similar uniforms, headed in the same direction: Watts.[51]

During the war era, Watts had become the hub of black settlement, the streetcar and the bus its primary means of conveyance. The area's most heavily used lines were the local Los Angeles Railway U car on Central Avenue and the Big Red Car interurban, or "express," from Watts to Long Beach (which traveled to the Long Beach Naval Shipyard, one of the biggest employers of blacks during the period). Twelfth and Central was the unofficial "Main Street" of black Los Angeles, where, "If you stood there long enough you'd meet every black in Los Angeles and greet all those who had just arrived from the South."[52] Bars and clubs sprawled all over the street. Jazz legends such as Johnny Hodges, Duke Ellington, Billy Holiday, Dinah Washington, and Ornette Coleman (to name but a few) would play regular gigs there. The street life of Central Avenue was infectious. As one former resident mused, "we used to sit right here in the alley and listen to the music," at a venue called the Downbeat Club.[53]

The high turnover rate and low pay of domestic work made access to a Red Car of the utmost importance.[54] Taking a drive down the streets of Los Angeles today gives one a clear sense of the public transit landscape of women's work in the city. From the east-west corridors of King and Venice Boulevards to the north-south arteries of Western and Broadway Avenues, bus-riding Latin and Central American women have largely replaced the streetcar-riding black domestic workers of the World War II and postwar eras. Indeed, a drive through South Central Los Angeles reveals the tremendous ethnic and racial flux of the region, Latino communities having sprung up in the wake of a shrinking black presence.[55] As in New York and other East Coast cities, where the numbers of West Indian women squiring around white charges continue to climb, domestic work is ever the province of immigrant women of color. In the wealthy West side enclaves of L.A., Salvadoran, Guatemalan, and Colombian women have moved in to fill the gap created by the growth of nominally better-paying service sector jobs increasingly occupied by native workers of color.[56]

Black domestic work helped smooth white women's path into the workforce during the wartime and postwar eras. Historian Jacqueline Jones has noted that black women often functioned as a "behind-the-scenes cadre of support workers for gainfully employed white wives."[57] In 1940, 60 percent of black women were domestic workers, compared to 10 percent of white women.[58] From 1940 to 1950 the numbers of black women in the workforce was 37 percent compared to white women's 24.5 to 28.5 percent.[59] This disparity in employment levels was naturally attributable to the chronic gap in earnings for both black men and women vis-à-vis that of whites. Women's work was not merely supplementary but mandatory to the livelihood of black households.[60] At the height of World War II, black women had "begun to feel the full impact of 'powerful forces at work...to repopulate the abandoned kitchens of Southern and Northern white women.'"[61] The pressure placed upon black women to form an auxiliary force for white homes vacated by new white women workers manifested itself in narratives evoking the age-old stereotype of black women's laziness. In a typical rendering of the grotesquely slothful black domestic, one white employer commented, "And the Negro maid...If you don't carry her back and forth in your car...she will not work...many of our white women...have husbands in the Army and must work, and they must have help in their homes if they are to keep bravely going. That's where the Negro maid is supposed to fit in."[62] In one fell swoop, the specter of black slothfulness, white female fortitude, and the instrumentality of the auto are linked in a melodrama of national/domestic crisis. This statement is particularly interesting because it illustrates the degree to which black female labor was integral to national production. By "fitting in" with the cause of white domestic stability, black women became part of the war effort, stepping into the breach of white feminine production in order to consolidate the well-oiled machine of white domesticity. The almost surreal evocation of the black female worker waiting to be ferried around from point A to point B is the subtext of the white family's march to first-world progress—delivered from the wartime threat of global fascism to postwar Ozzie and Harriet prosperity. In this scenario the car enabled white household stability, facilitating the use of black female labor in the service of white private space. The temporary aberration of white women in the workplace only served to strengthen a white patriarchy nourished by the specter of the fascist Other of Germany and Japan. During the next decade, as the development of the interstate highway system hastened the shifting axis of power from city to suburb, the growing schism between public and private transportation would play a major role in refocusing these notions of otherness back onto the black family and the inner city.

"LARY Hires Negro"

The issue of wartime national unity was a big factor in the *California Eagle*'s crusade against employment discrimination at the Los Angeles Railway during the 1940s. On December 11, 1942, the *Eagle* published an editorial decrying the impact that housing shortages, restrictive covenants, and transit discrimination were having on South Central. The newspaper then called for a mass meeting of "big guns of the East side," as represented by the NAACP, the Negro Victory Committee, and *The Los Angeles Sentinel*.[63] Aside from the politics of the meeting what interests most is its historical irony—namely the paper's decision to frame worsening conditions in the community as "sabotage of the war effort."[64] Throughout its campaign, the newspaper sounded the theme of national unity, emphasizing the role that East side workers would play in ensuring the victory of the United States:

> Eastside workers are predominantly employed in industries important to war production. Peacetime property restrictions force them into a tiny fraction of the city, an area removed from all major defense plants. When housing...cannot be occupied by war workers simply because of their race, a situation exists which endangers Los Angeles' contribution to victory.[65]

The first black newspaper in the city, the *Eagle* was founded in 1915. The tenor of the paper swung from unabashedly "progressive"—e.g., in its promotion of Communist rallies, unrelenting attack on the foot-dragging FEPC, and support of an independent presidential candidate—to retrograde (self-hating "darkie" cartoons and tons of ads for the latest line of skin lighteners and hair straighteners which were a staple of the paper's ad layout). The paper's appeal to an ill-begotten national unity illustrated the schizoid position of blacks in the context of a war in which they were still fighting in segregated units.[66]

The LARY had long been notorious for its refusal to hire blacks as motormen or conductors.[67] The public, LARY management opined, was just "not ready for the upgrading of black workers," preferring to see them acting in the more familiar capacity as janitors and car cleaners.[68] The restriction of blacks to menial positions was so entrenched in the structure of transit employment that it was one of the most stubbornly segregated fields in the municipal sector. Company policy was rigidly enforced by the Association of Street, Electric Railway, and Motor Coach operators, whose members threatened to strike if blacks received promotions.[69] White transit workers in Philadelphia and New York were also allied against black promotion. In 1944, 5,000 white Philadelphia transit workers walked off the job after the FEPC ordered the transit company to promote blacks to motorman positions.[70] On the heels of this ruling, the California Supreme Court declared segregated unions in a closed shop unconstitutional.[71] It is impossible to overvalue the role that unions had, not only in fostering white working-class solidarity (whipping up resentment about the "incursions" of blacks and other workers of color who were perceived as undermining white benefits), but in also allowing whites to become upwardly mobile.

Transit unionism in Los Angeles was crippled by the city's long-standing antiunion tradition.[72] During the 1920s, an organization called the Pacific Electric Club was intended as a kinder, gentler, management-sanctioned alternative to the unions.[73] In 1934, amendments to the *Federal Railway Labor Act* by Franklin Roosevelt led to the formation of the Pacific Electric Brotherhood of Railroad Trainmen.[74] The majority of American unions during this period were under the aegis of the AFL or CIO. Before their merger in the 1950s the AFL and CIO had followed different agendas vis-à-vis black employment. The CIO actively organized black workers and made some strides in improving black employment opportunities, despite the fact that it never succeeded in reconciling its avowed commitment to racial justice with the inner workings of its locals.[75] According to Keith Collins, "the CIO became a leading force in breaking barriers to black employment," helping blacks obtain jobs in aircraft plants and rubber factories while working to end segregated shifts.[76] AFL locals, on the other hand, segregated members by race and gender and were more susceptible to the red-baiting tactics of anti-Communist organizations. The CIO, in contrast, worked with the Communist Party to organize blacks.[77] Blacks were highly attractive to the Party in its efforts to consolidate its influence upon American grassroots politics. However, with the onset of the Cold War, the CIO severed its ties to the Party and dismissed unions with heavy communist ties, many of which, not surprisingly, had the highest black membership in the organization.[78]

The merger of the AFL and CIO defanged the CIO's stalwart pursuit of racial justice in the workplace.[79] At the convention to determine the organization's platform, the new merger didn't explicitly address the issue of workplace discrimination. By the 1950s the CIO retreated from its emphasis on racial equality, abandoning its efforts to organize blacks.[80]

Black employees' struggles against discrimination in the LARY occurred when the CIO's efforts to organize blacks were at a high point. Conditions at the railway were especially egregious because nearly a quarter of the company's positions were vacant.[81] According to Alonzo Smith, "It was stated that no blacks were utilized as conductors or motormen, although there were 2,500 jobs in the system, of which 600 were unfilled."[82] The *Eagle* recommended redress by the FEPC and the War Commission, maintaining that "The stupendous perversion of our war effort flaunted in the face of Los Angeles patriots by the railway firm turns its all from the gigantic common task, the crushing of Hitler."[83] The paper's willingness to exploit nationalist sentiment in the name of social justice illustrated the extent to which the black middle classes' investment in the American Dream fueled its trajectory in Southern California. The inconsistency of the United States' opposition to the Axis power regimes while continuing its maintenance of Jim Crow and de facto segregation did not escape the paper's editorial staff. However, the paper's desperate attempt to include blacks in the narrative of world conquest was a particularly schizoid gyration, one which painfully elides the issue of how "making the world safe" for democracy was predicated on the opposition of blackness to the very notion of American citizenship and civil rights.

The LARY impasse finally came to a head in 1944, when the FEPC ordered the company to admit blacks to motormen and conductor positions.[84] The company proceeded to upgrade fifteen black men to motormen and several black women to conductor.[85] According to Alonzo Smith, the 1944 ruling made municipal transit "the one occupation where blacks achieved solid gains in the Los Angeles area."[86]

These gains notwithstanding, marginal transit service deepened Watts's isolation from the rest of the city, undermining workers' efforts to keep jobs outside of the community. The most prominent case in point was that of workers at the Long Beach Naval Shipyard. One of the largest employers of blacks in Los Angeles (and the model for "Atlas Shipyard" depicted in Himes's novel), the Long Beach shipyard was a focal point for families in South Central. Most black workers were hired to work the graveyard shift from 12 midnight to 8 o'clock in the morning. The timing of the shift was especially difficult because streetcar and bus service was not scheduled for South Central communities late at night, making it necessary for workers to find other means of transportation for the ride to the plant.[87] Recalling his frustration over getting to work, one former shipyard worker observed:

> It took the Red Car a long time to go from Watts to Long Beach and the damn thing broke down a lot. And when it didn't break down it would have to wait until the freight train passed...It was a job getting a job, it was a job getting to the job; and I felt like the white man didn't want me to work so he could label me lazy.[88]

Bus, jitney, and taxi drivers would not go to the area out of fear of crime.[89] The absence of local black-owned businesses, large universities, and government offices made the situation in South Central even more desperate for black residents tethered to public transportation.[90] Indeed, the surge in migration to the area caused overcrowding on the U car line, leading to half-hour service lags that further compromised workers. Although another train—the "D" car—was put on the line to alleviate service lags, increased demand for service in the area was never addressed.

While 1942 represented a turning point for black employment, limited black mobility mitigated these gains. Because most black residents did not own cars, middling streetcar service reinforced the city's boundaries of exclusion and containment. While the wartime economy proved to be a temporary boon to the ailing street railways, postwar prosperity restored the automobile to its former glory. Thus, the decline of public transportation coincided with African Americans' loss of the semiskilled and skilled work and relatively high wages that they had obtained because of wartime labor shortages. As white men returned to home and hearth, blacks began to see most of the gains they had made in the workplace evaporate. More insidiously, this downsizing was concomitant with the shift of jobs from the central city to the suburbs.[91]

Suburban manifest destiny was in full bloom. With the end of the war, Los Angeles experienced a renaissance of highway development, its car obsession culminating in the inception of the most extensive system of freeways in the world. As early as 1944, the Interregional Highway Committee had proposed building a system of 39,000 miles of intercity highways. Although funding for the initiative was "preempted" by the war effort, the age of frontierism was well on its way to its most monumental expression yet.[92]

When Larry Aubry left Los Angeles to go into the military in 1952, the city had already scrapped the majority of its streetcar lines. Aubry recalls riding the "V" car line down Vermont Avenue to Los Angeles City College upon his return in the late 1950s, when he had acquired a 1932 Chevy, his first automobile. During that period, Aubry lived on Normandie near Manual Arts High School on Vermont, an area that had formerly been considered the West side, but, with the abolition of restrictive covenants, and increasing black settlement would in ten years be deemed as part of the East side.

Mr. Aubry came to L.A. from New Orleans on a Santa Fe train at the height of World War II. He recalled the atmosphere on the train as one of camaraderie, servicemen and civilians mingled with one another in the often crowded Jim Crow cars. Aubry and his family settled on Morgan Avenue on the East side. Morgan was one block away from a LARY stop, and a short distance away from the famed Dunbar Hotel on Central Avenue. Once considered a tony gathering place for the black elite, the Dunbar was the pride of the South Central, and the hub of the area's vibrant nightlife.

While the Central Avenue U car became a lifeline for many of the area's residents, car culture was also rapidly becoming a force in the community. Those few black residents who did own cars were a valuable resource to their fellow workers. During the war, gasoline rationing became a major point of contention within the community. Rationing strained the community's already tenuous transportation resources. One of the most vociferous critics of rationing was the *California Eagle*:

> The bulk of people living in the Negro ghetto are essential to the production of arms to lick Hitler. This vast, vital working group, faced with gas rationing find themselves removed by miles from the aircraft factories and shipyards at which they labor for America's victory.[93]

Gas rationing and erratic streetcar service forced many black Angelenos to come up with other means of getting around. Shipyard workers formed carpools, taking turns doing the twenty-minute drive to Long Beach. One auto mechanic actually restored old junkyard cars and put them on the road for carpoolers. In Himes's *If He Hollers Let Him Go*, Bob Jones drives a carpool to work every day:

> It was a bright June morning. The sun was already high. If I was a white boy I might have enjoyed the scramble in the early morning sun, the tight competition for a twenty-foot lead on a thirty-mile highway. But to me it was racial. The huge industrial steel plants flanking the ribbon of road—shipyards, refineries, oil wells, steel mills, construction companies—the thousands of rushing workers, the close hard roar of Diesel trucks and the distant drone of patrolling planes, the sharp, pungent smell of exhaust that used to send me driving clear across Ohio on a sunny summer morning and the snow-capped mountains in the background...didn't mean a thing to me. I didn't even see them; all I wanted in the world was to push my Buick Roadmaster in some peckerwood's face. (14)

For Jones, driving in Los Angeles becomes both a metaphor for the terroristic landscape of the city and an outlet for its exorcism. Speeding to work to avoid the inevitable reprisals from white supervisors for coming in late, Jones lives and breathes the contradictions of wartime United States Granted a deferment from fighting in the war because of his job at the shipyard, Jones's narrative resonates with his bitterness over the grinding injustice of being required to fight in a segregated army.[94] His gritty evocations of the shipyard, with their raw critique of the byzantine racial schema of white/black one-upmanship, reflect the schizoid workaday conditions of defense manufacturing. Musing on the heated choreography of worker relations, he inveighs, "As long as white folks hate me and I hate them we can earn the same amount of money, live side by side in the same kind of house, and fight every day" (88). Jones frequently dubs his white co-workers "peckerwoods" (a black term for whites) or "paddies" (a derogatory term for the Irish). Jones's portrayal of L.A. disrupts the picture of racial and ethnic homogeneity perpetuated by the Middle American myth of white Southern California. Jones's commentary on work relations in the shipyard—particularly that of jockeying for power among white supervisors contemptuous of and intimidated by his outspokenness—marks whiteness as a contested space. His identification of the hierarchy of white racial and ethnic identity foregrounds the construction of whiteness, and the way in which white racial indifference is obscured and normalized through the exercise of power in an industrial context. As he drives through the streets of L.A., Jones's critical gaze highlights the ways in which the cityscape reflects the production of power via whiteness. However, the character is nonetheless imprisoned by his desire to be seen by white men. The insidious aura of racial terror and violence that informs relationships between workers in the shipyard is played out in the male characters' verbal jousting and one-upmanship. Navigating the city's racial divide, Jones's contest with white masculinity is his perpetual compass. His misogyny becomes the backdrop for his desire to best white men, and ultimately precipitates a misbegotten attempt to retaliate for racist mistreatment at the plant.[95]

As with the men in Colleen McElroy's *Sister Detroit*, Jones's car is a form of cultural capital, a means by which the "emasculating" force of racism could be resisted. Here, Jones's mastery of the road is an expression of masculine agonism and affirmation. Negotiating the East side/West side axis, Jones re-enacts the rituals of masculine power and domination that inscribe white hegemony.

The East side/West side split continued to play a significant role in the mapping of racial space in the city after the war. When my grandfather and his family came to L.A. from Chicago (in the family Buick) in 1960, it was to a post–restrictive covenant city that was beginning to show the pattern of hypersegregation for which it has become renowned. Conceding to my grandmother's "obsession" with California, the family made the uncertain trip from the politics-driven landscape of Chicago, where "nightlife started at 11:00, and you ran into friends on the street," to a city with no discernible cultural center.[96] When the family landed in Leimert Park, several years after Genethia

Hayes's family, the white and Japanese families were still prominent, and "blacks had only gotten as far as Western Avenue."[97] Western, a street that was considered West side when Larry Aubry was growing up in the city during the 1940s, is now considered the East side. In the 1980s it emerged as a thriving Korean commercial district and home base for the Korean community.

Thus, as the East side/West side orientation of the city shifted, marking more communities as sites of racial otherness, the dismantlement of the streetcar system solidified the pattern of spatial inequality promoted by the institutionalization of the automobile. However, while the regime of auto and bus reinforced transit dependency in inner-city communities, riding the bus provided another means of envisioning the city. As the streetcar faded into memory, the bus became an unlikely symbol of the struggle for democracy within the "inner city."

CHAPTER SEVEN
Waiting for the Bus

> Every now and then—like now—Los Angeles is reminded that there is no such thing as a functioning city without mass transit. With near-pornographic glee, the Adam Smith boys have been of late trashing the very idea of publicly supported mass transit as not only unnecessary, but an economic catastrophe. The automobile and paratransit, claim these hyper-free marketeers, left to their own devices, can out-perform public transit...tell that to the half-million and more commuters left stranded Monday morning by the...walk-out...Standing in bewilderment on corners where no buses came, they confronted the Gordian knot of Los Angeles transit history—from which there is no escape.[1]
>
> —Kevin Starr (1994, M1)

Having been one of the "bewildered" waiting in the torrid August sun for a northbound 210 bus one afternoon on Crenshaw Boulevard in the summer of 1994, I vividly remember the well of frustration and outrage that neighborhood riders expressed toward a system that was already, in most people's minds, poorly managed and insensitive to the needs of neighborhoods with the heaviest ridership. Boarding an L.A. bus after a six-year hiatus was a surreal experience; the plodding lurch and tumble between stops, the dark, cave-like interior, and the seamy odor of the bus conjured a flood of associations and memories from when riding on the bus had literally been a lifeline to the web of the city. The bus was perhaps the most indelible symbol of public space in my daily encounters, stitching together the crazy quilt of L.A.'s communities for an eighty-cent fare. On weekends my best friend Heather and I caught the bus to Hollywood Boulevard on a long winding trip that took us from the hybrid sprawl of Crenshaw Boulevard. to the white, old money affluence of Rossmore Avenue in Hancock Park, to the manic glory of Vine past Sunset and Hollywood Boulevards. The city bus was a universe unto itself. Its uneasy mingling of class, age, and race made it a symbol of all the economies that drove L.A., from student to domestic worker, teacher to service worker, retiree to day laborer. In this regard, it was a window onto an "alternative" L.A. One that while true to its rigid social boundaries was nonetheless evocative of the urbanism that the city left behind. On the bus, the city's streetcar past was a delphic black-and-white reel. Its influence on the layout of the city was like a rumored wisp of lore and legend so at odds with the ubiquitous skein of road arteries and auto traffic that it had the odor of science fiction.

When I rode the bus during the 1994 bus strike after coming from the culture of the New York subway; the rhythms of the bus, and the working-class and elderly women who filled the majority of its seats were a vivid reminder of why the racial landscape of mass transit is absolutely central to L.A.'s conception as a posturban city. The MTA had only recently been revived in 1993 through the merging of the defunct Southern California Rapid Transit District (the agency that had been created to oversee the bus system when the streetcar system was finally dismantled in 1961) and the Los Angeles Transportation Commission. The organization manages the largest bus system in the country, and, with the development of the Red Line subway, is overseeing one of the largest and most controversial public works projects in United States history.[2] The 1994 bus strike centered on the mechanics' union's opposition to private maintenance contracting.[3] The MTA, faced with an impending lawsuit over alleged misuse of funds for its rail project, was further assailed for its failure to mete out contracts equitably to its own employees. While the strike was resolved a week later, the issues that it evoked bespoke the firestorm of controversy that erupted over public transportation in 1990s L.A., as the city struggled to recuperate its conflicted metropolitan heritage.[4]

The struggle between bus and rail in L.A. County has been at the very heart of the city's schizoid identity. While the city spent fifty years selling out the urban ethos of its rail heritage, it now looks to rail for redemption. Conferring the subway with the same rarefied cultural symbolism of the pyramids of ancient Egypt, Kevin Starr laments that the project's demise is as much a "matter of idea" as it is of politics.[5] For boosters such as Starr, the subway symbolizes the city's reach for civic greatness, the utopian promise that feeds the myth of the "California dream" that he has chronicled in his trilogy on the state's history. The subway "bespoke a vision of Los Angeles as a unified metropolis, possessed of a discernible, if subtle, civic unity and centered, more or less, on a downtown."[6]

The issues and alliances that have sprung up over the course of the MTA's downward spiral are so byzantine that they have shifted the political ground of the city, making strange bedfellows of longtime foes.[7] The mismanagement of the MTA has thrown the degree to which the city council determines the direction of municipal government into relief.[8] More importantly, it has renewed serious debate on the importance of the city's bus system to not only the livelihood of scores of low-income riders, but to alleviating the tremendous environmental and social burden that the city's inordinate dependence on the private automobile has imposed:

> In their panic about getting to work, commuters left high and dry by public transit did not have the luxury of the Adam Smith crowd's comparative statistics...They were discovering, among other things, that the vaunted automobile culture of greater Los Angeles is dependent on public transit. Put another half-million people on the road—as the MTA strike did—and the already overloaded freeway system edges toward gridlock.[9]

The "Adam Smith" crowd that Starr refers to would ostensibly have L.A. rewind the reel back to the Pacific Electric era, when public transportation was privately funded and managed and generally unaccountable to the public. It is important to recall that similar sentiments fueled support for the street traffic plans that ultimately undermined the viability of rail transportation and consigned L.A. to a generation's worth of mediocre bus service. Despite having been served with a federal court order to improve its service, the MTA still skirted its responsibilities to bus riders, cutting back nighttime service in the spring of 1998, well after the consent decree was approved. At that time, the city was considering breaking up the bus system and allowing "subregional" companies to run bus lines in each community. It also weighed the option of allowing the San Fernando Valley to create its own transit authority. These potential changes were further complicated by the ongoing soap opera of the agency's funding woes, board patronage scandals, and abortive attempts to get construction for the Red Line subway on course.[10] The 1994 strike was climactic because it illustrated—with a vengeance—for policymakers, municipal government, and diehard drivers who were heretofore indifferent to the city bus system the raw truth of Starr's observations that public transportation was indeed a vital element of the region's economy. In the years since, the MTA's egregious mishaps have remained under the spotlight of the city's bus riders. In 2002, the MTA board voted to appeal the landmark 1995 consent decree that required the agency to upgrade bus service to the Supreme Court. The court refused to hear the appeal, validating the Bus Riders Union's challenge to the two-tiered system of Los Angeles transportation politics.

Nationwide, other interracial coalitions have successfully linked the issue of transit dependency with institutional racism in the courts. In 1995 the New York City Straphangers' Campaign joined with the Urban League in an anti-discrimination lawsuit against the New York Metropolitan Transit Authority.[11] Using a strategy similar to that of the BRU, the New York coalition charged that bus and subway fare increases would have a disproportionate effect on the blacks, Latinos, and Asians, who make up the bulk of the system's riders.[12] In its suit against the MTA, the BRU's insistence that "improving the transit system is a civil rights issue because most commuters are minorities and have low incomes" went to the heart of the issue of how denial of access, and viable alternatives to privatized space, "others" communities of color. In Red Hook, Brooklyn, a low-income, mostly black and Latino neighborhood near the Gowanus Expressway, whose dock properties have become the subject of revitalization efforts by the city, the neighborhood's high-rise housing projects are virtually isolated by an industrial swath of bridge and highway development. Assessing the impact of the auto-industrial complex on urban development, critic Jane Holtz Kay cites Red Hook as a premier example of the isolating effects that inadequate public transportation and highway infrastructure inflict upon a neighborhood stripped of local industry. In 1996 I worked in Red Hook at the office of a construction contractor near the shore. My daily schlep on the bus went through a blight of waste management companies, incineration plants, and garbage dumps located near playgrounds, schools, and apartments. A half-mile walk from the nearest subway station, local residents must tread through expressway overpasses and high-traffic connectors to get to the subway station or a bus stop. Because of the neighborhood's industrial desolation, both options are potentially dangerous at night.

While federal welfare for autos has wreaked havoc on the social and economic well-being of neighborhoods such as Red Hook, the dynamic of "driving while black" informs the black driver's experience of spatial segregation in L.A. The Los Angeles uprising of 1992 clearly demonstrated that the social geography of the city has changed only slightly from the early period in the region's history, when "many public areas were partly or entirely closed to blacks, especially...suburban cities around L.A."[13] A drive through an "unauthorized" area of the city can be potentially hazardous for black motorists. The emergence of "racial profiling," in which black and Latino motorists are routinely stopped and apprehended by law enforcement without compelling reason, has further restricted the mobility of people of color. In L.A., where the city is symbolically divided into the "white" Westside, "black South Central" (i.e., *any* area east of La Cienega Boulevard that is predominantly black) and more "nebulous" areas east of downtown with large Asian and Latino representation, the landscape of racial otherness is strictly enforced by the knot of highways that crowd out the bus stops in the visual space of the car. In this respect, "[t]o ride a bus in Los Angeles is to know a city...different from its enduring image of uncircumscribed freedom," one radically separate from the hallmarks of auto development, in which distance becomes a function of time.[14] Riding the bus in L.A. is a parallel city, the purest expression of L.A.'s one-hundred-year dialogue of urban and antiurban. Its street plans enclose women with their packages, as they wait in front of hospitals, grocery stores, check-cashing places, and day care centers in the early morning crush. Some buses are so packed they do not even stop for more passengers. The thriving car cultures of South Central and Southwest L.A. flow past the majority of mass transit users, who are overwhelmingly poor women of color, both native-born and immigrant. Although the Lincoln Land Policy Institute estimates that only 4 percent to 5 percent of trips in the United States utilize public transportation, this figure does not adequately account for rates of use in so-called inner-city communities, where women depend heavily upon buses and subways for multiple, daily trips to the workplace, public agencies, and the homes of friends and relatives. Critiquing the disparity caused by transportation planning that privileges male travel within the city (where men typically, whether riding the bus or driving, make a round trip journey to work), Dolores Hayden notes:

> If the simple male journey from home to job is the one planned for, and the complex female journey from home to day care to job is the one ignored, it is easy to see how women's time disappears when they attempt to overcome the separation of home and work.[15]

If the daily travel of male workers is generally linear, the daily travel patterns of women are more "triangular."[16] In Los Angeles, the transition from streetcar to bus amplified this issue. In a city in which space has been conquered by time, the parallel time of the bus makes women's triangular journeys longer and more arduous. Whereas the Pacific Electric and the Los Angeles Railways were an integrated network of local and express service, the majority of MTA buses run locally except on major throroughfares such as Crenshaw Boulevard and Wilshire Boulevard. The absence of express service on most major north-south corridors in communities of color essentially ensures that the journey on a bus will often be twice as long (as opposed to roughly comparable on rapid transit) as that of the automobile.[17]

Crossroads

For black women in the postrailway era, the bus has historically been a site where the intersection of public and private highlighted the racial subtext of American notions of femininity. While public transportation has figured largely in the twentieth century's most important desegregation struggles (Plessy vs. Ferguson to Montgomery, Alabama), bus service has especially been seen as a symbol of the malaise of urban communities in general and of Los Angeles in particular. Despite municipal governments' early flirtation with buses as the savior for big-city transit, the figure of the bus, in its lumbering rhythm of stop and go, has come to be reviled as the stepchild of modern transportation technology. Devoid of rapid rail's elemental seductiveness and ostensible ability to transfigure time and space, the bus is a marginal figure within the American cultural imagination. Poorly maintained, slow, and, occasionally, missing in action, buses carry the stigma of backwardness within a social landscape that has condensed, and thereby "conquered" time via the medium of the expressway, the interchange, and the diamond lane.[18] While some transit critics hew to the notion that the "mass popularization of the auto democratized" transportation, this claim is in view of the fact that the hierarchy between public and private transit marks bus riders as second-class citizens.[19]

When Rosa Parks boarded the bus in Montgomery in 1955 she was part of a long legacy of working black women who protested the demeaning conditions under which they were forced to travel everyday. In many cities throughout the nation, black women form the backbone of ridership on city buses. Behind the wheel, I am temporarily removed from them, shorn of their markings, made over by the road, the chromium steel of the bumper raging forward. My gaze is transfixed by the yellow and white lines in a cyborg fantasy of omniscience, eating lanes, eating streets, eating corners in one great, big, ten-minute V-6 gulp. It is a fantasy that is interrupted by the specter of Rodney King sliding down the off-ramp in Simi Valley. It is a fantasy unraveled by the itchy trigger-finger slickness of a white policewoman's hands over my body after my friends and I are ordered out of one of their older brothers' car at gunpoint and surrounded by five police vehicles one evening on Hyde Park in Inglewood. He is ordered to lie face down on the ground. The car's backfire was mistaken for a gunshot, we are later told.

During the World War II era, as more and more women entered the workforce, the marking of the black female body as racial space was enacted on a daily basis within the context of the city bus. Despite the fact that greater opportunities opened up for women as a whole during this period, the realities of institutional racism/employment discrimination allowed white women and white families to make gains via semiskilled work, whereas black women were routinely assigned to menial jobs that white women considered beneath them. For example, in the garment, munitions, and railroad industries, which offered the highest wages, black women manufactured gas masks and worked as car cleaners and track repairers.[20]

The entry of greater numbers of white women into the labor force during this period was further facilitated by the discriminatory policies of organized labor. Although black women held some of the most undesirable jobs, laboring in some of the most odious working conditions, their presence in the workplace was viewed with hostility by white women. Many white women workers considered them a "reserve" labor force that bosses would exploit in the event of a strike.[21] Indeed, many AFL locals saw the "elimination of black women from the labor force to be in their own best interest."[22] White women's attitudes toward black female workers were a major impediment to their progress. As Darlene Clark

Hine explains, "white women...objected to sharing the settings, including hospitals, schools, department stores, and offices" with black women.[23] Locked out of the structure of racist union representation that had long hindered black men, black women workers were routinely dismissed after a union won a strike.[24] Thus, the shift in the gender composition of the American workforce during World War I and World War II was in many ways business as usual for black women, who as factory workers made half the wages of their white female counterparts.[25]

In addition to the reality that black women made less than their white counterparts, the stereotypes of black female labor and the black female "constitution" continued to reinforce the hierarchy of white and black femininity in the public sphere. Indeed, the experiences of black women workers in the North reflected the slavery-era inscription of black femininity as a hybrid space. Betwixt and between the categories of public and private, the black female worker was the double to the idealized space that white femininity has traditionally occupied within American social history. As Paula Giddings notes in her overview of black women's activism in the United States, "The satisfaction Black women received working in the mainstream of labor was tempered by their having to perform the dirtiest and most difficult tasks. The historical stereotypes assigned to Black women were largely responsible for this."[26] Under the Public Works Administration projects during the 1930s, black women were assigned outdoor jobs in the city's ditches, dumps and incineration plants that were normally given to men.[27] Similarly, "[t]he garment industry reserved the position of presser for black women because of the intense heat and because the work required 'unusual strength and endurance.'"[28]

The schism between black and white femininity—so critical to the Jim Crow economy of public and private space in the South—also informed perceptions about public transportation in the West. The influence of these constructs of femininity was powerfully reflected in the ad campaign for privately owned jitneys during the 1910s in Los Angeles. First introduced in L.A. in 1914, the jitney was a forerunner of the bus, designed to carry large numbers of passengers for the same nickel fare as the streetcars. Jitneys entered the breach between railways and automobiles just as the struggle for the soul of urban rapid transit was getting underway. Considered to be quicker and more convenient than streetcars by many passengers, the jitneys were nervously viewed by street railway officials as a potentially dangerous competitor for their already waning ridership. The success of the jitneys in L.A. spurred demand for jitney service in other cities across the country, and led to the creation of the first interurban bus lines between L.A.'s central city and its suburbs.[29]

In a 1917 ad campaign to convince white patrons to vote against the regulation of jitney service, the company exploited white fear of black riders:

To our jitney patrons:
Why should you vote for the jitney?
First....
Second...Because your wife and daughter are
not compelled to stand up while Negro men [sic]
and women sit down.[30]

Although Los Angeles's African American community was still a relatively small presence among the waves of white Midwestern newcomers and Asian and Mexican residents, black civil rights groups successfully challenged a city ordinance which allowed the whites-only jitneys to pose as public transportation.[31]

The racial mise-en-scène evoked by the jitney ad provides an important window into the landscape of public transportation in Southern California during this era. As under Jim Crow, white entitlement in the public sphere was represented by the specter of the white woman in need of protection from the encroaching black hoard. Within this equation, the preservation of white rights of access and white insulation from those baser elements of the body "public" secured whiteness as racially unmarked space. By yoking the comforts of jitney transportation with the unmarked white body (and, by extension, unsegregated public transit on the streetcars with the debasing/marking of the white body) the jitney ad underscored how public space was racialized. Using the white female body as its "selling point," the jitney ad traded on the historic connection between white femininity and the maintenance of white racial purity. In this scenario, white racial purity bore directly upon the maintenance of the white family. White femininity—and whiteness by extension—was produced and validated through this hierarchy of spatial relationships. The indignity of white women being required to stand up while black men and women sat threatened the very edifice of white subjectivity. Exploiting the white rider's sense of entitlement, the jitney ad foreshadowed the privileging of private space that propelled the ascent of the automobile in Southern California.

Thus, the ad vividly illustrated how the transition from public to private transportation complemented the monocultural vision of the good life that spurred white migration to the region. As the western oasis for the white Midwesterner looking to start anew in Eden, Southern California's transportation network repudiated the vision of the troubled, teeming immigrant urban centers with "equalizing" subways and elevateds that threw everyone together. The jitney was the antidote to the onerous egalitarianism of the public streetcar. Although the jitneys were eventually discontinued due to the poor conditions of the city's roads, their popularity with white L.A. residents foreshadowed the problematic transition between rail and the city bus in the late 1940s. The jitney ad is thus an important public artifact from the period when the city was beginning to codify its brand of de facto segregation, building upon the legacy of racialized, gendered figurations of space under Jim Crow. Its appeal comes from the most basic of Anglo American notions about how the maintenance of whiteness should be organized, and speaks, like the explosion of white activism and unrest over immigration in California in the 1990s, to the hysteria of racial displacement that has traditionally been embodied within the notion of the white family under siege.

When they were initially introduced in the 1920s and 1930s, buses were portrayed as innovative alternatives to the clamor and "chaos" of the streetcar. They were viewed as being particularly effective for streamlining downtown traffic. One ad for buses in downtown Philadelphia in 1957 skillfully conveys the biases of urban planning. The ad depicts two cars trailing an abysmally slow streetcar as the announcer intones, "Before the big change all but six of the city's main downtown arteries were handicapped with streetcar operations."[32] In the next frame a lone bus ferries past on the now unburdened, empty street, as "magic wand" music swells. In the rhetoric of the era, buses were "repeatedly described as cleaner, quieter, faster, more flexible and more maneuverable than rail vehicles."[33] Bowing to financial pressure, the Pacific Electric began relying increasingly on buses to serve 35 percent of its travelers as early as the 1930s.[34] Indeed, though it is difficult to imagine, "throughout the thirties and forties, buses were in the ascendancy, they were considered the wave of the future, and rail transit was slowly declining in terms of use, status and quality."[35] Insofar as they supplemented auto transit, buses were viewed as compatible with L.A.'s garden city vision. Because they were able to run without a motorman or conductor, did not rely on expensive rights-of-way, and were more "flexible" than trolleys, they were widely touted as superior to the streetcars.[36] Further, since they required less infrastructure adjustments and labor overhead than rail, buses were, first and foremost, a key component in the promotion of auto-oriented development. They were the perfect complement to the revolution in road design that had begun with rural road development during the Roosevelt administration. Buses further undermined the old radial axis of centralization that the streetcar system promoted.

As buses were gradually integrated into the public transportation network in United States cities, the number of trolleys in Los Angeles dropped from 721 in 1932 to 546 in 1939.[37] Faced with falling profits, buses became the focus of the Pacific Electric's strategy to arrest its downward spiral.[38] According to Martin Wachs, buses "became the symbol of modernity in contrast with the hated streetcar."[39] The glorification of the bus is hard to fathom in this era when bus systems have emerged as the antithesis of efficient transportation. Within the slow rhythms of the Los Angeles city bus system one can clearly detect the legacy of city planning's abdication of control over the development of urban public space.[40]

The Ontology of the Street

Appraising the systematic destruction of the Southern California landscape since World War II, Mike Davis has argued that a "selfish, even fanatical presentism ruled Southern California" during this period.[41] The region's rigid commitment to the private subdivision was the result of a generation's worth of public policy that rejected far-reaching plans for open space preservation.[42] In 1930 Frederick Law Olmsted Jr. and his partner Harland Bartholomew devised a plan to preserve park and recreation space in the city.[43] Opposed by the city's powerfully philistine homeowners associations, the Olmsted/Bartholomew plan was the first in a handful of open-space proposals to become a casualty of Southern California's romance with the automobile. Commenting on the fate of the report, Davis notes that

> [i]f their proposals had been implemented the results would have been revolutionary. The existing hierarchy of public and private would have been fundamentally overturned. A dramatically enlarged commons, not the private subdivision, would have become the dominant element in the Southern California landscape.[44]

Instead, highways and parking lots "have devoured...the crucial open-space buffer zones" of the city—eliminating parkland and greenbelt areas that would have undoubtedly contributed to a greater sense of civic life and community.[45]

The "fanatical presentism" and "devouring" of space that Davis identifies have determined the way subjects experience time in the posturban city. One's experience of time in much of the city is mediated by the rhythm of the freeways and the pulse of auto traffic on the street. Enfolded within the peculiar temporality of the automobile, "the moving body does not want to be arrested in space, it seeks pure forward thrust."[46] While the car has effectively accelerated time and condensed space, the city bus exists in a parallel universe in which the car's dictates of speed and disconnection from the environment are inverted. As an adjunct to the car—and the initial "victor" of the spoils of war between the auto and the streetcar—the bus draws upon the spatial relationships created by the car yet demands a large degree of connection with the environment. Fares are to be collected, aisles maneuvered, doors negotiated, other passengers observed. The bus's economy of movement is eminently tactile and utterly dependent upon an enactment of public space relationships that do not exist on the parking meter laden streets outside. As the interface between the hypertransit of the auto and the limited mobility of the pedestrian, the bus is at once isolated from and reinforcing of the rhythms of suburban sprawl that govern Los Angeles. On the bus, the "freeway-defined vector points" that mute the specificity of the street are bracketed and superseded by the rush of city life to which the rider must remain at least partly oriented.[47] Although Richard Sennett has characterized the moving body as a "pacified body," the circuitry of ridership is not that simple on a city bus.[48] Depending upon whether one is on a local or an express bus, the subject's attention to time is governed by the procession of bus stops—stringing one after the other on a local, or blurring past in a whirl of streetlights and intersections and passed up passengers on an express. The embodying influence of the bus is part and parcel of the tactility of the riding experience, the dynamism and suspension that ensues while waiting for one's stop throughout a choreography of delays, passenger boarding, and disembarking. On the 105 bus, one of the more elliptical lines that goes from Cudahy in the south of the city up north to West Hollywood, you memorize every turn of the bus, as it hangs a left onto the blacktop flatlands of King Boulevard in the Crenshaw District, and steams down Rodeo Road, past Village Green, the forerunning 1940s housing complex that sits in cool serenity off the street, shaded by giant trees.

As a stranger to the complex, I have walked and run on the edge of it and admired the landscaping, which peers out lushly from between the apartments. Designed in the same era as Levittown, Village Green (formerly Baldwin Hills Village) was modeled on a European standard of public housing that attempted to minimize the influence of the automobile.[49] Emphasizing shared space, such as common garages and a community center, the complex's design reflected a collective, less privatized version of housing which was intended to be more conducive for women and families.[50] According to Dolores Hayden, Baldwin Hills Village was unique because it "raise[d] the broadest issues in housing and urban design: the relationship of housing to jobs and social services, the need to design for diverse household types, the rights of female and minority workers to housing and jobs...the need for regulation of automobiles."[51]

Located on a "fast" automotive corridor in the predominantly black middle-class community of Baldwin Hills, the Village has an out-of-time flavor to it, the roads that run through it held in check by an extensive network of sidewalks. While residential streets harbor elderly walkers and students, pedestrian traffic remains a perfunctory affair in the city. A stone's throw away from the Village in Leimert Park, theaters, cafes, and art galleries have sprung up in the neighborhood's cultural hub of Degnan Avenue to meet a burgeoning black middle-class's demand for homegrown cultural venues. Pedestrian life is largely confined to either Degnan or the sprawling, parkway-esque Crenshaw Boulevard. A byway situated in a modest, village-like warren of streets that dam up in a small green on Crenshaw, Degnan has been the site of a concentrated revitalization effort. On Degnan, the social diversity of the Crenshaw District is vividly reflected in the wide array of classes—from blue collar to upper middle—that mingle in the street's stores. With their quaint, cottage-like windows and colorful displays, the shops on Degnan are an antidote to the more banally commercial development of strip malls, fast food places, banks, gas stations, and convenience stores that line Crenshaw. The area is serviced by the Hollywood–to –Torrance bound 210 bus, which runs down Crenshaw Boulevard to Vine; and the aforementioned 105. Both buses provide service to the neighborhood's landmark Baldwin Hills-Crenshaw Mall. Boasting the elegant Art Deco design from the original facade of its two flagship stores, the mall underwent an extensive makeover in the late 1980s, and has the distinction of being the only major mall in the country to be located in a predominantly black area.

Rolling through the Crenshaw District, the 210 bus is as critical to the flow of production and consumption in the area as the retail service stores. Because of the area's high concentration of low-income residents, the flow of pedestrian traffic generated from non–car owners patronizing the mall and surrounding stores is greater than that of more upscale malls located in the affluent communities of West L.A. (with the exception of the Santa Monica Galleria, which is adjacent to a promenade retail space that has become a popular shopping and walking hangout). At the intersection of King and Crenshaw Boulevards, where the bus stops in front of a chicken place that punctuates a notorious stretch of wig shops known as "wig row," pedestrian activity is almost exclusively bus-oriented; elderly shoppers mix with students from the local junior high school along with young women and men employed at the stores. Approaching it from the west, the intersection has a kaleidoscopic feel to it. The ebb and flow of auto traffic and the hoary jumble of small shops on the southeast corner are overcome by the mammoth unwieldiness of the mall, its uneasy marriage of Art Deco, Charles Foster Kane's Xanadu, and malltown USA flanked by the quiet expanse of middle-class single-family homes. Since the 1980s there have been a number of different incarnations on the corner; the mise-en-scène of the intersection as a whole has been defined by a billboard that typically features a public health service announcement intended to "raise consciousness." One such ad that has been prevalent in the Crenshaw District features the silhouette of a pregnant woman's stomach and the tagline "no smoking section." This faceless, potentially irresponsible representative of dysfunctional pregnancy overshadows the ostensibly beneficial message of preventing maternal risk behavior that jeopardizes the health of unborn children. By labeling the woman's body a "no smoking section," this ad reinforces the objectification of black motherhood, underscoring the social irresponsibility traditionally ascribed to pregnant black women. This kind of cultural representation is a less than subtle comment on the community's presumed pathology. During the height of the crack-cocaine crisis in the 1990s, a prominent billboard at this location featured the picture of a baby hooked up on life support, with the tag line "he couldn't take the hit." The evocation of substance abuse and reproduction on this particular corner underscores the way the black female body is yoked to the othering of public space.

Thus, at the corner of King and Crenshaw, where three out of five waiting passengers are female, the female face of the American public transit landscape is writ large. The buses' adjunct status has had particularly grave consequences for women. Spatially, the shift to buses, with their largely open-air stops and irregular hours, has been especially inhospitable to women, who are faced with the potential hazard of waiting for the bus at night in environments where what little pedestrian "city life" or "street culture" there is has been siphoned off by the automobile. The potential threat for female riders is amplified due to the transportation planning's bias toward linear, male-oriented travel.[52] In Los Angeles, this dynamic is further intensified by the paramilitarization of public space.[53] According to the Lincoln Institute of Land Policy, "[s]tudies have shown that women are more likely to shun mass transit and prefer driving alone."[54] This statistic is hardly surprising, given the conditions in which women are forced to travel in many cities where bus service is the sole means of public transportation. Insofar as it teeters between a stentorian private transportation system and an inequitably designed rail system, Los Angeles's bus system often enforces the racial hierarchy and gender inequality that underlies suburban "manifest destiny." In a perverse irony, the bus system—conveyance of the raced body, the transient, the low-income, the immigrant—has metamorphosed from being the 1930s model of "modern" transit infrastructure into an emblem of the postapocalyptic vision of third-world dystopia widely caricatured in films such as *Blade Runner* and *Falling Down*. These schisms are embodied within the built landscape of downtown, where the famed Bunker Hill has been transformed into a phalanx of sleek malls, office buildings, parking lots, and well-appointed coffee bars designed to insulate the white-collar workforce from the encroaching hoard of the older, more easterly parts of downtown. It is not a coincidence that the revitalized sections of downtown border the freeway, perpetuating the freeway's status as antidote to the white Angeleno's age-old fear of the city.

Indeed, the white-collar patrons and workers that downtown development seeks to insulate from the huddled masses are descended from the same constituency that pushed for the subsidization of auto traffic at the expense of the streetcar system. With its endless array of parking lots interspersed with metered parking of all time increments, downtown L.A. is very much the creation of the traffic war that was waged there seventy years earlier.[55] Though many of the east-west bus lines do dam up downtown like the streetcars did, their "trajectory" is clearly modulated by auto traffic. Creeping along from corner to corner, the buses are a reminder of the schizoid history of downtown in its eternal struggle to establish its relevance to the city. Waiting for the bus in Los Angeles is an exercise in how the decentralization of the city, concomitant with the early adoption of buses over rail transit, has furthered the cause of private transportation and strengthened the barriers to access for the city's poor. As one drives past the MTA bus stops on an early weekday morning "they"—the bus riders—are invisible to the street traffic, testimony to the otherworldly economy of L.A.'s sidewalks, to the now-cliched observation that "nobody" walks in L.A. After sixty years of the streetcar, to be car-less in L.A. is to be possessed of an intimate knowledge of the rhythms and cadences of the city's streets, the grinding commerce of each intersection and transfer point. The city bus imposes a certain burden of consciousness upon the individual rider, one that is manifest in an "unnatural" familiarity with one's fellow rider. During the streetcar era, this familiarity bespoke an onerous mingling of class, race, and ethnic boundaries. In the highway era, the auto rigorously protects against this threat. For, central to the convenience of being able to "go where one wanted, when one wanted," was the sense that the buyer of the automobile was essentially buying private space in time, ostensibly fulfilling one of the most important rights of American citizenship. In transit, behind the wheel, alongside the center divider, the prescribed social and racial boundaries of cityhood could be preserved.

However, whereas the superficial egalitarianism of the modern freeway temporarily unites and disembodies the driver in a genderless, raceless, classless orgy of speeding lanes and anonymity, the tactility of the street exacts embodiment, an embodiment that has been at the root of American hostility toward urban space. The street, as Paul Hampton Gamard notes, "has always served as not only a transportation network but a communication network as well, providing the means by which urban dwellers interact and convey the shared perspectives that defined collective life."[56] Waiting for the bus in L.A., the collective life that Gamard extols has been transmuted into the solipsistic logic of auto traffic. Within this logic "the city is experienced as a passage through space, with constraints established by speed and motion, rather than the static condition of...buildings that define the pedestrian experience of traditional cities."[57] Waiting for the bus, the otherness of the streetcar past collides with the autopian present, where the burdens of racial embodiment are amplified by the association of public transportation with second-class citizenship.

L.A.'s status as one of the most racially polarized cities in the United States is born of this otherness, this estrangement of the values that inform the collective life of the urban street. With the exception of prefabricated enclaves such as the Promenade in Santa Monica and Universal Walk in Universal City,

L.A. streets are viewed by the dominant culture as the province of the homeless, small goods vendors, and public transit patrons. As L.A. has arguably developed into the eminent model of the Jeffersonian ideal of urban retreat, the city's antipathy toward the street has become an enduring example of how the privatization of transit has informed the racial inscription of space in postwar United States The privatization of transit has degraded the street's historic function as the most basic unit of urban space, such that in many communities walking is widely perceived as unsafe. It is for this reason that the city bus system has become one of the few meaningful municipal symbols of L.A.'s potential to develop into a more deeply realized, robust urban center.

Reflecting on the influence of the streetcars makes one wonder how this translates into the way urban subjects experience time and space. The resurrection of the bus system is a compelling example of the bridge between public policy, equitable public access, and collective memory.

CHAPTER EIGHT

The Juggernaut

> Oil...became the basis of the great postwar suburbanization movement...it is the lifeblood of suburban communities...the twentieth century rightly deserves the title "the century of oil."[1]
>
> —Thomas Angotti (1993, 56)

> It is the roadside, entering from the periphery of vision, which causes a kind of visual friction by intruding into the quiet universe of highway slab and sky.[2]
>
> —Tunnard and Pushkarev (1963, 206)

Downshifting through the "new" downtown on the Harbor Freeway will ferry you right over the remains of the tunnels of the Pacific Electric Subway Terminal. Part of the freeway was built over the tunnel in 1947, before the Terminal itself was closed completely in 1955. One of the main arteries in the city, the Harbor was what the downtown corporate elite fought for. It is what has ultimately kept the Community Redevelopment Agency's vision of "first-world" capital consolidation from becoming obsolete. Hence, after the conflict over auto traffic, elevateds, Union Station, and the Red Line subway, there is still the redemptive promise of the freeway.

The freeway has been dubbed the postwar Main street experience, the "communion" of the liberated motorist. Although the byproducts of autopia have been universally decried by scores of planners, politicians, policy analysts, and ordinary American citizens as the bane of civilization, the reality remains that even in "rail-evangelical" centers like Portland, Oregon, the seduction of the automobile and the iron embrace of the auto-industrial complex continue to hold sway. Improbably, two generations after the last Red Car shuttled into oblivion, Los Angeles's new light- and fixed-rail systems have been designed to counter the effects of sprawl upon downtown by courting suburban residents and their consumer dollars back into the city. The MTA's elitist goal of providing state-of-the-art mass transportation for a select few, for whom sacrificing the comfort of their private automobiles would be otherwise unthinkable, has driven the BRU's focus on rail—rather than highway outlays. As theoretically seductive and surreal as the prospect of fixed-rail transit in Los Angeles is, for thousands of "inner-city" passengers, day-to-day bus travel is often onerous. The racial, demographic, and cultural asymmetry that has informed the landscape of the city since the Southern California Rapid Transit District was created from the ashes of the Pacific Electric and Los Angeles Railways in 1961 continues to govern the experiences of contemporary bus riders.

While the United States' car obsession is part and parcel of a broader cultural and ideological bias toward individualism, Western Europe, with its tradition of nationalized economies, exemplifies the social benefits of multimodalism. Higher gas prices, subsidized public transportation, fuel-efficient vehicles, and integrated transportation planning have created a climate where the social costs incurred by private transportation are far greater than that of the United States[3] In Stockholm, for example, suburbs are located near mass transit, a plan concomitant with the city's emphasis upon walking and open space.[4] In 1996, in Frankfurt, Germany, American architect Frank Gehry designed a public housing complex whose attention to landscape, pathways, and structural openness reflected the "garden city" ideal of community planning. In this scheme, social housing is not merely a "way station between the gutter and the suburbs" but a way of life.[5] American urban planning's downward spiral stands in high relief to the vigorous tradition of planning and cooperation between the public and private sectors that exists in Western Europe. The failure of planning in the United States "left urban development particularly vulnerable to the corporate strategy of opposing mass transportation."[6]

In 1998 the House of Representatives passed a $217 billion highway bill that earmarked $9 billion for highway demonstration projects and several million for mass transit.[7] The bill (which was in addition to the Transportation Appropriations Subcommittee's approval of a 10.4 percent increase in the federal transit program for fiscal year 1998[8]) was decried by the *Los Angeles Times* as a shining example of "pork politics" gone awry.[9] President Bill Clinton's appropriations for highways actually represented a 40 percent increase in funding. As *The Times* noted, "amid the gloating—every state succeeded in getting a little extra—lurks the big question of what federal programs would be cut to offset this budget buster."[10] The bill was the result of unrest about the condition of the nation's highways. Truckers (the linchpin of disputes over the conditions of highways because of the damage semis and other heavy commercial vehicles inflict upon roads) are among the most fervent advocates of modernizing the interstates. However, the arguments made in favor of improving highways typically criticize funding of mass transit.[11]

The "epic struggle between road and rail" has so deeply informed the American subject's experience of public space that the infrastructure costs of highway culture are deemed the necessary burden of society's "natural" preference for the private automobile. Generations of highway welfare have contributed to a situation in which "more land in this country is set aside for roads, driveways, ramps, parking lots, and garages than is dedicated to housing."[12] An estimated 60,000 square miles of United States land is paved land.[13] And with approximately $200 million dollars a day allotted for maintaining streets and roads, "nature" is now more properly represented by a paved road.[14]

As a result of its overinvestment in auto development, the United States also consumes 26 percent of the world's oil.[15] Indeed, as memory of the Arab oil embargo in 1973 fades from public consciousness, American reliance on imported oil has reached epic proportions.[16] The United States' century of oil has affected the built landscape in such a way that it is possible to occupy a residential community that has more parking space than sidewalks. In Southern California, a heritage of heavy auto use has given the city the dubious distinction of being one of the most polluted in the world (among a group that includes Mexico City and Houston, Texas). Two-thirds of the region's land is devoted to automobiles, "from the blue waves of the desilted Colorado River, to the reddish tides of the fish-depleted Pacific."[17]

These vaunted cultural values are the legacy of the Highway Trust Fund. Since its inception in 1956, the Fund has run rings around legions of other special interests as chief guzzler at the federal trough. Elbowing aside such petty interests as education, public housing, and health care, the highway-motor lobby is one of the most lavishly indulged recipients of the attentions of Congress. Before the fund was created, political anxiety over the diversion of highway revenues to other programs had become a virtual land mine for members of Congress in their home districts.[18] A "political version of a perpetual motion machine," the fund effectively insulated spending on highway infrastructure from the vagaries of politics and public opinion by guaranteeing yearly appropriations for construction and rights-of-way purchases.[19] Thus, "with one stroke, it satisfied those who wanted spending linked to revenues, those opposed to diversion, and congressmen, who would now have one less vote to justify at election time. It would become a sacred cow to which Congress would pay homage, even to the present day."[20] The fund derives its subsidies from gasoline taxes, tire sales, and other automobile-related expenses.[21] Because of this dynamic, the Highway Trust Fund has emerged as the least visible example of corporate/industrial welfare within the federal budget, prompting auto industry critics such as A.Q. Mowbray to label the fund "magical."[22] Of both magical and spiritual resonance, the fund inspires the most perverse forms of nonpartisan communion, drawing otherwise strange bedfellow Democratic senators and Republican governors into a virtual amen corner of support. In 1998, despite much ballyhooed congressional opposition to public spending, and criticism of the nation's rising deficit, the federal government allocated one billion dollars in excess of its yearly $4.4 billion allotment to the fund.

Generations of this kind of federal largesse have sabotaged all but the most tentative attempts to change automobile production. While a precedent-setting, zero emissions mandate passed the California Legislature in 1996, the auto industry summoned all the lobbying firepower it could muster to defang the initiative.[23] The funding inequity between road and rail is so deep, and the structural and environmental conditions in United States cities so dire, that most increases in federal appropriations for mass transit are nominal improvements.

In 1953, GM chair and Eisenhower secretary of defense Charles Wilson made the infamous comment that "What's good for our country is good for General Motors and vice versa."[24] Wilson's comment is just as prophetic now as it was then. The global might of General Motors continues to dwarf other United States corporations in sheer revenue and market presence (Brad Snell has estimated that if GM were a country it would be the sixth largest in the world). During the 1960s, when highway construction was at its peak, road propaganda from General Motors portrayed the project of road building as every citizen's social obligation. One such television ad depicts irate drivers sitting in a bumper-to-bumper traffic jam on the highway. As a volley of honking horns erupts, a squat, disgruntled white driver from central casting roars "We ain't goin' nowhere!" to the driver behind him. The narrator of the commercial then intones, "What's a citizen going to do? Don't honk your horn, raise your voice, ask for better highways and more parking space. *It's your country.*" The GM ad appeared at a time when highway departments across the nation were furiously prospecting sites for construction.[25] The highway dance would typically begin with an engineer selecting "desire lines"(routes delineated by the engineer), followed by a land survey of prospective sites.[26] Site choice often resembled an elaborate intelligence-gathering scheme. Engineers would frequently designate several sites then select the final one without community input. In a 1957 survey from *Better Roads*, one engineer stated, "I would run several lines and when I had decided which one I was going to use I would prepare the condemnation papers very secretly. Then I would drop them in the file all at once so that no one would have any advance notice."[27]

Perhaps the most infamous examples of such duplicity were committed under the aegis of "master builder" Robert Moses in New York City. Moses's status as "author" and architect of the vision of New York automobility that informs public space in the city is promoted in Robert Caro's landmark 1974 biography *The Power Broker*. To be sure, Caro's depiction of Moses's "vast genius" and "imagination broad enough so that it could take as its medium an entire city" fetishizes the latter's role as author of the city's roads. However, his portrayal is valuable for its illustration of the class and race discrimination that determined Moses's site selection.[28] For example, the construction of the Cross-Bronx Expressway in the East Tremont section of the Bronx resulted in the demolition of fifty-four homes and the displacement of thousands of poor Jewish, Irish, and German families.[29] As Caro reveals, the route was favored over another route (which would not have exacted so much human damage) that would have demolished a depot of the Third Avenue Transit Company, in which several Bronx Democratic politicians had "hidden interests."[30] The expressway is one of the many byways that one can take to other nodes in the Moses pantheon such as the Bruckner Expressway to Connecticut and the Major Deegan Expressway to upstate New York. It ferries the driver out of the quilt of arterials that form the city's expressway system and into the belly of suburbia—the northern slide to White Plains and Westchester, communities to which some of the people Moses displaced escaped after demolition.[31]

In his critique *All That is Solid Melts to Air* Marshall Berman contends that Moses's reconstruction of modern urban space edited the public and the city out of the frame of automobility.[32] Moses's version of urban modernity effectively "buried" the city. "To cross the Triborough Bridge," Berman observes, "is to enter a new 'space-time continuum' that leaves the modern metropolis forever behind."[33] A drive in the sea of thruways, knotted roads, toll bridges, and plainspoken freeways that form New York City's highway system results in a phantasmagoric misreading of the city. Behind the wheel, the city is captured in great iconic expanses that showcase the downtown skyline, the rash of brick factories on the rim of Harlem, the tiny, stitched-together headstones of a cemetery that creep from the earth on the way from Manhattan to Queens. Although Moses's antiurban authorship may have intended "these expensive illusionistic parkways...to make the experience of driving an auto a self-contained pleasure free of resistance," as Richard Sennett contends, the city ultimately triumphs.[34] In New York, the fact that "cars are present, but...do not have sole occupancy rights to the public realm" has always been the subtext of the city's motorscape, perpetually and mercifully beholden to the railway grid of the city.[35] The decidedly urban network of blacktopped roads in New York stand in high relief to those of Los Angeles. The billions of dollars in road subsidies that swell California's coffers each year are managed by Caltrans, the state's highway planning organization, whose slick calling cards dot the skeletons of new road developments as soon as they arise. Caltrans's defense of the California driver's god-given right to good roads guarantees tires an empyrean glide over roller rink–like stretches of blacktop.

The open horizon and fissured decay of New York freeways make negotiating them a visual and sensual experience that ultimately embodies the driver in a manner not dissimilar from that of riding the subway across the Manhattan or Williamsburg bridge—the city sprawled outside of the window, tantalizingly within reach. Here, the "city based on the moving body" is performed in the ambiguous boundary between car and driver.[36] The body cannot retreat from the corporeality of the city, looming in vertical abjection up into the sky, free from the constraints of retainer walls and un-artfully designed landscaping (the modern freeway's pale homage to Olmsted's parkway greenbelt). On New York expressways, overpasses sit in quiet anticlimax overhead, upstaged by the city, the river, the network of potholes that rise cankerously from the ground. In Los Angeles, automobility establishes its own mechanical economy of veering lane changes and cat-and-mouse tailgating. On the freeway, the car's feral back-and-forth between lanes becomes a kinetic regime unto itself, one impervious to the world that teems beyond the freeway's fortress-like retainer walls.

> On clear nights the cities are lights in motion. On boulevards and freeways there are solid banks of whitish lights going one way and solid banks of reddish ones going the other way in an unending procession of kilowatt hours.[37]

This "unending procession of kilowatt hours" has become one of the foremost means of experiencing time and space in autopias such as Los Angeles. The automobile is the primary medium through which the subject connects with the built landscape, in a literal rite of passage that defies connection. Movement from one private space to another becomes the dominant mode of social engagement with the outside. Moving from signpost to signpost, symbols of public space become a cinematic blur in the margins, jump cuts clarified by road signs. Here, "the city is experienced as a passage through space, with constraints established by speed and motion, rather than the static condition of...buildings that define the pedestrian experience of traditional cities. The resulting detachment further privatizes experience, devalues the public realm."[38]

These relationships are most vividly expressed in maps of the city that often marginalize municipal boundaries while foregrounding freeways in "wide red bands."[39] As a result, the freeway becomes the primary locus of orientation. Proximity to an on-ramp becomes one of the highest values of being in the city.[40]

The buildings that hover at the edges of the freeway sit as silent witnesses to the evolution of urban neighborhoods in the ghost age before the right-of-way was designated. The effects of highway siting have shifted since the Great Migration. The final generation of white "ethnic" inner-city dwellers has given way to the black and Latino heirs of an urban America disenfranchised by the postwar investment in suburbia. The construction of the Harbor Freeway in Los Angeles, which passes through downtown, initially involved the displacement of mostly white residents living in areas that had been bounded by restrictive covenants. The first leg of the freeway opened in 1952, and when the last segment was completed in 1970, the areas that the freeway passed through had changed significantly.

The Harbor

> When a highway slashes through a city, it is usually the low-income areas that suffer, often the Negro ghetto...this brutal, unjust shoving aside of black human beings to make highways for white motorists no doubt has played its part in nurturing the outrage against society that fires black revolt.[41]

A picture from the preconstruction days of the Exposition area near where the freeway was constructed shows a handful of prototypically quiet looking suburban streets with bungalow homes neatly arrayed side by side. Figueroa Boulevard, one of the main arteries of the community, and the street that parallels the freeway, possessed a streetcar line. Once dominated by car dealerships, the boulevard has developed into a paragon of roadside delectation—strip malls replete with fast food joints, convenience stores, and check cashing places serving the transient population of the University of Southern California and an older mix of working-class renters and homeowners. During World War II only a small pocket of black residents lived in the immediate area. However, by 1960 it had become almost entirely black.[42] Now the community is one of the many blips on the Harbor traveling downtown, to Pasadena, connecting with the Hollywood Freeway, or the Golden State Freeway, which shunts up to Northern California and through Washington State.

Woodrow Coleman, a self-described "professional agitator" and member of the BRU who lived downtown during the 1950s and 1960s is among the generation that saw manufacturing's wholesale abandonment of the city. In a phone interview with Coleman a few days after the BRU embarked upon a protest over cutbacks in nighttime bus service, he reflected on the disjunctions of the freeway system, and how easy it was to get around the city on the streetcar. Commenting on the construction of the Harbor Freeway, he remarked, "I was always concerned about that concrete; the amount of land that was moved; gobs of land wasted on on-ramps...when I got more sophisticated I saw that it only went through poor areas."[43] Coleman lived on Georgia Street, in one of the many Z-grade hotels that populated downtown (and were the grist for

Raymond Chandler's jaundiced portrayal of the area). The hotel's residents mainly consisted of black parolees, and the area was mixed with whites and Native Americans.

Growing up in Bakersfield, a northern suburb of Los Angeles that has long been the butt of Okie jokes about its provincialism, Coleman rode the trolleys frequently. In a lively conversation that took us from the twilight of the streetcar system to the birth of the Harbor Freeway, and the city's bus system, Coleman recounted how people felt safe riding the trolleys at night. Undoubtedly, one of the most important, as well as vibrant, aspects of metropolitan life for women is being able to ride public transportation safely at night. Coleman's vision of the city—in which men and women were comfortable hopping on the trolleys at all hours—contrasts sharply with the reality, in which the alien prospect of taking a city bus during the dead of night inspires abject terror among the car-driving public. Coleman, like his compatriot Sam Martin, who labeled reappraisals of the trolley nostalgic, painted a picture of the city as open, despite its segregation. The boundaries of the city extended to the nondriving public in ways that are inconceivable now, despite the presence of new rail lines that run to the remotest parts of the county. Coleman owned a car for a brief period but got rid of it in the 1960s. He wanted to be able to enjoy the "downtime" afforded by riding the bus, to read the newspaper, watch the world go by.

Coleman decries the absence of the kind of civility he experienced on the trolleys. He believes that the absence of recognition of shared public space among bus riders is largely due to the mediocre conditions on the buses. Coleman, who is in his seventies, is among the cadre of elderly riders who compose the other primary contingent of public transit ridership. Although the life span of people living in postindustrial Western countries promises to increase in the next millennium, the United States' wasteful housing and transportation policies will only make life more difficult for its rapidly aging population.[44]

* * * *

The transition from streetcars to buses was a tidal shift in the culture of public transportation in the city. My mother remembers them suddenly not being there, though she was in high school when the last line bowed out in 1961. Still, the sight of those last few trains ghosting through the streets, duking it out with '57 Chevies and tanker Cadillacs must have been something.

> The destiny of many trolleys was to be piled into big stacks, like toy trains, as they awaited scrapping. Other interurbans were ingloriously dumped into the ocean as experimental havens for marine life.[45]

Organizing in the Aisles

As I discussed in Chapters 1 and 7, the BRU's campaign to improve bus service in Los Angeles is based on the radical notion that navigability is a social right. The union's dedication to street-level organizing (the union trains organizers through its own civil rights action program) represents a version of the American Left that is not captured on the national radar, with its hoary promotion of white Eastern seaboard intellectuals from the print media and academia. Commenting on the degree of political commitment required to do the daily work of going from bus to bus, organizer Rita Burgos, who ran the union's training program in the late 1990s, said, "we're trying to shape the debate differently, give people the space to dream about things."[46] Over the years, the frontline status of Burgos and other women of color organizers such as Barbara Lott-Holland and Kikanza Ramsey makes this commitment to giving bus riders "a space to dream" (my spin on Burgos's take) a means of dreaming about space differently. When the MTA announced that it was cutting late-night service in January 1998, the BRU responded with a sit-in at the organization's board meeting. Members also began riding buses at night to encourage rider protest. The threat of further cuts in already scant nighttime service was more than a travesty—it was criminal. Women who work late shifts as janitors, security guards, checkers, or fast food workers must walk through deserted streets and wait at equally deserted bus stops, the majority of which have no shelters. The segregation of sidewalk space and the estrangement of the city street have had the most insidious effect on low-income black and Latino women, who are more likely to be victims of assault than are middle-class women of all races.

BRU member Lupe Hernandez expressed these concerns at a March 1998 meeting I attended shortly after nighttime service had been cut. The meeting was held in the new MTA wing at the edge of the recently renovated Union Station building. Within the past two years, Union Station has undergone a major facelift. Once desolate and forbidding, it has morphed into a space that ushers weary travelers through long, yawning corridors appointed with food vendors, fastidiously landscaped waterfalls, an aquarium, and other concessions to urbanity.

The building is something of a shock to the initiated, unaccustomed to a Los Angeles (particularly in downtown Los Angeles) public space built to take into account how architectural design affects the experience of time. The building also exemplifies a historical irony, because in many ways the 1926 referendum to construct Union Station was the death knell for truly equitable rail transit in Los Angeles. The installment of the rail-frenzied MTA on the station's premises is a bittersweet nod to the road not taken. Elevated lines could have stood in Union Station's place. Downtown could have boasted a string of bustling elevated platforms from the westernmost tip of the business district to the easternmost perimeter of Skid Row. Furthermore, Los Angeles could have been grappling with an entirely different set of issues than that of the current rail transit impasse. The city might have come to resemble a Chicago or Washington, D.C. with their robust downtowns.

When musing about Los Angeles's ostensible lack of urban culture, many Angelenos and non-Angelenos alike often wrongly assume that the dominance of the car precluded the possibility of developing a subway system. Now that the tide of transportation politics has turned, and the city's rail obsession has become symbolic of Los Angeles' urban discontents, many are now wondering why the city has chosen to develop a subway when the fiscal burdens of joblessness, welfare reform, unaffordable childcare, a severe affordable housing crisis, and deep cuts in health care have made the city virtually inhospitable to working people of color. The obscenity of this contradiction reverberated throughout the testimony I heard from citizens at the MTA board meeting I attended in March 1998. The meeting provided a good window onto the labored tempo of municipal politics, and the hurly burly of public advocacy. Waiting for the members of the MTA board to convene, BRU members milled around grumbling about the board's foot dragging, while the board discussed the morning's agenda behind closed doors. Sitting in the audience, I drifted in and out of impassioned discussions about the trajectory of the city post–Red Line. The audience composed a cross-section of rail naysayers, student documentary filmmakers, Legal Aid activists, "citizen advocates," and city officials. This wide array of factions reminded one of the unprecedented degree to which the development of rail has diversified transportation politics within the past decade.[47]

When the meeting finally resumed, board members went through a few perfunctory agenda items and allowed members of the audience to speak. Attorneys from the Legal Aid Foundation of Los Angeles rose to protest demolition for an eastside extension of the subway. The extension was slated to go through the Boyle Heights community. The representatives proposed developing affordable housing in the area. Aside from conservative County Supervisor Mike Antonovich's query (Antonovich has been one of the most vocal critics of the Red Line on the board) as to why the Red Line was continuing to receive appropriations in light of cutbacks in funding of nighttime service, the board's contribution to the debate over the MTA's mismanagement was typically obfuscatory. As various ancillary figures attended to the board table, adjusting microphones and laying out miscellany for the board, the performance of bureaucratic power was brought home by the aura of suspense lent by the board's decampment behind closed doors, as the citizenry milled anxiously about. Sam Martin was among those union members attending the meeting. As we waited, Martin reiterated his earlier point about how the Red Cars paralyzed downtown, ostensibly giving city leadership a "mandate" to downsize the trolleys.

Migration-era residents such as Coleman and Martin maintain that Los Angeles has become even more segregated now than it was during the streetcar era. Coleman recalled that during the early stages of the Southern California Rapid Transit District, Redondo Beach (a southerly community with a majority white population) restricted bus service because it did not want poor people commuting to the area. In this era of welfare reform, cutbacks in nighttime service highlight the degree to which (once again, àla the Watts Rebellion) public transportation and access to employment centers are inextricably linked. As more and more jobs are exported to the suburbs and exurbs, access is one of the most pressing concerns for a population that must first *get to* the low-paying jobs that city agencies require welfare recipients to take, before they can even seriously consider how to go about keeping them.

As the six-year Highway Appropriations Bill gold standard widens the commercial frontier over the next decade, the need for multimodalism for transit-dependent communities will become even more acute. Of course the flip side of "driving while black" has been the enormous toll that highway building has taken on the social cohesion of the so-called inner city.[48] Not only has the enterprise of road building been devastating to community cohesion but inner-city residents have historically shouldered the tax burden of this roadway renaissance, effectively subsidizing the exodus of white refugees.[49]

The impact of highway development on working-class communities of color is one of the many sleeping dogs of post-uprising Los Angeles. The issue has not been addressed as assiduously as necessary in the furor surrounding MTA appropriations for rail.[50] In the next decade, the construction of the Long Beach 710 freeway extension will seriously disrupt the predominantly black and Latino neighborhoods that lie in its path. The project will cost an estimated $1.4 billion for six miles of highway.[51] Meanwhile, in the city proper, Figueroa and surrounding communities exemplify the shifting cultural and racial ground embodied by the confluence of bus, rail, and highway projects in the eastern corridor of the city. A proposed extension of the Blue Line, a light-rail line that runs from Long Beach to downtown Los Angeles, has become a flashpoint issue in the transportation debate, as well as a target of BRU protests over MTA misappropriation of funds. The first light rail extension to be completed under the MTA's billion-dollar rail project, the Blue Line's diverse ridership vividly showcases the changing demographics of the region.

The Blue Line and the Return of the Subway

A streamlined, modern trolley that runs from Long Beach to downtown, the Blue Line serves neighborhoods that are heavily reliant on public transportation such as Watts and the predominantly Latino Pico Union district. Whereas the transition from streetcars to buses deeply informed the postwar black community's rites of passage in segregated Los Angeles, the "renaissance" of rail transit in Los Angeles is a subtext to the second phase of that development—namely, the transition of predominantly black neighborhoods to predominantly Latino. Similar to the bus system, the Blue Line represents a turning point in the city's demographic makeup, reflecting the heavy use of public transportation among immigrants, who constitute 42 percent of the region's users.[52] The growing influence of the Latino immigrant population throughout the urban United States in general, and in Southern California in particular, could very well be characterized as the third wave of American ethnic urbanization. Indeed, the ascent of Latino immigrant communities has become the most significant demographic shift to succeed the "christening" of the European immigrant in the late nineteenth and early twentieth centuries, and that of the Great Migration era black migrant from World War I to the 1960s.

Driving east down Washington Boulevard past the Harbor Freeway underpass gives one the first clear glimpse of the Blue Line's right-of-way. Wires crisscross the horizon in endless synchrony, sloping over and through an open station platform that looms up as though conjured out of thin air. The sheer incongruity of the sight of the platform slices into one's consciousness. When I saw it for the first time after returning to the city one summer, it evoked an eerie sense of reckoning. Inserted in the middle of the street across from a Burger King, it is both a figment out of time and a testament to the transforming power of urban form. The location of the platform in the middle of the street forces the city into confrontation with its buried heritage, when the city street was a vector of communitas and social interaction, rather than an extension of the highway. On its southern leg, the train runs interurban-style through old Pacific Electric territory in Watts (using some of the same right-of-way as that system), Long Beach, and along some of the same turf spanned by the Los Angeles Railway. On its northern leg the train stops a few miles shy of the heart of downtown, recalling the warp and woof of the city when the five-cent fare reigned supreme.

Running radially in relation to the old streetcars, the Blue Line is partly a means of addressing the toll that automobility has exacted upon downtown.

Despite the popularity of the line, the fact remains that less than 5 percent of jobs are located in the old CBD. Thus, in many ways, the Blue Line is a counterintuitive planning choice.[53] According to Martin Wachs, the rights-of-way of the Blue Line and Metrolink, its suburban counterpart, were "chosen for their availability" rather than their conformity with patterns of heavy travel.[54] Even so, the Blue Line and its tracks concretely evoke the daily drama of car and train that played out in cities across the nation from the 1920s until the postwar era. It evokes the vaunted urban dualities of garden city and metropolis that informed the contest between public transportation and automobility. Shuttling through the streets, the line is less coda to the streetcar era than a reminder of the contemptible hubris and crisis of leadership in a city that—after being hauled into court by the BRU—continues to hold taxpayer money hostage to a billion-dollar vanity project whose stations remain hauntingly empty in the thick of the afternoon.[55]

During the postwar debate over building a new rail system, the region's low population densities were often cited as one of the biggest factors limiting rail's viability. However, now that the county has swelled to several million inhabitants, a large share of whom are public-transit riding immigrants, this argument is patently absurd. Saddled with the costly inheritance of a perilously exurban landscape that has sucked the city of capital investment, public space in Los Angeles is being held hostage to the MTA's fantasy of the redemptive powers of rail. The trajectory of the "four-part transit plan" that gave birth to modern rail in Los Angeles is as loopy as a knot of cloverleaf lanes. Regional consensus for rail grew as a result of what Wachs has characterized as the growing belief among politicians and planners in the 1970s that rail could be a "modernizing" force for the region, one that would extricate the city from the environmental and fiscal morass of automobility.[56] Hence, "[f]rom being unable to reach a consensus on a single rail project prior to 1970, the Los Angeles region has again turned transportation politics on its head and is now pursuing...the most vigorous transit capital investment program...in the country, perhaps in the world."[57]

This phase of capital investment has intensified the postwar drain of jobs and services from low-income communities. The growth of a Latino underclass, with poverty rates that have eclipsed those of African Americans, and the failure of politically embattled affirmative action programs to make a dent in raising the income of workers of color, coupled with the onerous Workfare policies of Los Angeles County, underscore the fact that improved bus service is not an idle concern.[58] While rider fares account for only 11 percent of operating costs on the Blue Line, they account for up to 90 percent of costs on heavily traveled city bus lines.[59]

Board any downtown bus in the summertime and the egregiousness of the MTA's failure to comply with the consent decree is writ large. On the Olympic Boulevard line through Koreatown, most of the riders are Asian and Latino women, unceremoniously jammed into a reeking fossil on wheels. Juxtaposed with the cool, clean, marmoreal splendor of the Red Line terminal, this scene is an atrocity. As one rider noted about the notoriously overcrowded Crenshaw Boulevard 210 line, "They need to put more of them in the ghetto. They put, what, six lines on Wilshire Boulevard, but [here] they only got this one. It's ridiculous."[60]

Wilshire Boulevard, home to the original Miracle Mile, one of the United States' first automotive commercial corridors, has lost none of its driveby luster in the years since it became one of the busiest thoroughfares in the world. With the completion of the first leg of the Red Line, this legacy has assumed a new chapter, as the Wilshire and Western subway station has become a symbol of world-class modernity on the boulevard. Approaching the site by car, the station entrance is all parking lot, fenced off in the manner of an industrial park mercilessly swallowed up by the sun. Rimmed by a desultory garnish of palm trees, there are no benches or phones inside the station entrance for pedestrian use. The mode of conveyance seems expressly geared to facilitate seamless passage from car to subway train. The first level of the station is bounded by ticket vestibules that skate dully on the sidelines of a long pavilion that leads down to the subway platform.[61] What impresses one initially about the structure is its monolithic hugeness and impersonality. Like its Pershing Square counterpart, the Wilshire station seems poised to brook the storm of fierce rush hour crowds. Going down into the tunnel, the staircase appears to descend nearly one hundred steps deep. The strain of the boring equipment used to break ground ratcheted by earthquakes has left an almost audible imprint upon the sense of subterranean dislocation that the rider experiences. Similar to the station's entrance, there are no benches on the platform, no pay phones or means of support for waiting travelers other than the beams of the station. At mid-afternoon the station is virtually empty, echoing with the voices of high school students, happily initiated into the arcane thrills of the dark subway platform, right before the rush of the train...

Now the train comes, after a thirty-five-year chronicle of dead-end turns, soundless, mercenary, mocking every driver's daydream of speed in the valley of seconds between the red and green of the stoplight.

Good for People

Flapping from street light to street light up and down the eastern part of Hollywood Boulevard, the signs insinuate out to the driver with subliminal force, a lulling, semiconscious, asleep-at-the-wheel mantra. The MTA's shameless campaign to sell the moribund Red Line to a wary public has reached novel proportions with the introduction of "Good for People" signs onto major city streets in eastern Los Angeles. Although I grew up in Los Angeles, I cannot recall having ever seen any such "assuring" messages from a public agency, much less from the Southern California Rapid Transit District, notoriously hostile to both riders and errant motorists (in the 1980s frequent duels with the latter prompted the agency to plaster signs declaiming "If I don't cut in I'll fall behind" on the sides of its buses). The architects of the Red Line envisioned the new subway as a means of making L.A. into a world-class city, of conferring a patina of "urban" sophistication to a region parodied as one big, car-addled backwater. Rail would match the city's infamous "ethnic diversity" and cultural omnivorousness with a system that would simultaneously give the (suburban) commuter access and freedom of choice. Rail would redeem downtown commercial development, bringing the suburban consumer back to where it all began, before the incursions of cars on trolley rights-of-way, before the Rubicon of freeway development.[62] As this work has illustrated, the MTA's "nostalgia" (a nostalgia of the most cynical variety) for rail has merely reinscribed the hierarchies of the city's suburban bias. In this respect the Red Line embodies both the Progressive-era venality of the street railway companies and the land-hungry frontierism of automotive politics.

Thrown onto the pyre of public scorn, the MTA has been forced to be accountable (at least on paper) in a manner that is unbecoming for a municipal agency. In tacitly acknowledging citizen unrest, the "Good for People" signs represented a substantive change in the tenor of Los Angeles transportation planning and municipal politics, a realm that has often been insidiously insulated from public oversight. Though minor, the embattled agency's token effort to redeem its sorry reputation with the public by appealing to some abstract notion of the common good is a result of the efforts of the BRU.

By keeping buses at the forefront of their campaign for better inner-city transit, the BRU has set about untying the Gordian knot of Los Angeles transportation politics, highlighting the work that needs to be done to redress the inequity of the region's auto pathologies. Although the union's ongoing battle with the MTA has kept the agency's prejudices toward rail development in the spotlight, the issue of the auto-oil-rubber-nexus' virtual monopoly on taxpayer money has been obscured. The crux of the Red Line debate centers on the ways in which the goal of bringing white collar commuters and their dollars back into the city contributes to both the spatial dislocation and political disenfranchisement of inner-city riders. However, the impact of highway development on land use ultimately has more serious implications for intensifying racial segregation and further isolating workers of color. Critic Jane Holtz Kay has observed that big city feuds between bus and rail, "the underdogs of mobility," ultimately reinforce the social inequities of automobility.[63] Transit historian Glenn Yago takes a dimmer view. Far from being a viable alternative to rail he argues, the "bus strategy has proved to be...another step toward transit abandonment."[64] The BRU has politicized a once disaffected public by arousing mass recognition of the ways in which bus service is critical to the community. Now, a similar critical consciousness must spur social action over the region's overinvestment in the highway juggernaut.

If "urban visionaries have become the New Deal's orphan children,"[65] then the dismantling of social entitlement programs such as AFDC and federally funded public housing in the 1990s (under a Democratic president no less) has been the death knell for government commitment to the public sphere. This assault demands nothing less than the reconstruction of urban public space. Planners and landscape architects of the New Urbanist school advocate the creation of pedestrian-oriented communities with the centralized thrust and quaint trappings of Main Street USA Though designed to curb dependence on the automobile, New Urbanist developments in Florida and Maryland have been criticized for their failure to incorporate mass transit planning. Clearly, such a model would not be practical for exurban Los Angeles in the forseeable future. Moreover, some New Urbanist developments such as Celebration in Florida have been criticized as elitist for failing to incorporate affordable housing. Thus countering the effects of spatial segregation will require both responsible development as well as a politicized consciousness of how time and space are raced and gendered. In the twenty-first century, the egregious absence of affordable housing and access to public space in Los Angeles continues to reinforce the hierarchy between suburbs and more urbanized areas.

Throughout this book, I have argued that race is not only a social and political construct, but a spatial and temporal construct as well. The single-family home, the public housing project, the sidewalk, the city street, and the highway corridor all evoke an ontology of race and gender that has nurtured the construction of nationhood in very specific ways. As the first modern metropolis to be based on the ethos of American antiurbanism, Los Angeles has been a bellwether for the crisis of place and identity that informed both black Southern in-migration and white urban out-migration.

Thus, twenty-first-century Los Angeles is faced with the task of redesigning the built landscape so that it enables socially integrated modes of being. One of the ways this goal can be achieved is through the establishment of public paratransit—such as jitneys and vans—or "neighborhood-based transit" to serve transit-dependent low-income communities.[66] Paratransit works most effectively through connections with commercial and shopping districts during rush hour and late-night zones, as well as with the distribution of transit vouchers to low-income passengers. According to BRU organizer Rita Burgos, part of the consent decree for the MTA involves the creation of "pilot lines" that would test demands for new service in outlying areas.[67] The BRU developed seventeen pilot lines in an effort to move the MTA to neighborhood-based transit. Neighborhood-based transit, in addition to well-lit bus shelters at city bus stops, will facilitate travel for women during hours when street activity ebbs.

The most radical reconstruction of space in Los Angeles, however, will involve coordinating public transit development with housing. Nicholas Patsaouras has proposed the development of high-density housing along transportation corridors. He envisions planning housing development in such a way that it would preserve the integrity of neighborhoods rather than have them serve as conduits for auto travel. In this respect rail would become a crucial link to the reconstruction of central-city neighborhoods. Rail, unlike bus transit, has the potential to provide more numbers of people with both access and jobs.

Reflecting on this point during a discussion organized by the *L.A. Weekly*, Gloria Ohland (then of the Southern California Surface Transportation Project) observed:

> There's no question that the inner city isn't getting its fair share of transit money, but it's not just buses. We're not building more inner-city rail lines, and we're not building busways. We're not making that big public infrastructure investment our city needs. Instead, we're making the infrastructure investment out where it's going to benefit developers, and not here in the urban core. Whenever you make that significant public investment in an inner-city community, it leverages other investment, it attracts private investment, and it attracts more public investment...it creates jobs around that investment. But that's not happening...instead, we're making investments in the highway system to serve outlying suburbs.[68]

While Ohland's remarks are hardly revelatory, they neatly encapsulate the crisis of urban Los Angeles since the postwar era. To the extent that transportation issues reflect the downward spiral of the urban core, improvements in bus service are merely the tip of the developmental iceberg. Ohland, Patsaouras, and other planners such as Denise Fairchild of the Community Development Technologies Center believe that transit infrastructure could and should provide the shot in the arm that communities such as South Central—thrown the crumb of a shopping center in the aftermath of the uprising—desperately need.[69]

In his 1997 *Los Angeles Times* article examining the tenor of debate about the Red Line's role in Los Angeles's future, Kevin Starr wonders, "And what will the surviving fragment of the subway, already in operation, come to mean in that distant time, if the subway project is abandoned? Will it mean that a generation wised-up and corrected its mistakes? Or will it mean that a generation lost faith in itself, lost faith in the unforeseen gifts and legacies of great public works across time, lost faith in the City of Angels and stopped its future?"[70]

Even though Starr's lament reflects a teleological, rationalist view of planning's role in the modern city, the question of the future is not an idle one in a city based on the mythos of "becoming;" particularly in light of the fact that it is a city that has steadfastly problematized the very drive to wholeness that Starr extols. As I grew up in the 1970s and 1980s, midway between the death of the streetcars, and the birth of their ancestral rail lines—imagining an L.A. with trains opened another space of being in the city, of existing within the suspended time of metaphor. On a glorious, maniacally burning blue sky afternoon, heavy with the kind of dead, insectoid breeze that sucks at the skin, I started to leave the house for the library and happened to tell my brother in passing that I was taking the bus. "Why?" he asked, in a tone of profound incomprehension, as he made for his car, an old Buick Regal with the shambling serpentine body of one of the drag-strip icons that used to line Crenshaw Boulevard around the corner from my mother's house on Sundays, when young black and Latino men and women from all over would throng the side streets in clubs to display their vehicles in a car-culture orgy unequalled throughout the city. Going to the bus stop, this "why?" reverberated again and again as I walked through the empty streets of Leimert Park past oceans of lawns and driveways, and onto King Boulevard, a fast six-laner that buzzes west into the sun and east into the shadow of the Harbor Freeway.

From the railroad expansion of the 1880s to the resurrection of rapid rail in the 1990s, the "future tense" of Los Angeles has always been intertwined with transit, movement, passage; with a vision of the city that was at once panacea and rebuke to an urban subjectivity driven by the simultaneous recognition and disavowal of the other. As an iconic space, in which the telos of Anglo American racial indifference and the Jeffersonian ideal of private space were most eloquently expressed, Los Angeles refigured American national identity in the image of the suburban frontier. The mass production of the automobile in the 1930s and its wildfire acceptance in the fledgling, resource-poor city established a national model for the decentralized city of the future. This drive to futuricity, the conquest of space by time embodied in the near-fetishized figure of the automobile, has been the city's enduring contribution to American posturban subjectivity. As the most precious unit and commodity of being, speed has become the national elixir, the ever-elusive quantity that throws "difference" into relief. In the time of the freeway, the neighborhoods that blip past through the cracks of the retainer walls are not merely phantasmatic witnesses to the march of "progress" but living testaments to the transportation palimpsest that we live and breathe every day.

On the 10 Freeway east of Crenshaw Boulevard, I sometimes catch sight of a castle looming above the throat of congested rush-hour lanes. It is a lurid salmon-colored building with lonely broken windows, the crumbling home of a deposed emperor, the forbidden candy house that Hansel and Gretel stumble onto in the forest. I have never driven the street that this building is on. It is one of the many curiosities that perch on the edge of the freeway like cats on a city windowsill. Waiting for the red light to change in the entrance lanes, or making my way home through the mounting rush hour traffic, I stare up at the building in hungry snatches of wonderment, mindful of how drive-by culture allows the streets that adjoin freeways to remain aggressively obscure. Anonymity and voyeurism are some of the perversely delicious "privileges" of the drive-by culture of postmodernity. The rhythm of driving is colored by these fleeting mini-narratives, as, brick by brick, these images become part of the driver's montage memory of the city. Memory is by definition fetishistic in nature, and just as memory gains the power to haunt because it is based on what can't be seen or recovered, so driving gains resonance from what lies just beyond the driver's vision. One remains seduced by Los Angeles in peep show, the parts of hidden flesh suggested by a doorway, a street sign, an alley. I remain fascinated by its intimations and borrowings, by how, for example, the squalor of the corner of Western and Santa Monica Boulevard in East Hollywood evokes Brooklyn, New York, in one moment and Guadalajara, Mexico, the next.

The Los Angeles mystique beguiles in part because it steals from these lexicons and transforms them into something fleetingly recognizable, fragments of a dream dimly remembered. However, even as the vaunted fragmentation of L.A. makes the city's legacies of segregation and racial terrorism a way of life for Angelenos of color, the frontierism of driving nonetheless has seductive power for many of us. This dualism, then, is the uniquely American modality of L.A., the dialectic of freedom and repression that transit articulates, forging the space of a city created in the image of the Jeffersonian ideal. This dualism is imprinted on the body, the way it moves through the city, indebted to the buried histories of the streetcar at every corner that wait to be remembered.

Notes

Introduction: Crossings

1. Edward Carey, *Remembering: A Phenomenological Study* (Bloomington: Indiana University Press, 1987), 24.
2. "Lines of the Pacific Electric, Southern and Western Districts," *Interurbans Special* 60 (1975): 19.
3. Contrary to popular fiction, Rosa Parks was not just a "tired seamstress" worn out from a day at work when she boarded the segregated bus in Montgomery on December 1, 1955, but a secretary for the Montgomery NAACP who had refused to give up her seat to white passengers many times before.
4. Ibid., 262.
5. George Hilton and John F. Due, *The Electric Interurban Railways in America* (Stanford: Stanford University Press, 1960), 3.
6. David Brodsly, *Los Angeles Freeway* (Berkeley: University of California Press, 1981), 71.
7. Glen Yago, *The Decline of Transit* (New York: Cambridge University Press, 1984), 50–55.
8. Danny Howard, *Southern California and the Pacific Electric* (Los Angeles: J & R Lithography, 1980), 75.
9. bell hooks, *Black Looks: Race and Representation* (Boston: South End Press, 1992), 191.
10. Ibid.
11. Howard Klein, *Histories of Forgetting: Los Angeles and the Erasure of Memory* (London: Verso, 1996), 8.
12. M. Christine Boyer, *The City of Collective Memory: Its Historical Imagery and Architectural Entertainments* (Cambridge: The MIT Press, 1996), 137.
13. See chapter 1 for more elaboration on the particular transportation systems that have been identified as part of the palimpsest.
14. I use the term non-teleological in two senses. First as it pertains to the way in which being is inscribed by transit, and secondly as it pertains to the *textuality* of history. *Textuality* refers to the play of presence and absence that constitutes beingness. According to Jacques Derrida, being involves a simultaneous recognition and disavowal of difference. This dynamic makes the dichotomy between subject and object untenable.
15. Such biases are predicated on what Friedrich Nietzsche has dubbed the transcendental present or the illusion of a present uncontaminated by past and future.
16. Ronald Takaki, *A Different Mirror: A History of Multicultural America* (Boston: Little, Brown and Company, 1993), 148–151.
17. Ibid., 151–154.
18. Dick Nelson et al., "Unconventional Wisdom," *The Seattle Times*, October 31, 1999: B-9; Alex Fryer, "Regional Board Selects Station Sites, Alignment for Light-Rail Plan," *The Seattle Times*, November 19, 1999: 1+.

19. Brodsly, *Los Angeles Freeway*, 38.
20. Ibid.
21. The beating of Rodney King occurred in the heavily white community of Simi Valley, not far from the Foothill Freeway.
22. See Thomas Pynchon, "A Journey into the Mind of Watts," *New York Times Magazine*, June 12, 1966; Brodsly, *Los Angeles Freeway*.
23. Nietzsche has referred to metaphor as "the bringing together of what is near with what is far." Herman Rapaport, *Heidegger and Derrida: Reflections on Time and Language* (Lincoln: University of Nebraska Press, 1989), 41.
24. Ibid.
25. Ibid., 44. In his reading of Nietzsche's ubermensch, Rapaport notes that this privileging of time within the drive of the eternal return is predicated upon transience, re., "the always coming to be something other."
26. Jacques Derrida and Martin Heidegger have both unpacked this question of the radical alterity of "the now"; see Jacques Derrida, *Aporias*, trans. Thomas Dutoit (Stanford: Stanford University Press, 1993).
27. Many theorists have critiqued the ability of whiteness to "disappear" as a subject position, thus mimicking the drive of the sign in its deferment of meaning. Some of the more compelling work includes Dyer, 1988; Roediger 1991; hooks, 1991; Morrison, 1992; Ware, 1992.
28. Susan Anderson, "A City Called Heaven: Black Enchantment and Despair in Los Angeles," *The City: Los Angeles and Urban Theory at the End of the Twentieth Century*, ed. Edward Soja and Allen J. Scott (Berkeley: University of California Press), 337.

Chapter One: Dreaming of La Plaza

1. Joan Didion, *Play It as It Lays* (New York: Simon and Schuster, 1970), 17.
2. Greg Hise, *Eden by Design: The 1930 Olmsted-Bartholomew Regional Plan for the Los Angeles Region* (Berkeley: University of California Press, 2000), 15.
3. Brodsly, *Los Angeles Freeway*, 159.
4. Reyner Banham, *Los Angeles: The Architecture of the Four Ecologies* (Los Angeles: Harper & Row, 1971), 75.
5. Douglas Rae, "Geocratic America: *Plessy* on Foot v. *Brown* on Wheels," *ISPS Seminar on Race, Class & Politics* (Yale School of Management & Department of Political Science, January 1998), 1–25.
6. The *Plessy* decision enshrined "separate but equal" into law, while *Brown* sought to undo legal segregation in American schools.
7. See for example, Starr, 1985; Davis, 1991; Baudrillard, 1990; Chandler, 1940; Dick, 1968.
8. Edward Soja, *Thirdspace: Journeys to Los Angeles and Other Real-and-Imagined Places* (Oxford: Blackwell Publishers, 1996), 219.
9. Ibid.
10. Ibid., 220.
11. Ibid., 221.

Notes

12. Ibid.
13. Robert M. Fogelson, *The Fragmented Metropolis: Los Angeles, 1850–1930* (Cambridge: Harvard University Press, 1967), 66.
14. Ibid., 72.
15. Brodsly, *Los Angeles Freeway,* 74; see also Soja and Scott, *The City,* 222.
16. Klein, *History of Forgetting,* 55–59.
17. Ibid.
18. Ibid.
19. Hazard Adams and Leroy Searle, *Critical Theory Since 1965* (Gainesville: University of Florida Press, 1986), 137.
20. Dolores Hayden, *The Power of Place* (Cambridge: MIT Press, 1995), 43.
21. Robin Kelley, *Race Rebels: Culture, Politics and the Black Working Class* (New York: Simon and Schuster, 1996), 57.
22. Interview with Barbara Lott-Holland, October 2001.
23. Erin Aubry, "Hell on Wheels," *Los Angeles Weekly* July 18, 1997, 32; Moore is one of a group of USC planners who have criticized the MTA as monopolistic, insisting that privately operated and managed transit companies are the cure for what ails Los Angeles
24. Jon D. Markman, "Study Contends That MTA Based 20–Year Transit Plan on Faulty Data," *Los AngelesTimes* June 25 1996, Sec. B: 1. The Reason Foundation questioned the MTA's overemphasis and overexpenditure on rail and recommended that the agency improve the bus system, expand carpooling options and introduce bus-only freeway lanes.
25. "Riding Momentum," *Los AngelesTimes* December 31, 1996, Sec B: 1.
26. Aubry, "Hell on Wheels," 25.
27. For further discussion see Pulido, *Mexican American Women Activists,* 178–186.
28. Ralph Rugoff, "The Last Freeway," *Los Angeles Weekly,* December 31, 1994, 23.
29. Brodsly, *Los Angeles Freeway,* 2. Brodsly has remarked that the primacy of the freeway to the landscape of Los Angeles is such that, for Los Angeles residents, *freeway* is used to refer to the entire freeway system. Accordingly, I will use that parlance here.
30. Chester Liebs, *From Main Street to Miracle Mile: American Roadside Architecture* (Boston: Little, Brown and Company, 1985), 4.
31. Spencer Crump, *Ride the Big Red Cars: How Trolleys Helped Build Southern California* (Corona Del Mar, CA: Anglo-American Books, 1966), 33.
32. Martin Wachs, "The Evolution of Transportation Policy in Los Angeles: Images of Past Policies and Future Prospects," from Soja and Scott, *The City,* 135.
33. Ibid., 134–36.
34. Ibid., 137.
35. Sy Adler, "Why BART but No LART? The Political Economy of Rail Rapid Transit Planning in the Los Angeles and San Francisco Metropolitan Areas, 1945–52," *Planning Perspectives* 2 (1987): 171.
36. See Kevin Starr, "What MTA Debate Is Really About," *Los Angeles Times,* September 7, 1997, sec. M: 1+.
37. For further discussion see chapters 7 and 8.

38. Jon D. Markman, "Senate Panel to Investigate Subway Project," *Los Angeles Times*, June 14, 1996: 1+.
39. Ibid., 79.
40. The Southern Pacific, whose chairperson was Collis Huntington, uncle to Henry Huntington, was the parent company of the Pacific Electric. The PE was able to function despite its heavy debt burden because of subsidies from Southern Pacific. See, Crump, *Henry Huntington and the Pacific Electric* (Glendale: Trans-Anglo Books, 1978).
41. Richard G. Lillard, *Eden in Jeopardy (Man's Prodigal Meddling with His Environment: The Southern California Experience)* (New York: Alfred Knopf, 1966), 165.
42. Ibid., 164.
43. The Lincoln Institute of Land Policy, *Alternatives to Sprawl* (Cambridge: The Lincoln Institute of Land Policy, 1995), 3.
44. Ibid., 4. I will discuss this issue in greater detail in chapter 2.

Chapter Two: Whiteness and the City

1. Barnor Hesse, "White Governmentality: Urbanism, Nationalism, Racism," in *Imagining Cities: Scripts, Signs, Memory*, ed. Sallie Westwood and John Williams (London: Routledge, 1997), 86.
2. Jane Holtz Kay, *Asphalt Nation: How the Automobile Took Over America and How We Can Take It Back* (New York: Crown Publishers, 1997), 36.
3. Toni Morrison, "City Limits, Village Values: Concepts of the Neighborhood in Black Fiction," in *Literature and the Urban Experience*, ed. Michael Jaye and Ann Chalmers Watts (New Jersey: Rutgers University, 1981), 37.
4. Ibid.
5. Ibid., 87.
6. James Kunstler, *Home from Nowhere: Remaking Our Everyday World for the Twenty-First Century* (New York: Simon & Schuster, 1996), 41.
7. Ibid.
8. See Joel Tarr, "From City to Suburb: The 'Moral' Influence of Transportation Technology," in *American Urban History*, ed. Alexander B. Callow Jr. (New York: Oxford University Press, 1973), 208–9.
9. David Harvey, "Between Space and Time: Reflection on the Geographical Imagination," in *Annals of the Association of American Geographers* 80 (1990): 423.
10. Leo Marx, *The Machine in the Garden: Technology and the Pastoral Ideal in America* (London: Oxford University Press, 1964), 197.
11. Ibid., 198–209.
12. Ibid., 208–29.
13. Ibid., 229–38. Marx notes that "Like Thomas Jefferson, Emerson is confident that science and technology can be made to serve the rural ideal."
14. Ibid., 238.
15. Martin Heidegger, *Basic Writings*, trans. David Ferrell Krell (San Francisco: Harper Collins, 1977), 47.

16. Ibid., 64.
17. Ibid., 61; see also Harvey, "Between Space and Time," 430.
18. hooks, *Black Looks: Race and Representation* (Boston: South End Press, 1992), 34.
19. For further elaboration on the "uses" to which blackness is put in the American psychic landscape, see Toni Morrison's excellent *Playing in the Dark: Whiteness and the Literary Imagination* (Cambridge: Harvard University Press, 1992), 53. In propounding a new criticism to engage with the evocation of blackness as "surrogate" for white subjectivity, Morrison shows how certain types of American narrative contrive the "construction of a history and a context for whites by positing history-lessness and context-lessness for blacks."
20. See Richard Dyer, "White," *Screen* 29 (autumn 1988): 44–64; Heidegger, *Basic Writings*, 71–87 on logos/appearance; see also Jacques Derrida, *Of Grammatology*, trans. Gayatri Chakravorty Spivak (Baltimore: Johns Hopkins University Press, 1976), on appearance and dissimulation.
21. For more on the spatial and temporal architecture of meaning see Rapaport, *Heidegger and Derrida*, 38.
22. Morrison, *Playing in the Dark*, 5.
23. Ibid., 39, 47.
24. Ibid., xxi–9.
25. Ibid., preface; David Roediger, *The Wages of Whiteness: Race and the Making of the American Working Class* (London: Verso, 1991); Sikivu Hutchinson, "Viral Signs: A Critical Reading of Don DeLillo's *Libra*" (master's thesis: New York University, 1994).
26. Morrison, *Playing in the Dark*, 48–53.
27. Ibid.
28. Ibid., 48.
29. Roediger, *The Wages of Whiteness*, 35.
30. Ibid.
31. Ibid.
32. Ibid.
33. This is a somewhat rhetorical flourish; I mean to suggest how the stigma of other or "subaltern" status attends living in the central city and how the transition to the suburbs was a form of cultural deliverance for non-Anglo second- and third-generation whites.
34. Kevin Starr, *Material Dreams: Southern California through the 1920s* (New York: Oxford University Press, 1990), preface.
35. Thomas Angotti, *Metropolis 2000: Planning, Poverty, and Politics* (London: Routledge, 1993), 30.
36. Michael Dear, "In the City, Time Becomes Visible: Intentionality and Urbanism in Los Angeles, 1781–1991," in Soja and Scott, *The City*, 79.
37. Boyer, *The City of Collective Memory*, 8.
38. Stephen Nathan Haymes, *Race, Culture, and the City: A Pedagogy for Urban Struggle* (Albany: State University of New York Press, 1995), 4.
39. Angotti notes that "the term central city has taken on the qualities of myth; it has become synonymous with low-income African-American communities. This equation is only

partially valid as other low-income racial groups occupy the central cities, and some inner suburbs become ghettoized."

40. Christine Boyer, "The Language of City Planning" (Ph.D. diss., Massachusetts Institute of Technology, 1972), 87–90.
41. Peter Marcuse, "Housing in Early City Planning," *Journal of Urban History* 6.2 (February 1980): 168–70.
42. Ibid., 170.
43. Tarr, "The Moral Influence of Transportation Technology," 202.
44. Ibid., 204.
45. Ibid., 205.
46. For example, in the 1890s U.S. Commissioner of Labor Carroll D. Wright identified improved public transportation as a "social and an ethical question." See Tarr, "The Moral Influence of Transportation Technology," 203–6.
47. Mark S. Foster, *From Streetcar to Superhighway: American City Planners and Urban Transportation 1900–1940* (Philadelphia: Temple University Press, 1981); see also Tarr, "The Moral Influence of Transportation Technology," 203–6.
48. Boyer, "The Language of City Planning," 88.
49. Marcuse, "Housing in City Planning," 169.
50. Ibid., 168.
51. For further elaboration on the radial path of the streetcars and their threat to the development of Los Angeles, see Scott Bottles, *Los Angeles and the Automobile* (Berkeley: University of California Press, 1987); on the primacy of the "auto-oil-rubber nexus" to national infrastructure see Yago, *The Decline of Transit*.
52. Sy Adler, "The Transformation of the Pacific Electric: Bradford Snell, Roger Rabbit, and the Politics of Transportation in Los Angeles." *Urban Affairs Quarterly* 27.1 (September 1991): 51–86. Adler pinpoints the rise of "place competition" as the precipitating factor in the demise of Los Angeles's streetcars. For further discussion see also Bottles, *Los Angeles and the Automobile*. Berkeley: University of California Press, 1987; and Brodsly *Los Angeles Freeway*.
53. Adler, "The Transformation of the Pacific Electric," 55.
54. Ibid.
55. Foster, *From Streetcar to Superhighway*, 34.
56. Ibid., 33–36; Marcuse, "Housing in Early City Planning," 159.
57. Marcuse, "Housing in Early City Planning," 161.
58. Ibid., 159.
59. Ibid., 161–62.
60. Ibid.
61. Ibid.
62. Ibid.
63. Angotti, *Metropolis 2000*, 30.
64. Sam Bass Warner, *The Urban Wilderness: A History of the American City*. New York: Harper & Row, 1972; see also Angotti, *Metropolis 2000*.
65. Foster, *From Streetcar to Superhighway*, 31–32; Warner, *The Urban Wilderness*, 37.

66. Warner, *The Urban Wilderness*, 15.
67. Ibid., 18.
68. Daniel Patrick Moynihan, *The Negro Family: The Case for National Action* (Washington D.C.: U.S. Labor Department, 1965); Hortense Spillers, "Mama's Baby, Papa's Maybe: An American Grammar Book," *Diacritics* (summer 1987): 65–81.
69. Crump, *Ride the Big Red Cars*, 132.
70. Ibid., 133
71. "Another Instance of Mass Transportation Policy," *Pacific Electric Magazine* 11 (July 10, 1926): 7; Crump, *Henry Huntington and the Pacific Electric*, 17.
72. Crump, *Ride the Big Red Cars*, 134.
73. Ibid., 133.
74. Ibid., 143.
75. Ibid.
76. Fogelson, *The Fragmented Metropolis*, 186–92.
77. Joseph Lilly, "Metropolis of the West," *North American Review* 232 (Sept. 1931): 232.
78. Clifton Hood, *722 Miles: The Building of the New York Subways and How They Transformed New York* (New York: Simon and Schuster, 1993), 25.
79. Ibid., 27.
80. Ibid., 93.
81. Warner, *Urban Wilderness*, 181.
82. Ibid.
83. Joshua Freeman, *In Transit: The Transport Workers Union in New York City 1933–1966* (New York: Oxford University Press, 1989), 27.
84. Ibid.
85. In this scheme, "native" Prostestant/English, speaking European immigrants were heavily represented in jobs requiring specific mechanical training and skills. Conversely, porter jobs, unskilled and the lowest paid, were almost exclusively filled by blacks, who had nominal representation in the company unions.
86. Freeman, *In Transit*, 14.
87. Ibid., 24.
88. Ibid., 25.
89. Ibid., 26.
90. Hood, *722 Miles*, 127.
91. Ibid.
92. Ibid., 128.
93. Toni Morrison has proposed that white subjects are inscribed as unraced; whiteness being the normative and thus unmarked subject position within the economy of difference that structures the binary. See *Playing in the Dark*.
94. Freeman, *In Transit*, 30.
95. Ibid.
96. Ibid., 31.

97. L.H. Whittemore, *The Man Who Ran the Subways: The Story of Mike Quill* (New York: Holt, Rinehart, and Wilson, 1968), 19–25.
98. Ibid.
99. Freeman, *In Transit*, 46.
100. Ibid., 43.
101. Ibid., 42; Whittemore, *The Man Who Ran the Subways*, 21–33.
102. Freeman, *In Transit*, 42.
103. Whittemore, *The Man Who Ran the Subways*, 22, 34; Quill became a high-ranking Congress of Industrial Organizations official and an advocate of civil rights within the organization. See Philip Foner, *Organized Labor and the Black Worker* (New York: Praeger Publishers, 1974), 312–13.
104. Freeman, *In Transit*, preface.
105. Ibid.
106. DuBois held that white skin privilege constitutes a "wage" for white subjects, in effect ensuring certain social and material benefits a priori. See Roediger, *The Wages of Whiteness*, 13.
107. Ibid.
108. Ibid., 10.
109. David Roediger, *Towards the Abolition of Whiteness: Essays on Race, Politics, and Working Class History* (London: Verso, 1991), 66.
110. Ibid., 192.
111. Earl Ofari Hutchinson, *Blacks and Reds: Race and Class in Conflict 1919–1990* (East Lansing: Michigan State University Press, 1995), 9, 49–51.
112. August Meir and Elliot Rudwick, "Communist Unions and the Black Community: The Case of the Transport Workers Union, 1934–1944," *Labor History* 23 (spring 1982): 170.
113. Ibid., 175.
114. Ibid., 173.
115. Ibid.

Chapter Three: The Northern Drive: Black Women in Transit

1. Sharon Harley on activist Anna Julia Cooper. See "Anna Julia Cooper: A Voice for Black Women," *The Afro-American Woman*, ed. Sharon Harley and Rosalyn Terborg-Penn (London: Kennikat Press, 1978), 91.
2. Peter Theroux, *Translating Los Angeles* (New York: W.W. Norton & Company, 1994), 154.
3. Darlene Clark Hine has written that black women were often motivated to leave the South out of "the desire for freedom from sexual exploitation, especially rape by white men, and to escape from domestic abuse within their own families." See "Black Migration to the Urban Midwest: The Gender Dimension, 1915–1945," *The Great Migration in Historical Perspective*, ed. Joe William Trotter Jr. (Bloomington: Indiana University Press, 1991), 138.
4. Toni Morrison, *Jazz* (New York: Penguin Books, 1992), 10.
5. Richard Wright, *American Hunger* (Harper and Row, 1977), 2.

6. Morrison, *Jazz*, 34.
7. Ibid., 35.
8. Soja, *Thirdspace*, 104.
9. See Jane Jacobs on the "social structure of sidewalk life." *The Death and Life of Great American Cities* (New York: Random House, 1966), 55–73.
10. Elizabeth Wilson, *The Sphinx in the City: Urban Life, The Control of Disorder, and Women* (Berkeley: University of California Press, 1992).
11. Malaika Adero, *Up South: Stories, Studies, and Letters of This Century's African-American Migrations* (New York: New Press, 1993), 117.
12. Hazel Carby, "Policing Black Women's Bodies in an Urban Context," *Identities*, ed. Anthony Appiah and Henry Louis Gates (Chicago: University of Chicago Press, 1995), 115–16. Carby has noted that the Great Migration was actually the culmination of a stream of black migration to urbanized areas first in the South, and later in the North; this stream included the underground railroad.
13. Catherine Barnes, *Journey from Jim Crow: The Desegregation of Southern Transit* (New York: Columbia University Press, 1983), 9.
14. Ibid., 11–12.
15. Ibid., 11.
16. Ibid., 10.
17. George S. Schuyler, "Traveling Jim Crow," *American Mercury* 20 (August 1930: 424).
18. Barnes, *Journey from Jim Crow*, 15.
19. Ibid., 428.
20. Morrison, *Jazz*, 30.
21. Jacqueline Jones, *Labor of Love, Labor of Sorrow: Black Women, Work, and the Family from Slavery to the Present* (New York: Basic Books, 1985), 152.
22. Nicholas Lemann, *The Promised Land: The Great Black Migration and How It Changed America* (New York: A. A. Knopf, 1991), 15; Lawrence B. De Graaf, *Negro Migration: 1930 to 1950.*" Ph.D. diss., UCLA, 1962
23. Nicholas Lemann, *The Promised Land*, 11.
24. Paula Giddings, *When and Where I Enter: The Impact of Black Women on Race and Sex in America*. New York: William Morrow and Company, Inc., 1984.
25. See chapter 6 for further discussion on the AFL's stance toward blacks.
26. Giddings, *When and Where I Enter*, 140.
27. Sharon Harley, "The Politics of Black Women's Labor History," *Women and Work: Exploring Race, Ethnicity, and Class*, ed. Elizabeth Higginbotham and Mary Romero (London: Sage Publications, 1997), 34; Jones, *Labor of Love*, 59–63.
28. Jones, 75.
29. Countering the prevailing notion that slavery "emasculated" black men, bell hooks has argued that black women were effectively masculinized in the labor roles that they were forced to assume during slavery. Whereas men were never systematically forced to do domestic work, women had to do both domestic and fieldwork. See bell hooks, *Ain't I a Woman* (Boston: South End Press, 1981), 22–23.
30. Darlene Clark Hine, "Rape and the Inner Lives of Black Women in the Middle West: Preliminary Thoughts on the Culture of Dissemblance," *Unequal Sisters: A Multi-*

Cultural Reader in U.S. Women's History, ed. Ellen Carol DuBois and Vicki L. Ruiz (New York: Routledge, 1990), 293.
31. Lawrence DeGraaf, "Negro Migration to Los Angeles," 15.
32. Lemann, *The Promised Land,* 45.
33. Jones, *Labor of Love,* 160.
34. James R. Grossman, "The White Man's Union: The Great Migration and the Resonance of Race and Class in Chicago, 1916–1922," *The Great Migration in Historical Perspective*, ed. Joe William Trotter Jr. (Bloomington: Indiana University Press, 1991) 88.
35. Ibid.
36. Adero, *Up South,* preface.
37. Ibid.
38. Ibid.
39. Ibid., 54.
40. Ibid., xviii.
41. See Lemann, *The Promised Land*; see also, St. Clair Drake and Horace Cayton, *Black Metropolis* (New York: Harcourt, Brace, 1945).
42. DeGraaf, *Negro Migration,* 9–20.
43. Hine, "Black Migration," 140.
44. Jones, *Labor of Love,* 160; Hine, "Black Migration," 139.
45. Hine, "Black Migration," 133.
46. Ibid.
47. See Patricia Hill Collins, *Black Feminist Thought* (Cambridge: Unwin Hyman, 1990), 56; Giddings, *When and Where I Enter,* 204. These arrangements were made all the more perilous by white employers who refused to pay for work, or white men who sexually assaulted the women who worked in their homes.
48. Harley, "The Politics of Black Women's Labor History," 45.
49. Giddings, *When and Where I Enter,* 154.
50. Ibid.
51. Carby, "Policing Black Women's Bodies," 117; Harley, "The Politics of Black Women's Labor History," 28–52.
52. Harley, "The Politics of Black Women's Labor History," 38.
53. Carby, "Policing the Black Woman's Body," 117. Carby draws on the work of Stanley Cohen: "[S]ocieties appear to be subject every now and then, to periods of moral panic. A condition, episode, person or group of persons emerges to become defined as a threat to societal values and interests; its nature is presented in a stylized and stereotypical fashion by the mass media; the moral barricades are manned by editors, bishops, politicians and other right-thinking people." See *Folk Devils and Moral Panics: The Creation of Mods and Rockers* (London: Hutchinson, 1972), 9.
54. See Carby, 115–32. Carby uses the work of Frances A. Kellor, "Southern Colored Girls in the North: The Problem of Their Protection," *Charities* (March 18, 1905): 584–85.
55. Carby, "Policing the Black Woman's Body," 118.

56. Bonnie Thornton Dill, "Our Mother's Grief: Racial Ethnic Women and the Maintenance of Families," *Journal of Family History* 13 (1988): 422.
57. Jones, *Labor of Love*, 59; see also hooks, *Ain't I a Woman*, 55–56, 62.
58. Jones, *Labor of Love*, 149.
59. Ibid.
60. Ibid.
61. Jane Lazarre, *Beyond the Whiteness of Whiteness: Memoir of a White Mother of Black Sons* (Durham: Duke University Press, 1996), 7; Hazel Carby has noted that the "institutionalized rape of black women has never been as powerful a symbol of black oppression as the spectacle of lynching." *Reconstructing Womanhood: The Emergence of the Afro-American Woman Novelist* (New York: Oxford University Press, 1987), 39.
62. Spillers, "Mama's Baby, Papa's Maybe," 65–81.
63. Hazel Carby, "It Jus Be's Dat Way Sometime: The Sexual Politics of Women's Blues," *Unequal Sisters: A Multi-Cultural Reader in U.S. Women's History*, ed. Ellen Carol DuBois and Vicki L. Ruiz (New York: Routledge, 1990), 238–49.
64. Ibid., 242.
65. Ibid.
66. Ibid., 243.
67. Ibid.
68. Carby points out that the "Railroad Blues" was actually a comment on going to urban Alabama, and reflected the "ambivalent position of the blues singer caught between the contradictory impulses of needing to migrate North and the need to be able to return."
69. Virginia Scharff, *Taking the Wheel: Women and the Coming of the Motor Age* (New York: Free Press, 1991), 5.
70. Ibid., 7.
71. Wolfgang Schivelbusch, "Railroad Space and Railroad Time," *New German Critique* 14 (1978): 34.
72. Ibid.
73. Michel Foucault, "On Other Spaces," *Diacritics* 2 (1980): 35–45. Foucault refers to heterotopias as in-between spaces that condense/idealize "normative" social relations, such as cemeteries and parks.

Chapter Four: Driving While Black

1. Kunstler, *Home from Nowhere*, 58.
2. Sallie Westwood and John Williams, ed. *Imagining Cities: Scripts, Signs, Memory* (London: Routledge, 1997), 9.
3. Collen McElroy, "Sister Detroit," in *Centers of the Self: Short Stories by Black American Women from the Nineteenth Century to the Present*, ed. Judith A. and Martin J. Hamer (New York: Hill and Wang, 1994), 264–76.
4. Ibid., 27, 43.
5. "Four Wheels and Off to New Horizons," *The New York Times* May 30, 1997, sec. C: 1+.
6. The World Resources Institute, *Car Trouble* (Washington, D.C.: The World Resources Institute, 1987), ix.

7. Ibid., x.
8. Bradford C. Snell, "American Ground Transport: A Proposal for Restructuring the Automobile, Truck, Bus, and Rail Industries," report presented to the *Subcommittee on Antitrust and Monopoly of the Committee on the Judiciary,* U.S. Senate, February 26, 1974. Snell's thesis has been the subject of vociferous criticism by such transit scholars as Adler, 1991, and Wachs, 1996.
9. Kunstler, *Home from Nowhere,* 27.
10. Ibid., 43.
11. Yago, *The Decline of Transit,* 51.
12. Liebs, *From Main Street to Miracle Mile,* 17; see also Kenneth T. Jackson, *Crabgrass Frontier: The Suburbanization of the United States* (New York: Oxford University Press, 1985), 159–60.
13. Jackson, *Crabgrass Frontier,* 161; Martha May, "The Historical Problem of the Family Wage," in DuBois and Ruiz, 283.
14. Martha May, "The Historical Problem of the Family Wage," *Unequal Sisters: A Multicultural Reader in U.S. Women's History.* ed. Ellen Carol DuBois and Vicki Ruiz (New York: Routledge, 1990). 284–85.
15. Jackson, *Crabgrass Frontier,* 160.
16. Ibid., 10–15; see also Kay, *Asphalt Nation,* 178–79.
17. Raymond S. Tompkins, "The Troubled Trolley," *American Mercury* 13 (1928): 402
18. Bottles, *Los Angeles and the Automobile,* 22–51; see Wachs, "The Evolution of Transportation Policy in Los Angeles," 118; for a riveting take on the cutthroat politics of the streetcar industry see Theodore Dreiser, *The Financier* (1912; Reprint New York: Dell Books, 1961).
19. *Los Angeles Record,* December 10, 1912.
20. *Los Angeles Times,* April 5, 1926.
21. Tompkins, "The Troubled Trolley," 403.
22. Ibid., 402–4; Yago, *The Decline of Transit,* 53–54.
23. Yago, 53–54.
24. "Proves Street Car Need in Mass Transit," *Pacific Electric Magazine* 11.3 (August 10, 1926): 13.
25. Tompkins, "The Troubled Trolley," 405; Wachs, "The Evolution of Transportation Policy in Los Angeles," 123–24.
26. See "Proves Street Car Need in Mass Transit," 13.
27. *Pacific Electric Magazine* Vol. 11.5 (October 10, 1926): 8.
28. Wachs, "The Evolution of Transportation Policy in Los Angeles," 118.
29. Bottles, *Los Angeles and the Automobile,* 24–27.
30. Ibid.
31. Ibid., 26.
32. Ibid.
33. Ibid., 28.
34. Ibid., 132.
35. I discuss the station in more detail in chapter 8.

36. For further discussion on the politics of the Red Line see chapters 7 and 8.
37. Bottles, *Los Angeles and the Automobile*, 126; Wachs, "The Evolution of Transportation Policy in Los Angeles," 119; Brodsly, *Los Angeles Freeway*, 85–88.
38. Brodsly, *Los Angeles Freeway*, 132; Wachs, "The Evolution of Transportation Policy in Los Angeles," 122.
39. Wachs, "The Evolution of Transportation Policy in Los Angeles," 122.
40. Bottles, *Los Angeles and the Automobile*, 131.
41. Ibid.
42. Wachs, "The Evolution of Transportation Policy in Los Angeles," 122; Fogelson, *The Fragmented Metropolis*, 178.
43. Fogelson, *The Fragmented Metropolis*, 176.
44. See Wachs, "The Evolution of Transportation Policy in Los Angeles," 113; "Los Angeles would not repeat the 'mistakes of the past' and would instead be kept a 'city in a garden...'"
45. Wachs, "The Evolution of Transportation Policy in Los Angeles," 123; Bottles, *Los Angeles and the Automobile*, 138, 152–156.
46. Davis, *City of Quartz:Excavating the Future in Los Angeles* (London: Verso, 1981), 114.
47. Bottles, *Los Angeles and the Automobile*, 152.
48. Crump, *Ride the Big Red Cars*, 168; Bottles, *Los Angeles and the Automobile*, 152.
49. Davis, *City of Quartz*, 118.
50. Ibid., 119.
51. Ibid.
52. Crump, *Ride the Big Red Cars*, 168.
53. Crump, *Ride the Big Red Cars*, 166; Wachs, "The Evolution of Transportation Policy in Los Angeles," 122–23.
54. Bottles, *Los Angeles and the Automobile*, 137.
55. Ibid., 152; Crump, *Ride the Big Red Cars*, 168.
56. Bottles, *Los Angeles and the Automobile*, 156.
57. Ibid. One of the objections to erecting a rapid rail system was that it might increase pedestrian traffic downtown, 159; according to Crump, Southern California placed a premium on eliminating the need for walking—auto occupancy 2.76 as opposed to 7.03 in New York City, 208.
58. Bottles, *Los Angeles and the Automobile*, 152.
59. See Jackson, *Crabgrass Frontier*, 170: "Thus Americans taxed and harassed public transportation even while subsidizing the auto like a pampered child."
60. Bottles, *Los Angeles and the Automobile*, 156.
61. Ibid., 159.
62. Ibid., 123.
63. Kay, *Asphalt Nation*, 177.
64. According to Crump, "The slowness of the public and public officials to grasp the fact that the role of providing transportation could not be filled by private enterprise." *Ride the Big Red Cars*, 208.

65. Paul Shoup, "Buses Can Best Serve When Linked with Electric Railway Carriers," *The Life and Times of the Pacific Electric* (Perris, CA: Orange Empire Trolley Museum, 1988), 44; the Pacific Electric began operating buses in 1917. Shoup also makes it known that the Pacific Electric itself had 160 buses in operation at that time of his speech.
66. Ibid., 45.
67. Ibid.
68. Kay, *Asphalt Nation*, 120–21. Kay factors in parking costs, police protection, and auto insurance in her estimate, noting that the American Bureau of Labor Statistics has concluded that American households spend nearly a fifth of their budgets on car ownership and maintenance.
69. Tompkins, "The Troubled Trolley," 400; Stephen Goddard, *Getting There: The Epic Struggle between Road and Rail* (New York: Harper Collins, 1994), 110.
70. Keith Collins, *Black Los Angeles: The Maturing of the Ghetto, 1940–1950* (Saratoga, CA: Century Twenty One Publishing, 1980) 11.
71. Goddard, *Getting There*, 110.
72. Ibid.; for more on MacDonald's influence see Tom Lewis, *Divided Highways: Building the Interstate Highways, Transforming American Life* (New York: Penguin Books), 1997, 8–24.
73. U.S. Senator Kay Bailey Hutchison has been among those active in pushing for legislation to save Amtrak (which teetered yet again on the brink of obliteration in 2002) decrying its status as a "[T]wenty-six year old experiment, not a viable passenger rail system," *Passenger Transport* (April 21, 1997): 1.
74. Goddard, *Getting There*, 113.
75. Ibid., 114.
76. Kay, *Asphalt Nation*, 175–77.
77. Goddard, *Getting There*, 114; Yago, *The Decline of Transit*; see Jackson *Crabgrass Frontier*; World Resources Institute, *Car Trouble*, 4–6.
78. Goddard, *Getting There*, 114.
79. Ibid., 115.
80. Ibid., 148–49.
81. Foster, *From Streetcar to Superhighway*, 115.
82. Ibid.
83. Kay, *Asphalt Nation*, 177.
84. Kunstler, *Home from Nowhere*, 59.
85. Ibid., 43.
86. Michael Omi and Howard Winant, *Racial Formation in the United States: From the 1960s to the 1980s* (Routledge: New York, 1986), 65.
87. Morrison, *Playing in the Dark*, 59.
88. Rae, "Geocratic America: *Plessy* on Foot v. *Brown* on Wheels." *ISPS Seminar on Race, Class, & Politics* (Yale School of Management & Department of Political Science, January 1998), 11.
89. Hesse, "White Governmentality: Urbanism, Nationalism, Racism." *Imagining Cities: Scripts, Signs, Memory*. ed. Sallie Westwood and John Williams (London: Routledge, 1997), 90.

Notes

90. It is my position that whiteness is in part based upon its seeming transcendence of the boundaries of time, and that the beingness of whiteness can be read through transit metaphors, i.e., the road as a signifier of both a spatial and temporal transcendence which makes it impossible to see whiteness as a racial category unto itself or to assign it racial "presence."
91. Barnes, *Journey from Jim Crow*, 11–12.
92. Ibid., 12–13, 16–19.
93. Ibid.
94. Ibid.
95. Ibid., 17.
96. Ibid.
97. Ibid., 18.
98. I use *site* in the manner that it is deployed in Omi and Winant, *Racial Formation in the United States*, 67: "We conceive of a site as a region of social life with a coherent set of constitutive social relations...thus in the advanced capitalist social formation, the liberal democratic state, the capitalist economy, and the patriarchal family may be considered sites in that each may be characterized by a distinct set of 'rules of the game' for participation in practices."
99. Ian F. Haney Lopez, *White by Law: The Legal Construction of Race* (New York: New York University Press, 1996), 23.
100. Ibid., 2–3.
101. Ibid., 27.
102. Ibid., 23.
103. Westwood and Williams, *Imagining Cities*, 9.
104. See Schuyler, "Traveling Jim Crow," 423–32.
105. Barnes, *Journey from Jim Crow*, 212–13.
106. Ibid.
107. Liebs, *From Main Street to Miracle Mile*, 4.
108. Ibid.
109. Brodsly, *Los Angeles Freeway*, 68; Crump, *Ride the Big Red Cars*, 115–19.
110. Brodsly, *Los Angeles Freeway*, 69.
111. Westwood and Williams, *Imagining Cities*, 26.
112. Warner, *The Urban Wilderness*, 63.
113. Bottles, *Los Angeles and the Automobile*, 93.
114. Ibid.
115. DeGraaf, *Negro Migration*, 10.
116. Ibid., 10–11.
117. Ibid.
118. Warner, *The Urban Wilderness*, 32–36; Fogelson, *The Fragmented Metropolis*, 139.
119. Ibid., 71; Crump, *Ride the Big Red Cars*, 63.
120. Bottles, *Los Angeles and the Automobile*, 32.
121. Ibid., 39–48; 95–97.

122. Ibid., 77.
123. Scharff, *Taking the Wheel*, 154.
124. Ibid., 155.
125. Ibid., 155–56.
126. *Los Angeles Record* April 17, 1920.
127. Scharff, 146.
128. Ibid., 48.
129. Ibid.
130. Bottles, *Los Angeles and the Automobile*, 237–38; Crump, *Ride the Big Red Cars*, 201.
131. Adler, "Why BART and No LART?" 80.
132. For a more complete examination see Adler, "Why BART and No LART?"; see also Goddard, *Getting There*.
133. Crump, *Ride the Big Red Cars*, 208.
134. Yago, *The Decline of Transit*, 193–94.
135. Crump, *Ride the Big Red Cars*, 208.
136. See Adler, 1991; Brodsly, 1981; Hilton, 1974.
137. Ibid., 81.
138. Ibid.
139. Brodsly, *Los Angeles Freeway*, 4.

Chapter Five: Little Patch of Green

1. Carey McWilliams, "Myths of the West," *North American Review* 232 (1931): 423–32.
2. David Lowenthal, *The Past Is a Foreign Country* (Cambridge: Cambridge University Press, 1985), 8.
3. Virginia Woolf as quoted in Lowenthal, *The Past Is a Foreign Country*, 74.
4. Klein, *Histories of Forgetting*, 4–13.
5. See Mike Davis on *Grapes of Wrath*, Okie workers analogy. "The Empty Quarter," *Sex, Death, and God in Los Angeles* ed. David Reid (Berkeley: University of California Press, 1992), 56–57.
6. Soja and Scott, *The City*, 459.
7. Crump, *Ride the Big Red Cars*, 145–50.
8. Ibid. According to Crump, in 1916 highway appropriations in California alone totaled $10 million.
9. Ibid.
10. Lillard, *Eden in Jeopardy*, 178.
11. National Public Radio Broadcast, June 1998.
12. Howard, *Southern California and the Pacific Electric*, 5.
13. This is to say that the superficial ease with which blacks can travel through the city by car is offset by the terrorism of "driving while black."
14. Steve Proffitt, "On Restoring Los Angeles through Public Transit," *Los Angeles Times*, September 21, 1997, sec. M: 3.

15. Jim Klein and Martha Olsen, prod. *Taken for a Ride*, Point of View Documentary, PBS,. WGBH, Boston, 1996.
16. David Ferrell Krell, *Of Memory, Reminiscence and Writing on the Verge* (Bloomington: Indiana University Press, 1990), 93.
17. See Derrida, *Of Grammatology*.
18. Lowenthal, *The Past Is a Foreign Country*, xix, 13; Klein, *Histories of Forgetting*, 8.
19. Maurice Merleau-Ponty, *Phenomenology of Perception*, trans. Colin Smith (New York: Humanities Press, 1962), 15, 60.
20. Ibid.
21. Erin Aubry, "Legacy of the Eastside Boys," *Los Angeles Times Magazine* (July 20, 1997): 12+.
22. Ibid., 28.
23. See, for example, Lewis Mumford, *The Highway and the City* (New York: Mentor Books, 1963).
24. As critic Alex Ross so sagely notes, "To talk about California as blank slate is no longer intellectually honest—perhaps never was. To begin with, you have to be aware of the sometimes overpowering presence of the past. Far from disappearing overnight, California history never seems to go away. Nothing there ever decays completely." Hold Every-thing," *The New Yorker* (February 23, 1998): 21.
25. Kevin Lynch, *What Time is This Place?* (Cambridge: MIT Press, 1972), 40.
26. See Joel Tarr on how the desire to be free of the "yoke" of public transportation affirms American individualism. "The Moral Influence of Transportation Technology," 202–12.
27. In spite of this fact, the majority of Americans continue to use their cars as their primary means of transportation.
28. See for example, Samuel G. Freedman, "Suburbia Outgrows Its Image in the Arts," *New York Times*, February 28, 1999, sec. 2: 1+.
29. Rapaport, *Heidegger and Derrida*, 42.
30. "Some have felt that Southern California has been a racial Eden for African-Americans, while others have argued the opposite. It seems that both views have a kernel of truth." Gerald Horne, *Fire This Time: The Watts Uprising and the 1960s* (Charlottesville: University Press of Virginia, 1995), 23.
31. Collins, *Black Los Angeles*, 22: "The economic conditions for blacks in California and Los Angeles during World War II seemed especially inviting when compared with other sections of the nation. Few areas experienced greater industrial expansion or so acute a shortage of manpower...Blacks had a larger share of defense production jobs in relation to their population in California than in Southern urban areas." See also Anderson, "A City Called Heaven," 340–42.
32. Collins, *Black Los Angeles*, 25; DeGraaf, *Negro Migration to Los Angeles*, 83; in 1940 black migration to Los Angeles was 2.7 percent, a figure which rose to 5.2 percent in 1950, with Los Angeles County receiving one third of the state's black population. Ong and Blumenthal, "Income and Racial Inequality in Los Angeles," *The City: Los Angeles and Urban Theory at the End of the Twentieth Century,* ed. Edward Soja and Allen Scott (Berkeley: University of California Press, 1996), 324.
33. Collins, *Black Los Angeles*, 23.

34. Horne, *Fire This Time*, 31.
35. Collins, *Black Los Angeles*, 20.
36. Ibid., 18. Collins notes that the Southern Pacific "abandoned its policy of enlisting Southern blacks in favor of hiring Mexican nationals."
37. Ibid., 43.
38. I will pursue this issue further in chapter 6. Chester Himes protagonist Bob Jones leads a carpool for his fellow workers to a navy shipyard in the South Bay. *If He Hollers Let Him Go* (New York: Thunder's Mouth Press, 1945). See also Alonzo Smith, "Blacks and the Los Angeles Municipal Transit System," *Urbanism Past and Present* 6 (winter-spring, 1981): 25–28; Collins, *Black Los Angeles*, 56–58.
39. Crump, *Ride the Big Red Cars*, 225.
40. Mel Scott, *Metropolitan Los Angeles: One Community* (Los Angeles: The Haynes Foundation, 1949), 97.
41. Ibid.
42. Ibid., 151.
43. Bottles, *Los Angeles and the Automobile*, 206.
44. Ibid., 98; Wachs, "The Evolution of Transportation Policy in Los Angeles," 126.
45. Wachs, "The Evolution of Transportation Policy in Los Angeles," 126.
46. Brodsly, *Los Angeles Freeway*, 101.
47. Ibid.
48. Wachs, "The Evolution of Transportation Technology in Los Angeles," 131.
49. Soja and Scott, *The City*, 428.
50. Raphael Sonenshein, *Politics in Black and White: Race and Power in Los Angeles* (Princeton: Princeton University Press, 1993), 27.
51. Wachs, "The Evolution of Transportation Technology in Los Angeles," 129.
52. See Richard Weinstein, "The First American City," 30, from Soja and Scott, *The City: Los Angeles and Urban Theory at the End of the Twentieth Century*, (Berkeley: University of California Press, 1996); Soja and Scott, *The City*, 446. According to Soja, "A recent national survey has shown that Los Angeles contains both the richest and the poorest predominantly African-American communities in urban America."
53. Collins, *Black Los Angeles*, 25; also DeGraaf, *Negro Migration*, 87. "The absence of any celebrated cases or overt outbreaks of racial hostility perpetuated the impression of Los Angeles as a city of comparatively liberal racial attitudes."
54. Collins, *Black Los Angeles*, 25. The decline in demand for "low-wage" unskilled labor drove black unemployment to an all-time high. Anderson, "A City Called Heaven," 240. By the 1960s black Los Angeles had become the most prosperous black community in the country, enjoying some of the best wages and highest rates of home ownership. This enduring paradox, i.e., that many blacks were prospering on the cusp of the Watts Rebellion, would be one of the many paradoxes of the post–Great Migration period. While Susan Anderson contends that "This sense of well-being persisted for many generations and formed the ontological core of black experience from the city's earliest days," black gains would always be edged with unrest and a resistance to the bitter inequality of the racial that boundaries governed movement within the city.
55. Weinstein, "The First American City," 28.

56. That is, in white America, many white women returned to the homefront after their first foray into the workplace. Black women, on the other hand, did not have this luxury because their income was often critical to their families' livelihood. See Jacqueline Jones, *Labor of Love, Labor of Sorrow,* and Paula Giddings, *When and Where I Enter.*
57. For another take on this dynamic, see Walter Mosley, *A Red Death* (New York: Norton, 1991).
58. Sam Bass Warner compares Southern California prosperity with the economic depression of central-city New York. *Urban Wilderness,* 148; see also Davis, *City of Quartz,* 18.
59. The American Communist Party boasted a substantial black membership during the 1940s and 1950s. Horne, *Fire This Time,* 5; Hutchinson, *Blacks and Reds*; and Davis, *City of Quartz,* 8.
60. During the 1990s California was at the forefront of anti-immigrant and anti-affirmative action legislation, which represents a conservative backlash against the increasing influx of immigrants of color, and the attendant eclipse of the white majority by Latino and Asian populations.
61. Interview with Larry Aubry, 1997.
62. Horne, *Fire This Time,* 29. Langston Hughes's remark that "Los Angeles seemed more a miracle than a city, a place where oranges sold for one cent a dozen, ordinary black folks lived in huge houses with 'miles of yards' and prosperity seemed to reign despite the Depression" is a famous example; Himes, *If He Hollers Let Him Go.*
63. Dolores Hayden, *Redesigning the American Dream: The Future of Housing, Work, and Family Life* (New York: W. W. Norton Company, 1984), 8.
64. Bruce Lambert, "At 50, Levittown Contends With Its Legacy of Bias," *The New York Times,* December 28, 1997, sec. B: 1+.
65. Hayden, *Redesigning the American Dream,* 8.
66. Westwood and Williams, *Imagining Cities,* 12.
67. Lambert, "At 50, Levittown Contends with Its Legacy," 1.
68. Richard Sennett, *Flesh and Stone: The Body and the City in Western Civilization* (New York: W. W. Norton, 1994), 368; Angotti, *Metropolis 2000,* 45–52.
69. Gerald Leinwald, *Negro in the City* (New York: Washington Square Press), 1968, 8. During this period there was an estimated 1.3 million decline in New York's white central city population.
70. See Klein, *Histories of Forgetting,* 85.
71. John Cassidy, "The Comeback," *The New Yorker* (February 23, 1998): 126. Cassidy cites an AT&T/City of Los Angeles research analysis project which identifies Los Angeles County as one of the biggest manufacturing centers in the country; a considerable number of its firms having been founded by immigrants within the past fifteen years.
72. This irony has not escaped some transit industry critics of the Los Angeles Bus Riders Union, who argue that the organization has unfairly fixated on rail development, while failing to challenge disparities in highway funding.
73. For an excellent discussion on the implications of homeowners' associations to the demographic and spatial development of the city since the World War I era, see Davis, *City of Quartz,* 160–69.

74. Davis, *City of Quartz,* 162; Anderson, "A City Called Heaven," 342–43.
75. See chapter 6 for further discussion.
76. *The California Eagle,* September 25, 1947.
77. Davis, *City of Quartz,* 161.
78. Ibid.
79. Ibid.; Anderson, "A City Called Heaven," 340–45. Anderson, however, holds that the 1920s were perceived as the "golden era" because of the greater availability of jobs and housing for black Angelenos. This dynamic still informs the politics of community and demographic boundaries in contemporary Los Angeles. During the postwar era the "eastside" of Larry Aubry's young adulthood began inching westward, because of a 1948 Supreme Court ruling against restrictive covenants in Los Angeles which allowed blacks to settle in heretofore white westerly suburbs such as Leimert Park, Baldwin Hills and Inglewood; Soja and Scott, *The City,* 430–31.
80. Smith, "Blacks and the Los Angeles Municipal Transit System," 27.
81. Jackson, *Crabgrass Frontier,* 343.
82. Ibid.
83. Soja and Scott, *The City,* 448; see also Rae, "Geocratic America," 22. Rae studied residential patterns among lower-income white and black families in Missouri and found, unsurprisingly enough, that lower-income white families were able to find housing in high-end communities at a margin of 1,446 to 0. "Far beyond the mere force of income inequality, segregation is a powerful fact...on geocratic American nationality."
84. Edward Soja has identified these areas as West Adams-Baldwin Hills-Leimert Park districts, and the unincorporated areas of Westmont, West Compton, West Athens and View Park-Windsor Hills neighborhoods. Within the past decade black out-migration to outlying suburbs such as those of San Bernardino and Riverside Counties—in large part because of low housing prices and the perception that these areas are safer and generally have more hospitable living conditions than the city—have dramatically increased, as has black migration back to the South; see also, "In a Reversal, More Blacks Are Moving to the South," *The New York Times,* January 31, 1998.
85. Jason DeParle, "Slamming the Door," *The New York Times Magazine* (October 20, 1996): 52+; M. Patricia Fernandez-Kelley, "Migration, Race, and Ethnicity in the Design of the American City," *Urban Revisions: Current Projects for the Public Realm,* ed. Russell Ferguson, *Los Angeles Museum of Contemporary Art* (Cambridge: Harvard University Press, 1996), 18–30.
86. Fernandez-Kelley, "Migration, Race, and Ethnicity," 21.
87. Anderson, "A City Called Heaven," 345.
88. *California Eagle* January 13 1939: "The FHA supported equally by white and black citizens, openly segregates and discriminates against Negroes..while the tax burden upon the Negro of means is equal to that of his white comrade on the same economic level, the colored property holder cannot borrow over a designated amount which FHA officials tacitly set as the highest sum for which black Americans can petition. He cannot select a home from any federal group as can his Caucasian next-door neighbor."
89. *The Negro and the City,* 7.
90. Wachs, "The Evolution of Transportation Policy in Los Angeles," 124.
91. Ibid.

92. Foster, *From Streetcar to Superhighway*, 65–75.
93. Ibid., 75.
94. See Angotti, *Metropolis 2000*, 30. While private capital, the market, and public monopolies determine the nature of planning, city planners are usually unable to challenge these interests because "The U.S. metropolis is thus a relatively pure expression of minimally regulated twentieth century capitalist urban development."
95. Foster, *From Streetcar to Superhighway*, 71.
96. Ibid., 102.
97. Kunstler, *Home from Nowhere*, 43–46; Angotti, *Metropolis 2000*, 42.
98. Foster, *From Streetcar to Superhighway*, 70.
99. Kunstler, *Home from Nowhere*, 43.
100. Wachs, "The Evolution of Transportation Policy in Los Angeles," 119; David G. Gebhard and Robert Winter, *Los Angeles: An Architectural Guide* (Salt Lake City: Gibbs Smith, 1994), xxiii. In 1941 the commission drew up twenty-five-year guidelines whose emphasis was the development of single-family housing, complemented by mass auto use.
101. Foster, *From Streetcar to Superhighway*, 89.
102. See Angotti, *Metropolis 2000*, 30; Warner, *The Urban Wilderness*, 51. City planners reinforced the hold of "outworn values of the private land market and the outmoded traditions of seventeenth-century land law."
103. Rae, "Geocratic America," 14.
104. Ibid.; Warner, *The Urban Wilderness*, 31; Angotti, *Metropolis 2000*, 29; Kunstler, *Home from Nowhere*, 110.
105. Rae, "Geocratic America," 15. "This could never have occurred before the rise of automobiles, because the slowness of variable-path transport made intermingling of land uses all but imperative on efficiency grounds. One does not *walk* to the big-box retail center."
106. Warner, *The Urban Wilderness*, 31–36; Angotti, *Metropolis 2000*, 43. According to Angotti, planners have used zoning and subdivision regulations to prevent construction of low-income housing, effectively promoting racial segregation.
107. Warner, *The Urban Wilderness*, 31.
108. Ibid.
109. Fogelson, *The Fragmented Metropolis*, 147; Rae, "Geocratic America," 19. Blacks' confinement to the central city has had devastating implications for their access to jobs and social services, as Douglas Rae explains, "[T]he chain of connections to jobs, investment opportunities, credit…is linked to place in a geocratic system. The most obvious instance of this—known to economists as the 'spatial mismatch' between skills and geographically accessible employment opportunities—directly limits the income potential of people whose mobility limits them to central-city locations."
110. Yago, *The Decline of Public Transit*, 181–91; see Goddard, *Getting There*, 123, on heavy subsidies made to autos.
111. Rae, "Geocratic America," 10.
112. Yago, *The Decline of Public Transit*, 190.
113. Adler, "The Transformation of the PE."

114. Wachs, "The Evolution of Transportation Policy in Los Angeles," 135; Adler, "Why BART and No LART?" 170. According to Adler, San Francisco was unique in that the county was the most significant governing body in the region. Hence, the "BART success was possible because the governmental structure of the Bay region permitted disaggregation as well as alliance-building based on transit system design."
115. Adler, "The Transformation of the PE," 52–54. In refuting Bradford Snell's controversial *American Ground Transport* study, Adler makes the argument that place competition was the most compelling factor in the decline of American public transportation systems.
116. Adler, "Why BART and No LART?"153.
117. Ibid., 54.
118. Yago, *The Decline of Transit*, 57.
119. Bottles, *Los Angeles and the Automobile*, 206.
120. Ibid.
121. Ibid.; Brodsly, *Los Angeles Freeway*, 91.
122. Bottles, *Los Angeles and the Automobile*, 206.
123. Rapid Transit Action Group, "Rail Rapid Transit Now!" (Los Angeles Chamber of Commerce, February 1948).
124. Ibid.
125. Ibid., 1.
126. For further discussion see chapter 8.
127. Wachs, "The Evolution of Transportation Policy in Los Angeles," 133.
128. Ibid.
129. Ibid.
130. Ibid.
131. Wachs, "The Evolution of Transportation Policy in Los Angeles," 126–33.
132. Foster, From Streetcar to Superhighway, 52; "Proves Street Car Need in Mass Transit," 13.
133. Crump, *Ride the Big Red Cars*, 198; Foster, *From Streetcar to Superhighway*, 123; Wachs, "The Evolution of Transportation Policy in Los Angeles," 124. Wachs observes that buses were being used in the area as early as 1917.
134. Haymes, *Race, Culture, and the City*, 81.
135. See Davis, *City of Quartz*, 169. Davis outlines how fiscal zoning precipitated migration of industries to suburbs and Orange County.

Chapter Six: Station to Station

1. Collins, *Black Los Angeles: The Maturing of the Ghetto*, 58.
2. Mary S. Pardo, *Mexican American Women Activists: Identity and Resistance in Two Los Angeles Communities* (Philadelphia: Temple University Press, 1998), 25.
3. Ibid., 61. Driving through the neighborhood, Pardo noted that "I often lost my way in the maze of dead-end streets that stop at a freeway and pick up somewhere on the other side." Rodolfo Acuna also notes that "the construction of freeways and the bulldozing of

homes incorporated the barrios into the rest of the city." *Anything but Mexican: Chicanos in Contemporary Los Angeles* (London: Verso, 1996), 45.
4. Vicki L. Ruiz, "A Promise Fulfilled: Mexican Cannery Workers in Southern California," in *Unequal Sisters: A Multicultural Reader in U.S. Women's History,* ed. Ellen Carol DuBois and Vickie L. Ruiz (New York: Routledge, 1990), 264–70.
5. Ibid., 266.
6. Ibid., 264–66.
7. Ibid., 268. The union gained notoriety as "communist influenced" and was eventually expelled from the CIO. It folded in 1950.
8. Ibid., 269.
9. Pardo, *Mexican-American Women Activists,* 54–55. After eight years of community marches and hearings, and formal protest from then City Council member Gloria Molina, the proposal was defeated.
10. Davis, *City of Quartz,* 230.
11. See Laura Pulido, "Multiracial Organizing among Environmental Justice Activists in Los Angeles," *Rethinking Los Angeles,* ed. Michael Dear, H. Eric Schockman, and Greg Hise (London: Sage Publications, 1996), 171–89. Pulido unpacks the difficulties of multiracial organizing between blacks and Latinos, examining how issues of language, raced space, and class have often prevented long-term relationships between the two groups.
12. See Acuna, *Anything but Mexican,* 45. This trend is evidenced in San Fernando Valley as well, which saw a big increase of Latino residents during the 1980s. As Acuna notes, "Chicanos were spreading throughout the city, and the automobile gave them, and especially youth, more mobility."
13. Chester Himes, "Lunching at the Ritzmore," *The Collected Stories of Chester Himes* (New York: Thunder's Mouth Press, 1990), 16.
14. Howard, *Southern California and the Pacific Electric,* 75–76.
15. Ibid., 77.
16. W.W. Robinson, *The Story of Pershing Square* (Los Angeles: Title Guarantee and Trust Company, 1931), 1–9.
17. Ibid., 11.
18. Ibid., 14.
19. Davis, *City of Quartz,* 228–36; I will discuss the implications of this dynamic in more detail in chapter 7.
20. Ibid. The city's regimentation of bus shelters to deter the homeless from sleeping on bus benches has been one of the more egregious *design* features that bolsters Los Angeles's hierarchy of urban public space.
21. Boyer, *The City of Collective Memory,* 3, 11–21.
22. Alexander Cockburn, "On the Rim of the Pacific Century," *Sex, Death and God in Los Angeles,* ed. David Reid (Berkeley: University of California Press, 1992), 17. Cockburn amusingly observes, "It is difficult to visualize that millions of people once used this tunnel to get to work...there are pygmy stalagmites in the recesses of the old cable channels and manholes...two-thirds of a mile from the mouth and fifty feet under the Harbor Freeway, the tunnel abruptly floods with water and ends in silent enigma."
23. I will discuss this dynamic further in chapter 8.

24. Trevor Boddy, "Underground and Overhead: Building the Analogous City," *Variations on a Theme Park: The New American City and the End of Public Space*, ed. Michael Sorkin (New York: Hill & Wang, 1992), 135.
25. Anastasia Loukaitou-Sideris and Gail Sansbury, "Lost Streets of Bunker Hill," *California History* 74 (1996): 403.
26. Ibid., 396.
27. Ibid.; Soja, *Thirdspace*, 12. Soja compares the area (when it was in decline) to Manhattan's Lower East Side.
28. For an extensive discussion on the politics of the inception of the Community Redevelopment Agency, see Mike Davis, "Chinatown, Part Two? The 'Internationalization' of Downtown Los Angeles," *New Left Review* 164 (July/August 1987), 65–86. Davis chronicles the CRA's role in shaping the corporate complexion of downtown by displacing thousands of poor residents from their homes to make way for high-priced condos and office buildings.
29. Ibid., 71. Davis estimates that 75 percent of downtown is foreign-owned; Soja and Scott, *The City*, 214; Gary A. Dymski and John M. Veitch, "Financing the Future in Los Angeles," in Dear, Schockman, and Hise, 47–49. Dymski and Veitch chronicle the rise of East Asian capital in downtown proper and in Los Angeles County in general. They have dubbed Koreans as the "Iowans of late 20th-century Los Angeles" for their creation of "ethnic" lending networks that have fueled development similar to that of the early suburbanization period.
30. See Davis, "Chinatown, Part Two?" 71–72, on the array of downtown investors.
31. Soja, *Thirdspace*, 215; Klein, *History of Forgetting*, 51.
32. Klein, *History of Forgetting*, 58.
33. Ibid., 55.
34. Giddings, *When and Where I Enter*, 237; DeGraaf, *Negro Migration to Los Angeles*, 114.
35. The FEPC was hardly the panacea for employment discrimination against people of color. The committee only investigated a handful of discrimination claims and was not mandated to address those issued before its inception. Similarly, the U.S. Employment Service and the War Manpower Commission had a nominal role in working to improve job conditions for blacks. See Collins, *Black Los Angeles*, 21; DeGraaf, *Negro Migration*, 114; with the backing of the FEPC, black railway workers were able to overturn the racially discriminatory "Washington Agreement" in the 1940s. See Foner, *Organized Labor and the Black Worker*, 243–45.
36. DeGraaf, *Negro Migration*, 198; Horne, *Fire This Time*, 32–35; Collins, *Black Los Angeles*, 26.
37. *California Eagle*, June 16, 1933; Himes, *If He Hollers Let Him Go*, 52. One bourgeois character in the novel complains that, "Southern Negroes are coming in here and making it hard for us."
38. Horne, *Fire This Time*, 14.
39. Ibid., 27. According to Horne the area was routinely referred to as "Nigger Heaven."
40. Ibid.
41. Collins, *Black Los Angeles*, 28; Robert C. Weaver, *The Negro Ghetto* (New York: Harcourt, Brace & Co., 1948), 219–22.
42. Weaver, *The Negro Ghetto*, 219–22.

43. Ibid., 214–15.
44. The suburb was incorporated in order to increase the tax base for the Owens Valley aqueduct, the city's main water source.
45. Sonenshein, *Politics in Black and White: Race and Power in Los Angeles*, 27; Horne, *Fire This Time*, 27.
46. My mother's family was one of the first to live in Imperial Courts when it opened in 1953.
47. Klein, *History of Forgetting*, 56. The housing project proposal also became the target of a red-baiting campaign which branded public housing "communist."
48. Sonenshein, *Politics in Black and White*, 27.
49. The westward movement of middle-class (blacks facilitated by the abolition of restrictive covenants in 1948) and the confinement of working class blacks to central areas deprived of social services would bedevil black political coalitions and preclude wider prospects for black economic mobility. See Sonenshein, *Politics in Black and White*, 30–35, for a discussion on the trajectory of early black and multiracial politics in Los Angeles.
50. Jones, *Labor of Love, Labor of Sorrow*, 262; *California Eagle*, January 19, 1939. According to the newspaper, only 5 percent of Los Angeles black women were employed in clerical occupations during the late 1930s. January 19, 1939; Collins, *Black Los Angeles*, 38, 44.
51. Collins, *Black Los Angeles*, 53.
52. Dolores Hayden, *The Power of Place* (Cambridge: MIT Press, 1995), 132.
53. Aubry, "Legacy of the Eastside Boys," 22.
54. Collins, *Black Los Angeles*, 54.
55. Since 1980, the once-solid 11 percent black makeup of the county has been reduced by black out-migration to the South and other counties near Los Angeles such as the Inland Empire.
56. Even so, the contemporary shift in the racial makeup of domestic work in the U.S. economy as a whole and Los Angeles in particular is the result of improving conditions (white women having been among the biggest beneficiaries of affirmative action policies) for both black and white women in both blue- and white-collar employment. See Roger Waldinger, *Still the Promised City? African-Americans and New Immigrants in Postindustrial New York* (Cambridge, MA: Harvard University Press, 1996).
57. Jones, *Labor of Love, Labor of Sorrow*, 237.
58. Ibid., 200.
59. Ibid., 262.
60. Ibid., 265; "Because of the financial status of black men, even middle class families remained just a paycheck away from financial disaster." See also Paul Ong and J. Eugene Grigsby III "Race and Life Cycle Effects on Home Ownership in Los Angeles 1970–1980," *Urban Affairs Quarterly*, 23.4 (1988): 608.
61. Jones, *Labor of Love, Labor of Sorrow*, 256; Giddings, *When and Where I Enter*, 237.
62. De Graaf, *Negro Migration*, 145.
63. *California Eagle*, December 11, 1942.
64. Ibid.
65. Ibid.

66. This was duly noted in a 1942 editorial: "The Negro cannot be blamed if he senses the irony of fighting for democracy abroad when he does not enjoy its full fruits at home." *California Eagle,* November 19, 1942.

67. Collins, *Black Los Angeles* 21-22; DeGraaf, *Negro Migration*, 118; see also the *California Eagle* on the issue of the closed shop and attempts to keep blacks out of firemen, brakemen positions, November 5, 1942; March 3, 1943; *Los Angeles Times* August 2, 1944.

68. Smith, "Blacks and the Los Angeles Municipal Transit System," 28.

69. Collins, *Black Los Angeles*, 22.

70. DeGraaf, *Negro Migration*, 190–91; Collins, *Black Los Angeles*, 22; Smith, "Blacks and the Los Angeles Municipal Transit System," 25; Foner, *Organized Labor and the Black Worker*, 266–67.

71. DeGraaf, *Negro Migration to Los Angeles*, 191.

72. See Crump, *Ride the Big Red Cars*, 128; Fogelson, *Fragmented Metropolis*, 107, 131.

73. Crump, *Ride the Big Red Cars*, 128.

74. Ibid., 131.

75. DeGraaf, *Negro Migration*, 191; Collins, *Black Los Angeles*, 22; Hutchinson, *Blacks and Reds*, 173; Sumner Rosen, "The CIO Era: 1935–1955," *Black Workers and Organized Labor*, ed. John H. Bracey Jr. et al. (Berkeley: Wadsworth Publishing Co., 1971), 173.

76. Collins, *Black Los Angeles*, 22; Jones, *Labor of Love, Labor of Sorrow*, 211, 265.

77. Rosen, "The CIO Era," 174; Hutchinson, *Blacks and Reds*, 169; Foner, *Organized Labor and the Black Worker*, 215–37.

78. Rosen, "The CIO Era," 177.

79. Ibid., 173, 183.

80. Ibid., 171.

81. *California Eagle,* December 11, 1942; Smith, "Blacks and the Los Angeles Municipal Transit System," 28.

82. Smith, "Blacks and the Los Angeles Municipal Transit System," 28.

83. *California Eagle,* December 3, 1942.

84. Smith, "Blacks and the Los Angeles Municipal Transit System," 29.

85. Ibid.

86. Ibid.

87. The absence of public transportation to South Central at night resonated in the 1998 dispute over cutbacks in nighttime service waged by the Los Angeles Bus Riders Union.

88. Collins, *Black Los Angeles*, 57.

89. Ibid., 56.

90. Ibid., 58.

91. Sally Jane Sandoval, *Ghetto Growing Pains: The Impact of Negro Migration on the City of Los Angeles, 1940–1960*, master's thesis, history, CSU Fullerton, 1973.

92. Kunstler, *Home From Nowhere*, 56. Kunstler has observed that the "mature auto suburb of our time is the reenactment of life on the frontier. The landscape of the auto suburb is the new wilderness. The outside doesn't matter, except as excess space. Everything outside is to be traversed and endured. The freeway-scape is exactly this sort of

wasteland...the regime of mass car use is an offshoot of our historical aversion to civility itself." Wachs, "The Evolution of Transportation Policy in Los Angeles," 130.
93. *California Eagle,* December 11 1942.
94. Himes, *If He Hollers Let Him Go,* 120–21.
95. Ibid., 123. Jones's "undoing" is ultimately his desire to "have" a white woman at the shipyard who called him a racial epithet during a confrontation. After enduring a racist joke about a black woman from a white coworker, Jones's anger over the exchange with the white woman is re-enflamed, and he thinks, "To rack her back or to cuss her out...wasn't going to be enough...I was going to have to have her. I was going to make her as low as a white whore in a Negro slum...all I could see was her standing there between me and my manhood."
96. Hutchinson interview.
97. Ibid.

Chapter Seven: Waiting for the Bus

1. Kevin Starr, "Ultimate Car Culture Was Built on Public Transport," *Los Angeles Times,* July 31, 1994, sec. M: 1+.
2. William Fulton, "But Is It a Matter of Rich (Rail) vs. Poor (Bus)?" *Los Angeles Times,* July 31, 1994, sec. M: 1+.
3. Starr, "Ultimate Car Culture," 6.
4. See Sherry Bebitch Jeffe, "Tug of War," *California Journal* (July 1997): 30. Former Los Angeles mayor Richard Riordan was at the forefront of this movement.
5. Kevin Starr, "What MTA Debate Is Really About," *Los Angeles Times,* September 7, 1997, sec. M: 1+.
6. Ibid.
7. These bedfellows include ultraconservative city supervisor Mike Antonovich and the progressive Bus Riders Union.
8. Los Angeles city government has historically been defined by a "weak mayor" form of government that privileges council district constituencies. The charter was amended to expand the mayor's powers in 2000.
9. Starr, "Ultimate Car Culture," 6.
10. Sigrid Bathen, "The MTA: Los Angeles' Transit Nightmare," *California Journal* (July 1997): 34–41.
11. Kay, *Asphalt Nation,* 41.
12. Ibid.
13. DeGraaf, *Negro Migration to Los Angeles,* 22.
14. Aubry, "Hell on Wheels," 25; Brodsly, *Los Angeles Freeway,* 35.
15. Hayden, *Redesigning the American Dream,* 152.
16. Ibid.
17. This estimate is based wholly on personal experience.
18. See Brodsly, *Los Angeles Freeway,* 35, on "distance as a function of time."

19. Brodsly, *Los Angeles Freeway*; Bottles, *Los Angeles and the Automobile*; Lillard, *Eden in Jeopardy*, 182. Lillard said it best: "To have no car is to be poor and vagrant and criminally inclined."
20. Jones, *Labor of Love, Labor of Sorrow*, 168.
21. Ibid.
22. Ibid.
23. Hine, "Black Migration," 140.
24. Jones, *Labor of Love, Labor of Sorrow*, 211.
25. Ibid., 208.
26. Giddings, *When and Where I Enter*, 144.
27. Jones, *Labor of Love, Labor of Sorrow*, 219.
28. Ibid., 210.
29. DeGraaf, *Negro Migration*, 49.
30. Ibid., 21.
31. Anderson, "A City Called Heaven," 341.
32. Klein and Wilson, "Taken for a Ride."
33. Wachs, "The Evolution of Transportation Policy in L.A," 124.
34. Ibid.
35. Ibid.
36. Crump, *Ride the Big Red Cars*, 198; Wachs, "The Evolution of Transportation Policy in Los Angeles," 124.
37. Crump, *Ride the Big Red Cars*, 88.
38. Ibid., 198.
39. Wachs, "The Evolution of Transportation in Los Angeles," 123.
40. See discussion of zoning in chapter 5. This legacy is etched in the very streets of Los Angeles, an "arena" that is world-renowned for lacking the pedestrian traffic that is commonly the hallmark of a city with a well-developed public transportation system.
41. Davis, "Cannibal City: Los Angeles and the Destruction of Nature," *Urban Revisions*, 41.
42. Ibid., 40–57.
43. Ibid.; the Olmsted plan proposed the development of more public parks, transit parkways, and greenbelts. It was rejected by the same coalition of interests that eventually helped defeat the railroads' elevated plan in 1926. During the 1970s, Gerald Ekbo drafted a report on open space under the California Legislature. His report recommended a less "exploitative" use of open/public space that would emphasize community use over development.
44. Ibid., 42.
45. Ibid., 57.
46. Richard Sennett, "The Powers of the Eye," *Urban Revisions*, 61.
47. Brodsly, *Los Angeles Freeway*, 25–30.
48. Sennett, "The Powers of the Eye," 61.
49. Hayden, *Redesigning the American Dream*, 10.

50. Ibid., 7–8, 12. Hayden contrasts the design of Baldwin Hills Village with that of Levittown, which was intended to provide a haven for the returning World War II patriarch.
51. Ibid., 12.
52. Ibid., 154. Hayden notes that feminist groups in Milwaukee and Madison started a paratransit service for women as part of their rape prevention center.
53. For a detailed discussion on how the increasing regimentation of public space in downtown Los Angeles—a phenomenon which prompted Mike Davis to coin the term "Fortress Los Angeles"—furthers the marginalization of homeless and poor residents from white-collar workers, see *City of Quartz,* 228–36.
54. Lincoln Institute of Land Policy, *Alternatives to Sprawl,* 14.
55. Starr, "Ultimate Car Culture," 1. Starr notes, "Not surprisingly, the City of Angels pioneered the one-way street, the traffic island and the rigid restriction of left turns into on-coming traffic."
56. Paul Hampton Gamard, *Engaging the Freeway As Urban Space: Finding Legibility and Order in the High Speed Landscape,* (master's thesis, Rice University, 1993), 79.
57. Richard S. Weinstein, "The First American City," Soja and Scott, *The City,* 35. Weinstein writes that the "resulting detachment further privatizes experience, devaluing the public realm."

Chapter Eight: The Juggernaut

1. Angotti, *Metropolis 2000,* 56.
2. Christopher Tunnard and Boris Pushkarev, *Man-Made America: Chaos or Control?* (New Haven: Yale University Press, 1963), 206.
3. J. Allen Whitt and Glen Yago, "Corporate Strategies and the Decline of Transit in U.S. Cities," *Urban Affairs Quarterly* 21.1 (September 1985): 56.
4. A. Q. Mowbray, *Road to Ruin* (Philadelphia: J.P. Lippincott & Co., 1969), 79.
5. Herbert Muschamp, "In the Public Interest," *The New York Times Magazine* (July 21, 1996): 41+.
6. Whitt and Yago, "Corporate Strategies," 51.
7. "Hogging the Road," *Los Angeles Times* April 3, 1998, sec. B: 6.
8. *Passenger Transport,* 55.26 (June 30, 1997): 1.
9. *Los Angeles Times,* April 3, 1998.
10. Ibid.
11. Thomas J. Donahue, "Preserving America's Highways," *Journal of Commerce* (July 16, 1996): 6.
12. World Resources Institute, *Car Trouble,* 12.
13. Kunstler, *Home from Nowhere,* 67.
14. Ibid.
15. World Resources Institute, *Car Trouble,* 11.
16. According to *The New York Times,* daily oil consumption in 1996 rose above 18 million barrels for the first time since 1979. Agis Salpukas, "Suburbia Can't Kick the Nozzle,*"* *The New York Times,* July 23, 1996, sec. D: 4+.

17. World Resources Institute, *Car Trouble*, 23, 12; Lillard, *Eden in Jeopardy*, 182.
18. Goddard, *Getting There*, 192.
19. Mowbray, *Road to Ruin*, 21, 98; Goddard, *Getting There*, 192; Whitt and Yago, "Corporate Strategies," 56; for a point-by-point discussion on the merits of Western European investment in mass transit, see Goddard, 278–80; see also Kunstler, *Home from Nowhere*, 73. Kunstler extols the merits of European planning.
20. Goddard, *Getting There*, 192.
21. Mowbray, *Road to Ruin*, 21.
22. Ibid., 18.
23. The mandate would require 10 percent of all manufactured vehicles to be electric powered. The industry claimed that it could not reach the technological standard set under the initiative—i.e., develop a long-range electric battery—by the enforcement deadline; auto industry critics such as James Kunstler and Jane Holtz Kay believe that the zero emissions vehicle is merely a smokescreen response to the larger problem of the social and spatial inequities that private transit causes.
24. Goddard, *Getting There*, 116.
25. Mowbray, *Road to Ruin*, 33. It is estimated that over 90,000 people annually have been displaced by highway construction since the advent of the *Interstate Highway Act*.
26. Ibid., 62, 104.
27. Ibid., 104.
28. Robert A. Caro, "The City-Shaper," *The New Yorker* (January 5, 1998), 38–55.
29. Ibid.; see also, Marshall Berman, *All That Is Solid Melts to Air: The Experience of Modernity* (New York: Penguin Books, 1982), 291–95.
30. Caro, "The City-Shaper," 49.
31. Ibid., 50.
32. Berman, *All That Is Solid Melts to Air*, 307.
33. Ibid.
34. Sennett, *Flesh and Stone*, 361.
35. Kunstler, *Home from Nowhere*, 283.
36. Ibid.
37. Lillard, *Eden in Jeopardy*, 8.
38. Weinstein, "The First American City," 35.
39. Brodsly, *Los Angeles Freeway*, 23.
40. Ibid., 24; Gamard, "Engaging the Freeway as Urban Space," 30.
41. Mowbray, *Road to Ruin*, 34.
42. Sandoval, "Ghetto Growing Pains," 29, 48.
43. Interview with Woodrow Coleman, March 1998.
44. See Kay, *Asphalt Nation*, 29. In 1992, senior citizens' activist group the Gray Panthers charged that the federal government's overinvestment in highway infrastructure and downsizing of public transit impaired public access for the elderly.
45. Crump, *Ride the Big Red Cars*, 101.
46. Richard Simon, "Bus Riders Protest MTA Cuts," *Los Angeles Times*, December 19, 1997, sec. B:1.

Notes

47. To the degree that there is a greater consciousness and sense of outrage over how transit funding has been hijacked by the unholy alliance of big business and city government, public transit activism in Los Angeles perhaps hearkens back to the pre-World War I period before streetcar companies began to experience their first major slump after World War I, and the regulatory oversight of public utility and public service commissions had inhibited public participation in transportation politics. Glen Yago has portrayed this development as the "first step in insulating transportation decisions from public pressures by the de facto disenfranchisement of the urban population." See *The Decline of Transit*, 53.
48. Wachs, "The Evolution of Transportation Policy in Los Angeles," 131
49. Lincoln Institute of Land Policy, *Alternatives to Sprawl*, 4
50. Participants in an interesting roundtable discussion sponsored by the *Los Angeles Weekly* addressed this issue. "Gridlock," *Los Angeles Weekly* (March 1998): 1–10.
51. Ibid., 4.
52. Ibid.
53. "Love for Car Still Top Roadblock for Mass Transit," *Los Angeles Times*, June 28, 1996, sec. B: 2.
54. Wachs, "The Evolution of Transportation Policy in Los Angeles," 140.
55. Richard Simon and Jon D. Markman, "Future of Subway Project Questioned by MTA Officials," *Los Angeles Times*, December 10, 1996, sec. A: 1+. One cent of every dollar of taxable goods in Los Angeles goes to the MTA.; see also, Bathen, "The MTA," 34–41.
56. Wachs, "The Evolution of Transportation Policy in Los Angeles," 136–37. This consensus was part and parcel of a gradual dwindling of highway projects by the late 1970s. According to Wachs, those who had once been engaged in highway development thereafter began to explore the potential of other options such as trains and monorails—which were then viewed as the cutting edge of transportation technology.
57. Ibid., 138.
58. Paul Ong and Evelyn Blumberg, "Income and Racial Inequality in Los Angeles," in Soja and Scott, *The City*, 327. Ong and Blumberg estimate that 58 percent of Los Angeles' poor are Latino.
59. Wachs, "The Evolution of Transportation Policy in Los Angeles," 139
60. Aubry, "Hell on Wheels," 25.
61. The fare is based on an honors system
62. .
63. Kay, *Asphalt Nation*, 313.
64. See chapter 7; for further discussion on the dynamics of this corporate strategy, see Yago, *The Decline of Transit*, 202.
65. Davis, "Cannibal City," 57.
66. Interview with Rita Burgos, July 1998.
67. Ibid.
68. "Gridlock," 7.
69. Ibid., 10; *Los Angeles Times*, September 21, 1997, sec. M: 6.
70. Kevin Starr, "What MTA Debate is Really About." *The Los Angeles Times*, September 7, 1997, sec. M: 1+.

Bibliography

Acuna, Rodolfo. *Anything But Mexican: Chicanos in Contemporary Los Angeles.* London: Verso, 1996.

Adams, Hazard, and Leroy Searle. *Critical Theory since 1965.* Gainesville: University of Florida: 1986.

Adero, Malaika. *Up South: Stories, Studies, and Letters of This Century's African-American Migrations.* New York: New Press, 1993.

Adler, Sy. "The Transformation of the Pacific Electric Railway: Bradford Snell, Roger Rabbit, and the Politics of Transportation in Los Angeles. *Urban Affairs Quarterly* 27.1 (September 1991): 51–86.

———. "Why BART but No LART? The Political Economy of Rail Rapid Transit Planning in the Los Angeles and San Francisco Metropolitan Areas, 1945–57." *Planning Perspectives* 2 (1987): 149–74.

Anderson, Susan. "A City Called Heaven: Black Enchantment and Despair in Los Angeles." *The City: Los Angeles and Urban Theory at the End of the Twentieth Century,* ed. Edward J. Soja and Allen J. Scott. Berkeley: University of California Press, 1996.

Angotti, Thomas. *Metropolis 2000: Planning, Poverty and Politics.* London: Routledge, 1993.

"Another Instance of Mass Transportation Theory." *Pacific Electric Magazine* 11 (July 10, 1926): 5.

Atherton, Lewis. *Main Street on the Middle Border.* Bloomington: Indiana University Press, 1958.

Aubry, Erin. "Hell on Wheels." *Los Angeles Weekly.* (July 18, 1997): 25+.

———. "Legacy of the Eastside Boys." *Los Angeles Times Magazine,* (July 20, 1997): 12+.

Banham, Reyner. *Los Angeles: The Architecture of the Four Ecologies.* Los Angeles: Harper & Row, 1971.

Barnes, Catherine. *Journey from Jim Crow: The Desegregation of Southern Transit.* New York: Columbia University Press, 1983.

Bathen, Sigrid. "The MTA: Los Angeles' Transit Nightmare." *California Journal* (July 1997): 34–41.

Berman, Marshall. *All That Is Solid Melts into Air: The Experience of Modernity.* New York: Penguin Books, 1982.

Boddy, Trevor. "Underground and Overhead: Building the Analogous City." *Variations on a Theme Park: The New American City and the End of Public Space,* ed. Michael Sorkin, New York: Hill & Wang, 1992.

Bottles, Scott. *Los Angeles and the Automobile.* Berkeley: University of California Press, 1987.

Boyer, Christine M. *The City of Collective Memory: Its Historical Imagery and Architectural Entertainments.* Cambridge: The MIT Press, 1996.

———. "The Language of City Planning." Ph.D. diss., Massachusetts Institute of Technology, 1972.

Brodsly, David. *L.A. Freeway: An Appreciative Essay.* Berkeley: University of California Press, 1981.

Carby, Hazel. *Reconstructing Womanhood: The Emergence of the Afro-American Woman Novelist.* New York: Oxford University Press, 1987

———. "Policing Black Women's Bodies in an Urban Context." *Identities,* ed. Anthony Appiah and Henry Louis Gates, Chicago: University of Chicago Press, 1995.

———. "It Jus Be's Dat Way Sometime: The Sexual Politics of Women's Blues." *Unequal Sisters: A Multicultural Reader in U.S. Women's History,* ed. Ellen Carol DuBois and Vicki L. Ruiz, New York: Routledge, 1990.

Carey, Edward. *Remembering: A Phenomenological Study.* Bloomington: Indiana University Press, 1987.

Caro, Robert. "The City-Shaper." *The New Yorker* (January 5, 1998): 38–55.

Cassidy, John. "The Comeback." *The New Yorker* (February 23, 1998): 16+.

Cockburn, Alexander. "On the Rim of the Pacific Century." *Sex, Death, and God in Los Angeles,* ed. David Reid. Berkeley: University of California Press, 1992.

Collins, Keith. *Black Los Angeles: The Maturing of the Ghetto, 1940–1950.* Saratoga: Century Twenty One Publishing, 1980.

Collins, Patricia Hill. *Black Feminist Thought.* Cambridge: Unwin Hyman, 1990.

Crump, Spencer. *Henry Huntington and the Pacific Electric.* Glendale, CA: Trans-Anglo Books, 1978.

———. *Ride the Big Red Cars: How Trolleys Helped Build Southern California.* Corona Del Mar, CA: Anglo American Books, 1966.

Davis, Mike. "Cannibal City: Los Angeles and the Destruction of Nature." *Urban Revisions: Current Projects for the Public Realm,* ed. Russell Ferguson. Los Angeles Museum of Contemporary Art, Cambridge: Harvard University Press, 1996.

———. "*Chinatown*, Part Two? The 'Internationalization' of Downtown Los Angeles." *New Left Review* 164 (July/August 1987): 65–86.

———. *City of Quartz: Excavating the Future in Los Angeles.* London: Verso, 1981.

———. "The Empty Quarter." *Sex, Death, and God in Los Angeles,* ed. David Reid. Berkeley: University of California Press, 1992.

Dear, Michael. "In the City, Time Becomes Visible: Intentionality and Urbanism in Los Angeles, 1781–1991." *The City: Los Angeles and Urban Theory at the End of the Twentieth Century,* ed. Edward J. Soja and Allen J. Scott. Berkeley: University of California Press, 1996.

DeGraaf, Lawrence B. "Negro Migration to Los Angeles, 1930 to 1950." Ph.D. diss., UCLA, 1962.

DeParle, Jason. "Slamming the Door." *The New York Times Magazine* (October 20, 1996): 52+.

Derrida, Jacques. *Aporias*. Trans. Thomas Dutoit. Stanford: Stanford University Press, 1993.

―――. *Of Grammatology*. Trans. Gayatri Chakravorty Spivak. Baltimore: Johns Hopkins University Press, 1976.

Deutsche, Rosalyn. *Evictions: Art and Spatial Politics*. Cambridge: MIT Press, 1998.

Didion, Joan. *Play It as It Lays*. New York: Simon and Schuster, 1970.

Dill, Bonnie Thornton. "Our Mothers' Grief: Racial Ethnic Women and the Maintenance of Families." *Journal of Family History* 13 (1988): 415–31.

Donahue, Thomas J. "Preserving America's Highways." *Journal of Commerce* (July 16, 1996): 6.

Drake, St. Clair, and Cayton Horace. *Black Metropolis*. New York: Harcourt, Brace, 1945.

Dreiser, Theodore. *The Financier*. 1912: Reprint New York: Dell Books, 1961.

Dyer, Richard. "White." *Screen* 29 (Autumn 1988): 44–64.

Dymski, Gary A., and John M. Veitch. "Financing the Future in Los Angeles." *Rethinking Los Angeles*. ed. Michael Dear, et al. London: Sage Publications, 1996.

Fernandez-Kelley, M. Patricia. "Migration, Race, and Ethnicity in the Design of the American City." *Urban Revisions: Current Projects for the Public Realm*. ed. Russell Ferguson. Los Angeles Museum of Contemporary Art, Cambridge: Harvard University Press, 1996.

Fogelson, Robert. *The Fragmented Metropolis: Los Angeles, 1850–1930*. Cambridge: Harvard University Press, 1967.

Foner, Philip. *Organized Labor and the Black Worker*. New York: Praeger Publishers, 1974.

Foster, Mark S. *From Streetcar to Superhighway: American City Planners and Urban Transportation, 1900–1940*. Philadelphia: Temple University Press, 1981.

Foucault, Michel. "On Other Spaces." *Diacritics* 2 (1980): 35–45.

"Four Wheels and Off to New Horizons." *The New York Times*, May 30, 1997, C1.

Freedman, Samuel G. "Suburbia Outgrows Its Image in the Arts." *The New York Times*, February 28, 1999, sec. 2, 1+.

Freeman, Joshua. *In Transit: The Transport Workers Union in New York City 1933–1966*. New York: Oxford University Press, 1989.

Fryer, Alex. "Regional Board Selects Station Sites, Alignment for Light-Rail Plan." *Seattle Times*, November 19, 1999, 1+.

Fulton, William. "But Is It a Matter of Rich (Rail) vs. Poor (Bus)?" *Los Angeles Times*, July 31, 1994, sec. M: 1+.

———. *The Reluctant Metropolis: The Politics of Urban Growth in Los Angeles.* Baltimore: Johns Hopkins University Press, 2001.

Fynsk, Christopher. *Heidegger: Thought and Historicity.* Ithaca: Cornell University Press, 1986.

Gamard, Paul Hampton. "Engaging the Freeway as Urban Space: Finding Legibility and Order in The High Speed Landscape." Master's thesis, Rice University, 1993.

Garreau, Joel. *Edge City.* New York: Anchor, 1992.

Gebhard, David G., and Robert Winter. *Los Angeles: An Architectural Guide.* Salt Lake City: Gibbs Smith, 1994.

Giddings, Paula. *When and Where I Enter: The Impact of Black Women on Race and Sex in America.* New York: William Morrow and Company, Inc., 1984.

Goddard, Stephen. *Getting There: The Epic Struggle Between Road and Rail.* New York: Harper Collins, 1994.

"Gridlock." *Los Angeles Weekly* March 1998: 1–10.

Griffin, Farah Jasmine. *Who Set You Flowin': The African-American Migration Narrative.* New York: Oxford University Press, 1995.

Grossman, James R. "The White Man's Union: The Great Migration and the Resonance of Race and Class in Chicago, 1916–1922." *The Great Migration in Historical Perspective.* ed. Joe William Trotter Jr. Bloomington: Indiana University Press, 1991.

Harley, Sharon. "The Politics of Black Women's Labor History." *Women and Work: Exploring Race, Ethnicity, and Class.* ed. Elizabeth Higginbotham and Mary Romero. London: Sage Publications, 1997, 28–52.

———. "Anna J. Cooper: A Voice for Black Women." *The Afro-American Woman.* ed. Sharon Harley and Rosalyn Terborg-Penn, London: Kennikat Press, 1978.

Harvey, David. "Between Space and Time: Reflections on the Geographical Imagination." *Annals of the Association of American Geographers* 80 (1990): 418–34.

Hayden, Dolores. *Redesigning the American Dream: The Future of Housing, Work, and Family Life.* New York: W.W. Norton, 1984

———. *The Power of Place.* Cambridge: MIT Press, 1995.

Haymes, Stephen Nathan. *Race, Culture, and the City: A Pedagogy for Urban Struggle.* Albany: State University of New York Press, 1995.

Heidegger, Martin. *Basic Writings.* Trans. David Farrell Krell. San Francisco: Harper Collins, 1977.

Hesse, Barnor. "White Governmentality: Urbanism, Nationalism, Racism." *Imagining Cities: Scripts, Signs, Memory.* ed. Sallie Westwood and John Williams, London: Routledge, 1997.

Hilton, George and John F. Due. *The Electric Interurban Railway in America.* Stanford: Stanford University Press, 1960.

Himes, Chester. *If He Hollers Let Him Go.* New York: Thunder's Mouth Press, 1945.

———. *The Collected Stories of Chester Himes.* New York: Thunder's Mouth Press, 1990.

Hine, Darlene Clark. "Black Migration to the Urban Midwest: The Gender Dimension, 1915–1945." *The Great Migration in Historical Perspective.* ed. Joe William Trotter Jr. Bloomington: Indiana University Press, 1991.

———. "Rape and the Inner Lives of Black Women in the Middle West: Preliminary Thoughts on the Culture of Dissemblance." *Unequal Sisters: A Multi-Cultural Reader in U.S. Women's History,* ed. Ellen Carol DuBois and Vicki L. Ruiz. New York: Routledge, 1990.

Hise, Gregory, and William Deverell. *Eden by Design: The 1930 Olmsted-Bartholomew Regional Plan for the Los Angeles Region.* Berkeley: University of California Press, 2000.

Hise, Gregory. *Magnetic Los Angeles: Planning the Twentieth Century Metropolis.* Baltimore: Johns Hopkins University Press, 1999.

"Hogging the Road." *Los Angeles Times,* April 3, 1998, sec. B: 6.

Hood, Clifton. *722 Miles: The Building of the New York Subways and How They Transformed New York.* New York: Simon and Schuster, 1993.

hooks, bell. *Ain't I a Woman.* Boston: South End Press, 1981.

———. *Black Looks: Race and Representation.* Boston: South End Press, 1992.

Horne, Gerald. *Fire This Time: The Watts Uprising and the 1960s.* Charlottesville: University Press of Virginia, 1995.

Howard, Danny. *Southern California and the Pacific Electric.* Los Angeles: J & R Lithography, 1980.

Hutchinson, Earl Ofari. *Blacks and Reds: Race and Class in Conflict 1919–1990.* East Lansing: Michigan State University Press, 1995.

Hutchinson, Sikivu. "Viral Signs: A Critical Reading of Don DeLillo's *Libra*." Master's thesis, New York University, 1994.

"In a Reversal, More Blacks Are Moving South." *New York Times*, January 31, 1998, sec. 1: 12.

Jackson, Kenneth T. *The Crabgrass Frontier: The Suburbanization of the United States.* New York: Oxford University Press, 1985.

Jacobs, Jane. *The Death and Life of Great American Cities.* New York: Random House, 1961.

Jeffe, Sherry Bebitch. "Tug of War." *California Journal* (July 1997): 1993.

Jones, Jacqueline. *Labor of Love, Labor of Sorrow: Black Women, Work, and the Family from Slavery to the Present.* New York: Basic Books, 1985.

Jordan, Philip D. *The National Road.* Gloucester: The Bobbs-Merrill Company, 1966.

Kay, Jane Holtz. *Asphalt Nation: How the Automobile Took Over America and How We Can Take It Back.* New York: Crown Publishers, 1997.

Kelley, Robin. *Race Rebels: Culture, Politics and the Black Working Class*. New York: The Free Press, 1996.

Klein, Howard. *Histories of Forgetting: Los Angeles and the Erasure of Memory*. London: Verso, 1996.

Klein, Jim, and Martha Olsen. *Taken for a Ride*. Point of View Documentary Series, PBS. WGBH, Boston, 1996.

Krell, David Ferrell. *Of Memory, Reminiscence and Writing on the Verge*. Bloomington: Indiana University Press, 1990.

Kunstler, James. *Home from Nowhere: Remaking Our Everyday World for the Twenty-First Century*. New York: Simon & Schuster, 1996.

Lambert, Bruce. "At 50, Levittown Contends With Its Legacy of Bias." *New York Times*, December 28, 1997, sec. 2, 1+.

Lazarre, Jane. *Beyond the Whiteness of Whiteness: Memoir of a White Mother of Black Sons*. Durham: Duke University Press, 1996.

Lemann, Nicholas. *The Promised Land: The Great Black Migration and How It Changed America*. New York: A.A. Knopf, 1991.

Lewis, Tom. *Divided Highways: Building the Interstate Highways, Transforming American Life*. New York: Penguin Books, 1997.

Liebs, Chester. *From Main Street to Miracle Mile: American Roadside Architecture*. Boston: Little, Brown, and Company, 1985.

Lillard, Richard G. *Eden in Jeopardy (Man's Prodigal Meddling with His Environment: The Southern California Experience)*. New York: Alfred Knopf, 1966.

Lilly, Joseph. "Metropolis of the West." *North American Review* 232 (September 1931): 239–45.

Lincoln Institute of Land Policy. *Alternatives to Sprawl*. Cambridge: Lincoln Institute of Land Policy, 1995.

"Lines of the Pacific Electric, Southern and Western Districts." *Interurbans Special* 60 (1975): 18–20.

Lopez, Ian F. Haney. *White by Law: The Legal Construction of Race*. New York: New York University Press, 1996.

Louikatou-Sideris, Anastasia and Gail Sansbury. "Lost Streets of Bunker Hill." *California History* 74 (1996): 394–406.

"Love for Car Still Top Roadblock for Mass Transit." *Los Angeles Times*, June 28, 1996, sec. B2.

Lowenthal, David. *The Past Is a Foreign Country*. Cambridge: Cambridge University Press, 1985.

Lynch, Kevin. *What Time is This Place?* Cambridge: MIT Press, 1972.

Marcuse, Peter. "Housing in Early City Planning." *Journal of Urban History* 6 (February

1980): 153–76.

Markman, Jon D. "Study Contends That MTA Based 20-Year Transit Plan on Faulty Data." *Los Angeles Times*, June 25, 1996, sec. B: 1+.

———. "Senate Panel to Investigate Subway Project," *Los Angeles Times* June 14, 1996, sec. A, 1.

Marx, Leo. *The Machine in the Garden: Technology and the Pastoral Ideal in America.* New York: Oxford University Press, 1964.

May, Martha. "The Historical Problem of the Family Wage." *Unequal Sisters: A Multicultural Reader in U.S. Women's History.* ed. Ellen Carol DuBois and Vicki Ruiz. New York: Routledge, 1990.

McElroy, Colleen. "Sister Detroit." *Centers of the Self: Short Stories by Black American Women Writers from the Nineteenth Century to the Present.* ed. Judith A. and Martin J. Hamer. New York: Hill and Wang, 1994.

McWilliams, Carey. "Myths of the West." *North American Review* 232 (1931): 423–32.

Meir, August, and Elliot Rudwick. "Communist Unions and the Black Community: The Case of the Transport Workers Union, 1934–1944." *Labor History* 23 (spring 1982): 165–97.

Merleau-Ponty, Maurice. *Phenomenology of Perception.* Trans. Colin Smith. New York: Humanities Press, 1962.

Morrison, Toni. "City Limits, Village Values: Concepts of the Neighborhood in Black Fiction." *Literature and the Urban Experience,* ed. Michael Jaye and Ann Chalmers Watts, New Brunswick: Rutgers University Press, 1981.

———. *Jazz.* New York: Penguin Books, 1992.

———. *Playing in the Dark: Whiteness and the Literary Imagination.* Cambridge: Harvard University Press, 1992.

Mosley, Walter. *A Red Death.* New York: Norton, 1991.

Mowbray, A. Q. *Road to Ruin.* Philadelphia: J.P. Lippincott & Co., 1969.

Moynihan, Daniel Patrick. *The Negro Family: The Case for National Action.* Washington, D.C.: U.S. Labor Department, 1965.

Mumford, Lewis. *The Highway and the City.* New York: Mentor Books, 1963.

Muschamp, Herbert. "In the Public Interest," *The New York Times Magazine* (July 21, 1996): 41+.

Nelson, Dick et al. "Unconventional Wisdom." *The Seattle Times*, October 31, 1999, B-9.

Omi, Michael, and Howard Winant. *Racial Formation in the United States: From the 1960s to the 1980s.* Routledge: New York, 1986.

Ong, Paul, and Evelyn Blumberg. "Income and Racial Inequality in Los Angeles." *The City: Los Angeles and Urban Theory at the End of the Twentieth Century,* ed. Edward Soja and Allen Scott. Berkeley: University of California Press, 1996.

Ong, Paul, and Eugene J. Grigsby. "Race and Life Cycle Effects on Home Ownership in Los Angeles 1970–1980." *Urban Affairs Quarterly* 23 (1988): 601–15.

Pardo, Mary S. *Mexican American Women Activists: Identity and Resistance in Two Los Angeles Communities.* Philadelphia: Temple University Press, 1998.

Petry, Ann. *The Street.* Boston: Houghton Mifflin Company, 1974.

Proffit, Steve. "On Restoring Los Angeles through Public Transit." *Los Angeles Times*, September 21, 1997, M3.

"Proves Street Car Need in Mass Transit." *Pacific Electric Magazine* 11 (August 10, 1926): 13–14.

Pulido, Laura. "Multiracial Organizing among Environmental Justice Activists in Los Angeles." *Rethinking Los Angeles,* ed. Michael Dear et al. London: Sage Publications, 1996.

Pynchon, Thomas. "A Journey into the Mind of Watts." *New York Times Magazine* (June 12, 1966).

Rae, Douglas. "Geocratic America: *Plessy* on Foot v. *Brown* on Wheels." *ISPS Seminar on Race, Class, & Politics.* Yale School of Management & Department of Political Science, January 1998.

Rapaport, Herman. *Heidegger and Derrida: Reflections on Time and Language.* Nebraska: University of Nebraska Press, 1989.

Rapid Transit Action Group. *Rail Rapid Transit Now!* Los Angeles Chamber of Commerce (February 1948): 1–13.

"Riding Momentum." *Los Angeles Times.* December 31, 1996, sec. B, 1+.

Robinson, W. W. *The Story of Pershing Square.* Los Angeles: Title Guarantee and Trust Company, 1931.

Roediger, David. *The Wages of Whiteness: Race and the Making of the American Working Class.* London: Verso, 1991.

———. *Towards the Abolition of Whiteness: Essays on Race, Politics, and Working Class History.* London: Verso, 1994.

Rosen, Sumner. "The CIO Era: 1935–1955." *Black Workers and Organized Labor,* ed. John H. Bracey Jr. et al. Berkeley: Wadsworth Publishing Co., 1971.

Ross, Alex. "Hold Everything." *The New Yorker,* (February 23, 1998): 21+.

Rugoff, Ralph. "The Last Freeway." *The Los Angeles Weekly,* (December 31, 1994): 23.

Salpukas, Agis. "Suburbia Can't Kick the Nozzle." *New York Times,* July 23, 1996, sec. D, 3+.

Sandoval, Sally Jane. "Ghetto Growing Pains: The Impact of Negro Migration on the City of Los Angeles, 1940–1960." Master's thesis, CSU Fullerton, 1973.

Scharff, Virginia. *Taking the Wheel: Women and the Coming of the Motor Age.* New York: Free Press, 1991.

Bibliography

Schivelbusch, Wolfgang. "Railroad Space and Railroad Time." *New German Critique* 14 (1978): 31–40.

Schuyler, George S. "Traveling Jim Crow." *American Mercury* 20 (August 1930): 424–431.

Scott, Mel. *Metropolitan Los Angeles: One Community.* Los Angeles: The Haynes Foundation, 1949.

Sennett, Richard. *Flesh and Stone: The Body and the City in Western Civilization.* New York: W.W. Norton, 1994.

———. "The Powers of the Eye." *Urban Revisions: Current Projects for the Public Realm.* ed. Russell Ferguson, Los Angeles Museum of Contemporary Art, Cambridge: Harvard University Press, 1996.

Shoup, Paul. "Buses Can Best Serve When Linked with Electric Railway Carriers." *The Life and Times of the Pacific Electric,* Perris, CA: Orange Empire Trolley Museum, 1988.

Simon, Richard. "Bus Riders Protest MTA Cuts." *Los Angeles Times,* December 19, 1997, sec. 2, 1+.

Simon, Richard, and Jon D. Markman. "Future of Subway Project Questioned by MTA Officials." *Los Angeles Times* December 10, 1996, sec. A, 1+.

Smith, Alonzo. "Blacks and the Los Angeles Municipal Transit System." *Urbanism Past and Present* 6 (winter-spring 1981): 25–31.

Snell, Bradford C. "American Ground Transport: A Proposal for Restructuring the Automobile, Truck, Bus, and Rail Industries." *Subcommittee on Antitrust and Monopoly of the Committee on the Judiciary.* U.S. Senate, February 26, 1974.

Soja, Edward. *Thirdspace: Journeys to Los Angeles and Other Real-And-Imagined Places.* Oxford: Blackwell Publishers, 1996.

———. *Postmodern Geographies: The Reassertion of Space in Critical Social Theory.* London: Verso, 1989.

Soja, Edward, and Allen J Scott. *The City: Los Angeles and Urban Theory at the End of the Twentieth Century.* Berkeley: University of California Press, 1996.

Sonenshein, Raphael. *Politics in Black and White: Race and Power in Los Angeles.* Princeton: Princeton University Press, 1993.

Spillers, Hortense. "Mama's Baby, Papa's Maybe: An American Grammar Book." *Diacritics* (summer 1987): 65–81.

Starr, Kevin. *Material Dreams: Southern California Through the 1920s.* Oxford: Oxford University Press, 1990.

———. "Ultimate Car Culture Was Built on Public Transport." *The Los Angeles Times,* July 31, 1994, sec. M, 1+.

———. "What MTA Debate Is Really About." *The Los Angeles Times,* September 7, 1997, sec. M, 1+.

Takaki, Ronald. *A Different Mirror: A History of Multicultural America.* Boston: Little Brown and Company, 1993.

Tarr, Joel. "From City to Suburb: The 'Moral' Influence of Transportation Technology." *American Urban History*, ed. Alexander B. Callow Jr. New York: Oxford University Press, 1973.

The World Resources Institute. *Car Trouble*. Washington D.C.: World Resources Institute, 1987.

Theroux, Peter. *Translating LA*. New York: W.W. Norton & Company, 1994.

Tompkins, Raymond S. "The Troubled Trolley." *American Mercury* 13 (1928): 400–8.

Tunnard, Christopher, and Pushkarev, Boris. *Man-Made America: Chaos or Control?* New Haven: Yale University Press, 1963.

Wachs, Martin. "The Evolution of Transportation Policy in Los Angeles: Images of Past Policies and Future Prospects." *The City: Los Angeles and Urban Theory at the End of the Twentieth Century*, ed. Edward Soja and Allen Scott, Berkeley: University of California Press, 1996.

Waldinger, Roger. *Still the Promised City? African-Americans and New Immigrants in Postindustrial New York*. Cambridge: Harvard University Press, 1996.

Ware, Vron. *Beyond the Pale: White Women, Racism and History*. London: Verso, 1992.

Warner, Sam Bass. *The Urban Wilderness: A History of the American City*. New York: Harper & Row. 1972.

Weaver, Robert C. *The Negro Ghetto*. New York: Harcourt, Brace & Co., 1948.

Weinstein, Richard. "The First American City." *The City: Los Angeles and Urban Theory at the End of the Twentieth Century*, ed. Edward Soja and Allen Scott, Berkeley: University of California Press, 1996.

Westwood, Sallie, and John Williams, ed. *Imagining Cities: Scripts, Signs, Memory*. London: Routledge, 1997.

Whitt, J. Allen, and Yago, Glen. "Corporate Strategies and the Decline of Transit in U.S. Cities." *Urban Affairs Quarterly* 21 (September 1985): 37–65.

Whittemore, L.H. *The Man Who Ran the Subways: The Story of Mike Quill*. New York: Holt, Rinehart, and Winston, 1968.

Wilson, Elizabeth. *The Sphinx in the City: Urban Life, the Control of Disorder, and Women*. Berkeley: University of California Press, 1992.

Wright, Richard. *American Hunger*. New York: Harper and Row, 1940.

Yago, Glen. *The Decline of Transit*. New York: Cambridge University Press, 1984.

Newspaper Articles

California Eagle, September 25, 1947.

California Eagle, December 11, 1942.

Bibliography

California Eagle, November 5, 1942.

California Eagle, January 13, 1939.

California Eagle, June 16, 1933.

Los Angeles Record, December 10, 1912.

Los Angeles Record, April 17, 1920.

Los Angeles Times, April 5, 1926.

Los Angeles Times, August 2, 1944.

Pacific Electric Magazine 11.5 (October 10, 1926).

Passenger Transport 55 (June 30, 1997): 1.

Interviews

Interview with Larry Aubry, September 1997.

Interview with Woodrow Coleman, September 1997.

Interview with Earl Hutchinson Sr., September 1997.

Interview with Emola Vaughn, September 1997.

Interview with Sam Martin, March 1998.

Interview with Rita Burgos, July 1998.

Interview with Yvonne Hutchinson, February 1999.

Interview with Cynthia Rojas, September 2001.

Interview with Wanda Solomon, September 2001.

Interview with Barbara Lott-Holland, October 2001.

Interview with Genethia Hudley Hayes, December 2001.

THEORY AND PEDAGOGY
Kristi Siegel, General Editor

The recent critical attention devoted to travel writing enacts a logical transition from the ongoing focus on autobiography, subjectivity, and multiculturalism. Travel extends the inward direction of autobiography to consider the journey outward and intersects provocatively with studies of multiculturalism, gender, and subjectivity. Whatever the journey's motive—tourism, study, flight, emigration, or domination—journey changes both the country visited and the self that travels. *Travel Writing Across the Disciplines* welcomes studies from all periods of literature on the theory and/or pedagogy of travel writing from various disciplines, such as social history, cultural theory, multicultural studies, anthropology, sociology, religious studies, literary analysis, and feminist criticism. The volumes in this series explore journey literature from critical and pedagogical perspectives and focus on travel as metaphor in cultural practice.

For additional information about this series or for the submission of manuscripts, please contact:
> Peter Lang Publishing. Inc.
> Acquisitions Department
> P.O. Box 1246
> Bel Air, MD 21014-1246

To order other books in this series, please contact our Customer Service Department:
> (800) 770-LANG (within the U.S.)
> (212) 647-7706 (outside the U.S.)
> (212) 647-7707 FAX

Or browse online by series:
> www.peterlangusa.com